THE AUGUR'S DAUGHTER

Frontispiece: Bronze statuette of a girl. Paris, Bibliotheque Nationale

THE AUGUR'S DAUGHTER

A Story of Etruscan Life

Sybille Haynes

Foreword by Professor Massimo Pallottino

The Rubicon Press

The Rubicon Press Limited
57 Cornwall Gardens
London SW7 4BE

British Library Cataloguing in Publication Data

Haynes, Sybille
    The Augur's Daughter : A Story of
    Etruscan Life.
    I. Title II. Die Tochter des Augurs.
    English
    833'.914(F)   PT2668. A9/

Drawings by Juanita Homan
Designed and typeset by The Rubicon Press
Printed and bound by Biddles Limited of Guildford and King's Lynn

For Massimo and Maria

Foreword

If the world of the ancient Etruscans has been a constant source of inspiration for modern literature, it is above all because of the fascination of the 'mystery' that has grown up around it, a mystery compounded of the romantic adventure of its rediscovery, the unfamiliarity of its monuments, the enigmatic obscurity of the origins and language of the Etruscan people. Despite the continuous advances in our scientific knowledge, the myth of the 'mysterious Etruscans' continues to be widely diffused and deeply rooted among the general public.

Etruria as seen by writers of the past century and this - by novelists, poets and essayists - is history reflected in the transforming mirror of the imagination, a creation of the liveliest and most unbridled fantasy. It is a picture abounding in striking allusions and colourful descriptions, in interpretations as brilliant as they are chimerical, in theoretical speculation, whimsey, nostalgia, even humour (Cardan's, for example, in Aldous Huxley's *Those Barren Leaves*). An Etruria in short in which scientific truth is subordinated, and often sacrificed, to the creative urge or even to mere caprice.

Thus it strikes us as all the more significant when a professional archaeologist ventures into the field of narrative fiction without surrendering anything of her scholarly integrity and knowledge, there to acquit herself with all the skill and taste needed to ensure not only the intrinsic value of her work, but the pleasure and interest of her readers. This is something rare in the annals of the historical novel and quite exceptional so far as the literary evocation of the Etruscan world is concerned; but it is what the Etruscologist Sybille Haynes has achieved. Author of valuable studies in Etruscan archaeology, organizer of the Etruscan section of the British Museum, a member of the Florentine Istituto di Studi Etruschi ed Italici, she has now written the story of *The Augur's Daughter*, the subject of the present remarks.

It is a book written out of love for the shadows of a remote, yet familiar past, a past which the writer has recomposed after long study of its fragmentary remains and reanimated with the magic of *sympatheia*, the timelessness of human feeling. But its writing has also been an act of courage, for it required great seriousness and dedication to meet and overcome the difficulties involved in such a delicate task of historical reconstruction. I do not hesitate for a moment to affirm, as a veteran of Etruscan studies, that in its setting, sequence of events and characters the novel reflects with scrupulous fidelity all that excavation and research have so far taught us about the civilization of the Etruscans.

But I would like to add another consideration of more general relevance from the theoretical and critical point of view. Besides enthralling readers of novels and stimulating the interest of the educated public, the pages Sybille Haynes has written are also worthy of the attention of students of ancient history. I have, in fact, always thought and occasionally stated explicitly, that periods and aspects of ancient civilization that lack the living testimony of an abundant original literature (as is the case with Etruria, as opposed to Greece and Rome) cannot be truthfully or convincingly presented as historical reality so long as study of them is limited to schematic formulations or generalized speculation about chronology or institutions or other forms of life. To bring us near to the individual men and women whose actuality lies behind these abstractions, a controlled effort of the imagination is needed.

Although classified as a novel rather than history, this book is, in my view, a not insubstantial contribution to the understanding of the Etruscan world at one of the most crucial moments of its existence: the critical period between the end of the sixth century and the beginning of the fifth, when its economic and political power was challenged by the overwhelming opposition of Greeks and Carthaginians. The imaginary but entirely credible plot is concerned with the 'great families' of Caere, at a time when the vicissitudes of this city are glancingly illuminated by the remarkable gold tablets inscribed in Etruscan and Phoenician which came to light at Pyrgoi more than twenty years ago. And historical reality is further evoked by the rich series of illustrations of original

archaeological documents which the publisher (who deserves our
warmest praise for this publication) has enhanced the volume. This
is a work, then, which will not only afford pleasure to a great
many readers as a novel, but kindle their interest in Etruscan civilization by presenting a picture of it based on illuminating and
reliable evidence. In other words, it is a genuine contribution to
learning, and we wish it every success.

Massimo Pallottino
Professor of Etruscology and Italic
   Antiquities of Rome University
President of the Institute of Etruscan
   and Italic Studies, Florence

Introduction

In 1964, the Italian excavators of the Etruscan sanctuary at Pyrgoi, the main harbour of the ancient city of Caisra, discovered three gold tablets, two inscribed with Etruscan texts and the third with a parallel text in Phoenician. Though short (and in the Etruscan versions only partially understood), these records shed fresh light on a hitherto obscure and little documented period of the late sixth and early fifth centuries B.C., the major events of which had been known to us only through fragmentary and contradictory later sources. The newly found texts revealed that around 500 B.C. a ruler of Caisra by the name of Thefarie Velianas dedicated a shrine to the Phoenician goddess Astarte who was identified with the Etruscan goddess Uni. Not only did the inscriptions present us with a new historical personality, a contemporary of the celebrated Etruscan kings Tarquinius Superbus and Porsenna and of the Greek tyrant Aristodemos of Kyme, but they also pointed to an alliance between the city of Caisra and the Phoenician-speaking Carthaginians, both engaged at that period in a crucial trial of strength with the Western Greeks.

It is against this complex political background that the present novel is set. Through the eyes of its protagonist Larthi, the sensitive and wilful daughter of the chief augur of Caisra, we see the development of events as they may have happened in the lifetime of a generation doomed to witness the decline of Etruscan supremacy in the western Mediterranean. We follow the slow crumbling of the long-established rule of the aristocratic families of Etruria and the rise of tyrants such as Thefarie Velianas, borne on a wave of popular aspiration, and we see how changing economic conditions, dictated by far-reaching historical events, impinge on the life of the Matuna family and that of the royal Velchana family into which Larthi marries.

As almost everything we know about the material aspect of Etruscan civilization is based on excavated remains, extensive use has been made of archaeological evidence in order to create as vivid a picture as possible of the physical setting and intensely religious atmosphere of Etruscan daily life.

The dramatic incident towards the end of the novel, in which Larthi has a premonition of her husband's death in battle, is inspired by one of the most significant objects in the Etruscan collection of the British Museum, a bronze helmet, captured during the decisive sea-battle off Kyme (Cumae) and inscribed by the victorious Greek ruler of Syracuse, Hieron, the son of Deinomenes, with a dedication to Olympian Zeus.

The official known in Latin as an *augur* was a priest whose task it was to discover the will of the gods from omens of all kinds and advise accordingly on the conduct of public business. Such religious officials existed in Rome and Umbria and almost certainly in Etruria as well. As no Etruscan word corresponding to *augur* has come down to us, the Latin word has been chosen for the title of this novel, since it perfectly describes the priestly functions of Larthi's father.

Part I

1

Larthi, the augur's daughter, frowned and jumped up impatiently. 'This game's boring! Let's play something else!' she said to Ramtha, a friend of hers, who was still crouching on the beaten clay floor in the porch of Larthi's home at Caisra.

With great dexterity Ramtha snatched up the sheeps' knuckle-bones which Larthi had dropped in disgust at her own clumsiness. 'Look, it's so easy' she said, throwing them up and catching them with the back of her hand, 'just try it again.'

Larthi shook her head. It was no use attempting to beat Ramtha, she was too good with her hands. As usual, Ramtha gave in to her. 'Well, what would you like to do instead?' she said, getting up and smoothing her chiton. She looked at her expectantly.

'Wait!' Larthi exclaimed suddenly, 'I'll throw them as dice just once. If I'm lucky, perhaps Aunt Culni will let me wear my new mantle this evening.' She took up four of the knuckle-bones, stared at them hard while wishing, and tossed them into the air. They fell, widely scattered near the wooden pillars supporting the porch. The girls ran to look at the dice. Larthi at first could not believe her eyes: it was the best possible throw, the one called after Turan, the goddess of love - each of the four bones showing a different face.

'Oh, I'm so glad!' Ramtha clapped her hands delightedly. 'I'd love to see your mantle. What's it like?'

'It's of Milesian wool with a wide border and a lot of little lotus flowers embroidered on it.'

'It sounds beautiful! Where did you get it?'

'Father gave it to me. He brought it from Sybaris about three months ago.'

'Why ever haven't you worn it?'

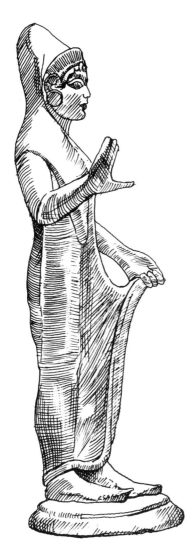

Bronze statuette of a woman.
Rome, Museo Nazionale delle
Terme

Larthi shrugged her shoulders. 'Aunt Culni wouldn't let me; she says I'm too young to put on such a precious garment.'

'But you are almost fourteen,' Ramtha protested.

'I know,' Larthi said indignantly, 'and I'm sure I have grown a lot recently.' She stood up against the corner-pillar and asked Ramtha to see if she now topped the notch, cut into its wood in the spring when she had last been measured. Ramtha had to stretch to make it out; although already fifteen, she was not so tall as her friend.

'You have outgrown it by about a finger's breadth,' Ramtha announced and then went on 'couldn't you at least just show me your mantle?'

'We might try and open Aunt Culni's clothes' chest,' Larthi said hesitantly, turning to listen. The hum of voices and clatter of cooking utensils came across from the kitchen quarter. 'She's gone there to supervise the slaves,' she whispered, 'we're having a feast tonight.'

'What feast?' said Ramtha, lowering her voice.

'It's to honour father's friend, Avile Spurinna from Ruma. He has brought his son Marce to be educated here.'

'Oh,' Ramtha breathed, 'what's Marce like?'

'Rather dull, I think. But then, I've hardly spoken to him, they only got here late last night.' She sounded indifferent.

As Ramtha went on to ask how old Marce was, Larthi pretended ignorance. She knew perfectly well he was fifteen, but his arrival had upset her. When her father had told her that Marce was going to live in their house so that he could teach him to read and write and to interpret the signs from heaven according to the sacred books, she had at once sensed a rival in him. So far, Larthi had been her father's only pupil. For some years now he had instructed her in the ancestral skills of discovering the will of the gods and the forms of ritual, which had been passed down in their family for generations. Ramtha might be clever with her hands, but she could not read or write, nor did she know the revelations which the sacred books of the prophet Tages and the nymph Vecui contained. Because of this, Larthi had felt apart from her friend, singled out for a special life. Marce's sudden arrival seemed a threat to her position, and she made up her mind to put this interloper, from a provincial place like Ruma, firmly in his place.

'If you want to see my mantle, we'd better walk on tiptoe, otherwise Aunt Culni will catch us out,' she said crossly to Ramtha. As she spoke, Larthi pressed her hand against her left temple and frowned again. She felt one of her headaches coming on. Violent stabs of pain warned her, as on many occasions in the past, that she was going to be haunted by a vision of future events. She suddenly knew that her father would tell her to put on her new mantle for the feast. A surge of joy swept through her, but it ebbed when followed by the insight that the evening was going to end in sorrow. Her mind strained to divine the cause of this coming affliction, when the vision ceased abruptly and only the pain remained with her, sharpened by a sense of impending doom.

'Careful,' she whispered uneasily, as Ramtha tiptoed towards the wooden clothes' chest, 'don't knock over any of the vases.' She kept rubbing her temple in a preoccupied way, while Ramtha lifted the heavy, bronze-sheathed lid. Aunt Culni was a passionate collector of Greek vases, and Larthi had often accompanied her to the quarter of Caisra called Agylla, where the Greek merchant Erasistratos had a depot and the foreign artisans their workshops. She, too, had liked these finely thrown vessels with their painted decoration in shiny black and red. But while Aunt Culni tended to choose vases with floral patterns, files of animals and dancers, Larthi preferred those depicting battle-scenes. Eagerly she would read the names written in Greek beside the individual figures and identify the heroes and gods they represented; for she knew all the old tales of the Greeks.

She differed from her aunt in other ways, too. Larthi sometimes wondered whether she had inherited her gift of foreseeing the future, and her love of excitement from her mother, who had died when she was born. Aunt Culni, the elder sister of Larthi's mother, was placid and domesticated and did not suffer from these sudden bursts of prophetic insight. Ramtha would have made a better niece for her, Larthi thought ruefully, while she watched her friend take the new mantle from the chest, unfold it and drape it neatly round her left shoulder. As Ramtha handled the soft wool admiringly and closely examined the embroidery, Larthi suddenly envied her. How easy and contented life was for Ramtha, untroubled as she was by painful visions of events to come. For a moment she longed to be like her friend, but quickly dismissed the thought. The lines of her life were laid down ineluctably - there was no escape from the fate allotted by the gods to each mortal. 'Yes, of course, you may,' she said listlessly to Ramtha, who had asked if she could copy the embroidered floral border onto a mantle of her own. 'I don't mind in the least.'

When they had put the garment back and shut the lid of the chest, Ramtha picked up the jugs and amphorae and rearranged them on top.

6

'Why has your aunt scratched letters on some of these pots?' she enquired.

'Mi Culnaial,' Larthi spelled out. 'That's to state that they belong to her. You see, she's only done it on her favourite ones.'

'I like this matching pair best. What fragile handles - they are as thin as ribbons!' Ramtha said, full of admiration, as she replaced the amphorae symmetrically. 'But now I must run. Anyway, you will be busy preparing for the feast.'

Larthi did not reply. She suddenly dreaded the return of her vision and wished that Ramtha would stay with her. But pride prevented her from admitting fear to her friend who had always looked up to her. She managed to smile and wave to Ramtha as she ran out into the cobbled street.

2

It was hot and noisy. The smell of beeswax from the candles burning on the tall bronze candelabra mingled with that of roast meat, fish and fresh bread-cakes. Laris Matunas' slaves, hurried to and fro between the kitchen and the great oblong room, flanked on

Banquet. Limestone relief from a cinerary urn. From Chiusi. Florence, Museo Archeologico

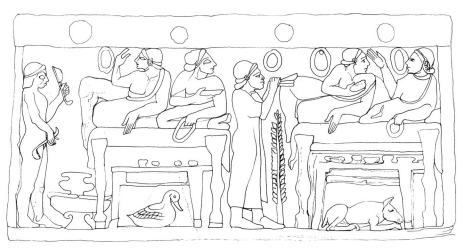

three sides by dining-couches. They called out to each other as they cleared away the dishes. The clatter drowned what conversation Larthi could have overheard between her father's guests. She was feeling bored. Absent-mindedly she brushed some crumbs off her mantle and bent forward to pick up a scrap of meat from the remains of the meal on the low, three-legged table in front of her couch. Krankru, her pet dog, looked up at her expectantly, beating his tail against the wooden couch-leg. Snatching the morsel thrown to him, he licked his muzzle and resumed his patient vigil. Warily he eyed a couple of geese who had found their way from the courtyard into the dining-room and were gobbling up debris of food fallen on the floor.

The fresh, green branches which adorned the frescoed walls and wooden pillars, began to wither in the heat. Larthi adjusted her banqueter's wreath and lifted her weary eyes towards the massive, smoke-blacked ridgebeam and the chequer-board pattern formed by the rafters and tiles on the slopes of the ceiling. She wondered why, after months of longing for her new mantle, she now took so little pleasure in wearing it. Was it because nobody seemed to have noticed it? Aunt Culni had handed it to her without objecting, though she had commended her to be careful of it during the meal.

Larthi suddenly felt warm affection for her aunt and began to observe her with a mixture of surprise and admiration. How magnificent she looked with her chestnut-coloured hair piled up high on the back of her head and bound in the coils of the tutulus. Large golden discs, patterned with minute granules of gold, glittered in her earlobes. Over a light sleeved chiton, dotted with red circlets, she wore a heavier red mantle with a wide green border. Her soft red leather shoes with up-turned points were standing next to the sandals of Marce's father on a footstool between the fretted couch-legs. Reclining beside him on a splendid striped mattress coverlet, she began toasting her kinsman. The meal was almost over and the slaves had begun to bring in the water-pitchers and towels for washing the hands of the diners. Larthi, who shared her own couch with Marce, noticed that he had at last stopped eating. So far they had not exchanged a single word, as Marce helped himself continuously to the delicacies piled on the table before him. He now looked round for the first time and fixed his gaze on his father and Aunt Culni.

'Did you know,' Larthi said, trying to draw him into conversation, 'that the golden fibula with which my aunt's mantle is pinned, is an heirloom from my great-grandmother through whom you and I are related.'

Marce looked at her blankly, as she went on 'Your father and Aunt Culni are both descended from her, and she came from the same family as Tanaquil, the wife of Lucumo Tarquin.'

Gold fibula decorated with powdery granulation. From the Tomb of the Lictor in Vetulonia. Florence, Museo Archeologico

'We don't consider women very important at home,' Marce said stiffly, 'and I know nothing of this relationship.'

Larthi was amazed by his lack of interest in the family's history. She had always felt sure that Aunt Culni's love of Greek vases and her own passion for everything to do with Greece was inherited from this line of her ancestors. As Marce pretended not to be aware of it, she told him that Tanaquil's husband, Tarquin, had been the son of a noble Greek, Demaratos of Corinth, who had settled in Tarchuna and married an Etruscan lady. Because Tanaquil resented the low esteem in which her half-foreign husband was held by her countrymen, she had persuaded him to move to Ruma and seek his fortune there. Larthi suspected that the present Tarquin and his sons and kinsmen did not wish to be reminded of their alien forebear, the family having been rulers of Ruma for generations now. But she herself took pride in the fact that it was solely due to Tanaquil's inspiration and prescient interpretation of the omens that the first Tarquin had reached Ruma and become its king.

9

'The people who matter in Roma,' Marce replied, casting a disapproving glance at Aunt Culni who was toasting his father again, 'would not like the way in which the Etruscans allow their women-folk to drink lying on a couch with men.'

'What a strange place Ruma must be,' Larthi said, feeling nettled, and thinking it likely that Marce's mother, who had been of Latin descent, had put such notions into his head. 'Remember that you are of Rasenna blood, too.'

Just to show him how little she thought of his prejudices, she called out to Elachsantre, the Greek cupbearer, to come over to their couch. Usually she avoided speaking to him, for he made her feel less certain of herself than she liked to be.

Larthi's father had bought the youth in the previous year from a local nobleman, one of whose ships had captured a Rhodian merchant vessel off Zankle with all her crew, passengers and cargo. Elachsantre, the son of the rich merchant who owned the ship, bitterly resented his enslavement; for months he remained sullen and unwilling to perform the tasks allotted to him. However, when he had managed to send messages to his father, the hope of being ransomed lifted his spirits. He was, in any case, treated kindly by Larthi's father and his duties were not arduous. Larthi thought that, in fact, he had become rather uppish recently.

Elachsantre lingered on purpose over filling his master's cup from the huge two-handled bronze vessel containing wine mixed with water. Then he slowly came over to Larthi's couch, not with the quick, lithe steps which become a cupbearer, but deliberately swinging the silver wine-strainer and ladle in his hands. He looked at Marce in a supercilious way.

'Elachsantre,' Larthi said awkwardly, 'give your master Marce some more wine.'

'My name is Alexandros, son of Timachidas,' he retorted, 'and if anyone is my master, it is Laris Matunas.' He jerked his head in the direction of Larthi's father.

'Haven't you been told that, while he lives in this house, you are to wait on Marce, the son of Avile Spurinna?' the girl asked, tossing back her brown curls indignantly.

Marce had half risen from the couch and glowered at the slave. Muttering something between his teeth, Elachsantre snatched the cup from Marce and took it over to the mixing-bowl.

Larthi sensed the threat of violence and a strange excitement seized her. The thought that Elachsantre and Marce might hate each other seemed not unpleasing. If they were to fight, Elachsantre was by no means certain to get the better of Marce; although sixteen and tall, he was of slighter build than Marce. With a sudden new interest she closely observed Elachsantre as he came back towards them. He wore nothing but a wreath on his dark, curly head; and now that his body hair had been plucked properly in the Rasenna fashion, she realized he was handsome. Marce was propping himself up on the bolster beside her again, when Elachsantre with a defiant expression on his face approached him to hand back the full cup. Stretching across the low tripod-table, he suddenly appeared to loose his balance and stumbled forward. The cup dropped from his hand spilling the wine all over Larthi and Marce.

The girl cried out in dismay. The cascade of red liquid seemed like a terrible omen to her. She started up and tried to shake the wine off her clothes. In vain - her new mantle was badly stained. The large patches of red looked like blood. Attempting to wipe the wine from his face and arms, Marce cursed Elachsantre for his clumsiness. There was a general commotion. Larthi's father called for more candelabra to be brought in, while Aunt Culni sent for her favourite slave, Peci, to help clean up and comfort the sobbing girl.

Some of the guests, heated by wine, laughed at the mishap. Larthi's distress grew. She felt that the air was vibrant with further disaster. As Peci took the stained mantle from her shoulders and wrapped a clean one round her, the tension in Larthi's body became almost unbearable. All her veins throbbing and half-blinded by stabs of pain in her head, she tried to catch her father's eye - surely he must sense the impending doom. But he had turned to talk to Marce's father and then called out that the dancers and flute-players should now be brought on.

She huddled miserably on her couch. As the slaves were hurrying about, clearing away the tables and sweeping the floor, the musicians and acrobats began to troop in. Amongst them Larthi was startled to discover her father's younger brother Caile. In the flickering candle-light he looked haggard and his travelling-clothes were crumpled and dusty. Larthi put out her hand and attempted to speak to him, but he ignored her and pushed his way forward towards her father. Why had he come home, Larthi wondered uneasily. He was supposed to be looking into some inheritance in the South and they had not expected him back for weeks. She watched as Caile addressed her father, who had turned towards him with a surprised and welcoming gesture. The hubbub of voices drowned what Caile said, but Larthi saw her father's face fall and then he lifted his fingers in the sign to avert evil. Clutching the bolster of the couch, she gazed at the two anxiously.

'Who's that, who's just come up to your father?' Marce nudged her. She shrugged him off impatiently:

'It's Uncle Caile. Just be quiet so that I can hear what the trouble is.'

Snatching off his wreath, her father got up and called for silence.

'Friends and kinsmen,' he said gravely, 'let us cease feasting. Caile has brought terrible news. A disaster has befallen the people of Sybaris. Let us sacrifice to the gods and implore them to save us from a similar destiny!'

Everyone exclaimed in horror and hands were raised to ward off such a calamity. Then there were shouts of 'What's happened?' 'Tell us about the fate of the Sybarites!' 'What will become of our business with them?'

They all crowded round to question Caile. But he took his time. Leaning against his brother's couch, he asked for wine and made the usual libation, pouring an offering from the cup from which he then drank himself.

'I am parched,' he sighed. 'I heard of the disaster in Poseidonia and thought it best to come straight back to bring the news to the Lauchume and you. The wind was contrary - I had to travel overland. It was a most tiring journey.' He emptied his cup and went on 'When I got to the king's house, they told me that he was away hunting, so I came here.'

Larthi's father nodded 'Cousin Velthur went boar-hunting after I had taken the omens.'

'What about Sybaris?' someone asked again, and everyone joined in demanding to know what had happened.

12

Larthi, deeply disturbed as she was by the truth of her fore-bodings, nevertheless felt a certain relief. The tension in her body lessened and she was able to concentrate on her uncle's report.

Caile chose his words deliberately, pleased to be the centre of attention.

'As you know, there has long been ill-feeling between Sybaris and Croton on account of their territorial ambitions and their rivalry in trade. The Crotonians envy the Sybarites not only their rich lands and mines, but also their safe and short land-route to their colonies Laos and Skidros, as well as Poseidonia, whence their goods reach us. The people of Croton have to go a long way round by sea to trade with the cities on the Tyrrhenian coast. And they have to contend with the Chalcidians, who control the traffic through the Straits, and also with pirates. The winds make the voyage most hazardous, too, and the Crotonians frequently suffer heavy losses. Their good fortune, therefore, is nothing compared with that of Sybaris.'

He stopped and asked for another cup of wine. Larthi listened impatiently and wished that her uncle did not like to hear himself talk quite so much. She felt he relished being the bearer of bad news, as it gave him, for a while, an importance which he other-wise did not possess. For the same reason he always mentioned the fact that their family was closely related to the Lauchume - as if the people of Caisra were not aware of the rank of our house, she thought disdainfully.

The old freedman Teitu now arrived with clean clothes and sandals for Caile and helped him change. Caile carefully coaxed the folds of his mantle into a pleasing curve before going on.

'I need not remind you of the intermittent civil strife in Sybaris itself. You all know that the city was founded both by Achaeans and by people from Troizen, who had formed hostile factions. The Achaeans finally drove out their fellow-citizens of Troizene descent, having deprived them of their share in the government. Recently a body of oligarchs was exiled from the city and fled to Croton, imploring help to regain power at Sybaris. Wanting to revenge themselves for the previous murder of some envoys of theirs, the people of Croton eagerly seized this oppor-tunity to go to war with their hated enemies. A battle took place in which the Sybarites were completely defeated. Following the rout of the army, Sybaris was besieged and sacked and most of the remaining inhabitants slain. But not content with that: such was the envious fury of the Crotonians that, after the destruction of their rival city, they deflected the course of the river Krathis to flow over the ruins of Sybaris, so that no trace of her should remain to be repopulated.'

Everyone moaned in horror and pity. Larthi, who had run up to her aunt, had a terrifying vision of slaughter and ruin. Culni clasped her in her arms and they both cried bitterly. Larthi knew that of the many different Greeks living in the South, the Sybarites had been the closest to the Rasenna in their habits and in their love of beautiful things. It was through them that precious stuffs from Miletus in Asia Minor and rare works of art from further East had reached their shores. She thought of her Milesian mantle again, so ominously stained by blood-red wine, and she sobbed inconsolably. Aunt Culni called for Peci to take the girl to bed. Larthi felt worn out and allowed herself to be led away. As they left the hall, she saw her father prepare for a sacrifice and she, too, prayed silently for her people to be spared a fate like Sybaris.

3

Torrential rain beat down on the roof-tiles of the augur's house. The only sound Larthi could hear above the rush of water outside was that of the double-flute, to which the slaves were rhythmically kneading dough in the kitchen. She felt life was heavy with boredom. Four days ago her father had set out, together with Caile, Marce and some slaves, to bring the news of Sybaris' destruction to the king. Larthi had expected to accompany them, but her father had refused to let her come. It was felt the going in the distant marshes, where the Lauchume was hunting, would be too rough for her, and nobody could foretell how long it might take them to find the royal party.

Listlessly Larthi picked up a wisp of carded wool from the tall wicker basket by her side. Aunt Culni, who was not feeling

14

well, had gone to lie down, and the girl sat in the darkening hall alone. She thought of sending for Ramtha to come and keep her company, but the violent drumming of the rain made her change her mind. Twirling the bronze distaff discontentedly with one hand, she wished she had been born a boy; working with wool was tiresome to her. How much more exciting it would have been to have ridden with the men into the coastal swamps, where water-fowl nested amongst the reeds and herons fished in the lagoon. She imagined Cousin Velthur and his hunters stalking the wild boar, she could almost hear the aggressive grunt of the sow, trapped with her squealing piglets in the undergrowth, while the dogs yapped furiously as the men stood waiting tensely with their spears poised for the kill.

Sighing, she turned to her wool-basket again. Even the dull and wooden Marce for company would be more cheerful than being left alone like this. With a pang of jealousy she realized that her father, having no son of his own, would in future always take Marce with him on such expeditions. Could that slight noise above the sound of the rain be them returning - or had someone else arrived? She listened attentively, but only the insistent rhythm of the flute could be heard beside the monotonous rush of water. She bent down to disentangle some wool which had dropped from the pile in the basket and got caught on the bronze decoration of her chair leg. As she settled back again to begin working in earnest, she suddenly noticed Elachsantre leaning in the doorway, his arms folded under his chlamys. Had he been standing there long - watching her? Larthi was taken aback and her heart started to race unaccountably. Before she went to bed, she had heard Aunt Culni tell Elachsantre to clean all the silver cups and vessels, surely he could not have finished that yet. She pretended not to notice him. Since he had ruined her mantle, she had not spoken to him at all, unable to make up her mind whether he had done it on purpose or not. Equally Elachsantre himself had seemed to avoid her.

The rain ceased all of a sudden and the sound of the flute penetrated the room powerfully; Larthi felt as though its rhythm beat in her very veins.

'It's a rare pleasure to see the Lady Larthi working with wool,' she heard Elachsantre's ironical voice quite close to her.

*Bronze incense-
burner. Karlsruhe,
Badisches Landes-
museum*

16

'You had better work yourself and clean the silver, as you were told,' she retorted. 'In any case, if you hadn't ruined my best mantle, there would be no need for me to start spinning the wool for a new one.'

'I did not mean to do it,' he protested in a pleading tone, which made her feel uneasy.

'Of course, you did, to get your own back on Marce for having to serve him. You just pretended to stumble.'

'I was terribly upset when I saw that lout sprawling next to you. I cannot bear to think of you and him together.' Elachsantre's voice sounded curiously strangled.

Larthi tried to think of something to say. As she put some more wool on her distaff, she warned him that he would have to get used to Marce living with them.

'His relations in Ruma, who know that we are better than any other people at interpreting the signs from heaven, want him to learn about it and about the laying out of temples and the foundation-rites of cities and all the necessary ceremonies. So you see, father has to teach Marce the whole of the ritual and what they call the Etruscan discipline in Ruma . . .'

She stopped, vaguely aware that Elachsantre was not paying any attention to her words. He now stood close behind her and she sensed that he was thinking of her in a way which frightened her. His curls touched her cheek, as he bent over the back of her chair. For a moment she was caught as if under a spell, unable to move. He then let his hand slide over her shoulder until it cradled her breast. Her face flushed, she pulled away from his searching grip and started up from her seat indignantly. Her distaff fell to the ground with a harsh clatter and in the stillness that followed she noticed that the flute had stopped.

Elachsantre was breathing deeply. Slowly he moved round to face her. Larthi did not look at him but kept her eyes fixed on the distaff at her feet. When they had stood silently for a while, Elachsantre finally bent down to pick it up. She took it from him without a word and sat down again, feeling weak at the knees, as if she had passed through some danger. Then she turned towards him and with a certain deliberation said:

'Why don't you tell me something about your home and people? I've been bored all day; the least you can do is to keep me amused, if you are too lazy to clean the silver.'

'You really are just as cruel as the Greeks always say your people are.'

'I don't know what you are talking about,' Larthi retorted.

'Remember what you people of Caisra did to the Phocaean citizens when you captured them in the battle of the Sardinian Sea?' he said.

Larthi looked down to avoid his gaze.

'You stoned them all to death without mercy, once you had landed them there!'

Larthi bit her lip; she knew that he spoke the truth. Her father and aunt had often told her about this outrage committed under the walls of their city and the divine punishment which followed it. But then, she consoled herself, all that happened a very long time ago - it must be almost thirty years now - and we did a great deal to appease .the gods and the spirits of the dead Greeks. Our family in particular went out of their way to make amends. It's not fair that Elachsantre should bring it up as if it was anything to do with me.

But he renewed his attack 'And you Tyrrhenoi are the most ruthless pirates in the whole Mediterranean, capturing the ships of peaceful merchants and selling free-born men into slavery!' His voice choked now and he turned away to hide his tears.

Larthi felt troubled and guilty. 'Alexandros,' she said gently, getting up again and touching his arm, 'it's not my fault that you are here as a slave.' For the first time since his capture he heard his name pronounced in the proper Greek way. He looked round slowly at her from under frowning brows.

'You know how much I like all things Greek,' she went on; 'I really do want to hear all about your family and your city - won't you tell me what they're like?'

When he looked less defiant and finally responded to her coaxing smile, she withdrew her hand from his arm and settled back into her chair, exulting in the knowledge that she could bend him to her will.

18

'How can I describe it all to you,' he said, leaning against the pillar, his knee bent with the foot resting on the wood behind, 'you can't possibly imagine it - Lindos is so much more beautiful than Caisra!' Irritating as she found it to hear him boast about his city in this way, Larthi kept quiet, for she was eager to learn more.

'First of all,' he began, looking into the distance, 'it has a splendid rocky acropolis and two perfectly sheltered natural harbours. When you stand up there on the citadel by the temple of Lindia, you might be a bird with the city at your feet, the open sea on one side and wooded mountains on the other. Your city here doesn't dominate land and water as Lindos does. From Caisra I can hardly ever see the sea - it's so far away; I feel quite cut off. I really can't understand how you manage to do all your commerce and piracy with no proper harbour within sight!'

'What nonsense!' she interrupted, 'You know very well that we have three excellent harbours where everyone comes, including the Greeks and Carthaginians.'

'You've obviously never set eyes on a good natural harbour like ours and that of the Syracusians, or the Tarentine one,' he said superciliously; 'yours are really nothing better than roadsteads with breakwaters.'

Baffled and incensed by his superior tone, Larthi tried to answer back.

'Oh, but I'm sure that your temples and houses are not nearly as fine as ours.'

'On the contrary, our temples are built of stone and beautifully proportioned, not at all like your heavy, wooden ones with all those garish facings of painted terracotta!'

'What can you mean by garish? Surely your temples have coloured decoration, too.'

'Ah, yes, there is some paint on the capitals and below the roof; but the stone is just rendered with fine plaster so that it looks like marble. And the only decoration which Kleoboulos put up on the temple of the goddess when he rebuilt it, were eight captured shields - they're still there, above the columns at the front and the back.'

'When did this Kleoboulos live? Was he your king?' Larthi

Antefix decorated with the head of a Gorgon. Polychrome terracotta from the Portonaccio-temple at Veii. Rome, Villa Giulia

asked, trying to imagine what a stone temple with columns at the back as well as the front would look like.

'No, he belonged to one of our great families and made himself tyrant when my father was a boy. Even today we still sing the song about the swallows which he wrote for the children of Lindos to sing while going round to raise support for the building.'

'Oh, could you sing that song for me?'

'I could' - he hesitated, 'but I won't - it would make me feel too sad.' He looked miserably homesick and Larthi would have liked to comfort him, but she did not know how to.

'Does your family live in a big comfortable house like ours?' she asked shyly, trying to distract him.

'No,' he said glumly, 'it's smaller than yours and everything is simpler.' He ran his eyes over the frescoed walls of the room, the colours of which were barely visible in the fading light.

'We don't have paintings like this and there isn't so much valuable furniture and silverware about - nor do we keep as many slaves as you seem to think necessary.' He began to pace about restlessly.

Ignoring the bitterness in his voice, she persevered. 'But how can your father do without slaves? Surely someone has to do all the work in the house and in the fields and in the mines?'

'Of course we have a couple of slaves about the house,' he said impatiently, 'but all the citizens are free; they are merchants and craftsmen and farmers and sailors who work on their own, and vote on all matters affecting the city.'

Larthi felt bewildered. How could there be anything but masters and slaves? And what did Elachsantre mean by vote? Not wanting to reveal her ignorance she changed the subject.

'Does your father travel a lot with his ships?'

'No, he always sent my uncles and me to Asia and to the West, because he has to spend his time in the market-place and in our warehouses by the harbour.'

'And I suppose your mother goes there with him?'

Elachsantre stared at her as if she had said the most outrageous thing.

'Of course, not!' he exclaimed; 'she would never think of going out as you do here. She stays at home in the women's quarter, as is proper.'

'Isn't that very boring for her?' Larthi asked, amazed. 'I hope she can see her friends and have them in to meals, at least.'

'A well-born woman does not dine with other people - only with her husband. And as for lying down to dinner on the same couch as other men, it's just not done! A lady sits up during the meal and waits on her husband. Only loose women and flute-girls join the men at a symposium.' He went on censoriously 'When I first came here it really shocked me profoundly to see you and your aunt behave like that - and twice a day, too!'

Larthi burned with indignation. For the second time in the last few days she had to put up with such ignorant criticism from a mere foreigner. To her it seemed absolutely natural that couples shared a couch and enjoyed their meals and dances together with their friends.

'There's no need to be insulting simply because our customs are different from yours,' she managed to say.

'I suppose after all you women are not as shameless as the Greeks believe, but . . .'

'What do you mean by shameless?' she interrupted, jumping up indignantly from her chair. Elachsantre hesitated.

'Go on say what you mean - or are you afraid of me?' Her dark eyes gazed at him challengingly.

'If you insist, I'll tell you what the Greeks think of you,' he said, giving her a sidelong glance, 'but you won't like it.'

'I don't care what you say.' She said folding her arms, trying to appear calm.

'Well, they believe that women are common property among you Tyrrhenians, and that men and women lie with each other indiscriminately and without any shame and bring up all the children thus born to them without knowing who their father is.'

Larthi was so taken aback that for a moment she just eyed him speechlessly. Then she burst out 'How dare you repeat such a lie to me? You know it isn't true!' Angry tears filled her eyes. 'I shall never speak to you again!' she shrieked and ran towards her aunt's room.

At that moment the dogs outside began to bark excitedly. Larthi knew that her father must have come home. She turned on her heel and rushed out into the courtyard, which still glistened with rain-water. Wet and mud-bespattered as Laris Matunas was, she threw herself into his arms and buried her face against his shoulder, sobbing helplessly. He stroked her back until she became calmer and had released him. Wiping her tear-stained cheeks, he looked at her questioningly. She was just about to tell him what had upset her so deeply, when Marce led in his mule and handed

*Banqueting couple.
Engraved bronze mirror.
Formerly Siena, Museo
Chigi*

the reins to Cupe, the stable slave. Marce did not even glance at
Larthi, but when Elachsantre suddenly slunk from the house and
ran past Teitu towards the slaves' quarters, Marce straightened and
stared after him until he was out of sight. Then he slowly turned
his eyes to Larthi; his expression was enough to tell her that it
would now be impossible to explain what had happened.

4

They were riding in Aunt Culni's carriage on their way to watch the games. Laris Matunas, accompanied by some of his slaves, had already set out the previous day to take the omens and perform the sacrifices with the other haruspices and priests in the presence of the king.

While negotiating the steep, stony road leading from the western gate of Caisra into the plain, Teitu guided the mules, but when they had reached the level road to the harbour, Marce, who sat in front, snatched the reins from the freedman. The morning was brilliantly sunny and the sea appeared as a sparkling blue stripe on the horizon beyond an expanse of dense, dark pine forests.

'I love the games!' Larthi exclaimed, looking excitedly at all the other vehicles full of brightly dressed people and the riders moving in the same direction; 'I only wish they came round more often.'

'But Larthi,' Aunt Culni admonished her, 'you should never forget what a serious occasion this is. Do not look upon the games as some feast to be enjoyed without a thought for the terrible events which led to their institution.'

'Oh, but I do remember; you have told me about it often enough!'

'Why do you hold these games, and such a long way from the town?' Marce asked.

'We were told to do so by the oracle of Apulu at Delphi in Greece,' Aunt Culni answered solemnly.

'But what have the Greeks and their oracle got to do with your games here?'

Larthi, who knew that her aunt loved to tell this story, quickly put in, 'Do explain it all to the poor ignorant provincial.'

Marce cracked the whip and the mules bounded forward nervously, making the carriage jolt over the deep ruts of the road. Larthi and her aunt had to grip the sides of the vehicle so as not to be thrown out. Culni had turned very pale. Running up from behind, Teitu seized the animals' bridles and calmed them with soothing noises. Larthi felt guilt-stricken. But Marce's dullness was too provoking; she simply could not help taunting him.

'If you would now leave the reins to Teitu,' Aunt Culni said quietly to Marce, 'I could show you the spot where we had the Greek prisoners buried and first held the games.' She pointed to a large, grass-covered mound rising in the distance. Shielding his eyes against the glare, Marce asked with growing interest 'Has there been a battle here?'

Two women in a carriage. Low relief from sarcophagus. From Vulci. Boston, Museum of Fine Arts

'No,' Aunt Culni replied; 'the battle was fought at sea, with the Phocaean Greeks on one side and us and the Carthaginians on the other. Everyone suffered heavy losses, but as many as forty Phocaean ships sank, and our sailors captured most of the crews and landed them here on the coast. You see,' she went on, 'these Phocaeans, who had left their homeland in Asia Minor when the Persians besieged their city, joined some of their fellow-country-men, who had earlier settled at Alalia on Corsica. They had all done much harm to their neighbours on the island and to the people of Caisra by intercepting ships and by plundering-raids. So we were angry with these Greeks for all the damage done to us in the past and during the sea-battle, and instead of bringing the Phocaean prisoners up to Caisra as slaves, our sailors stoned them all to death. They just left them unburied without the necessary rites, over there by the road leading to Pyrgoi. Afterwards, when sheep or oxen, or even men from Caisra passed by the spot, their bodies became distorted, or they were seized with palsy and lost the use of their limbs.'

This part of the story always made Larthi feel uncomfortable and she noticed that Marce, too, looked somewhat uneasy.

'What impiety not to have given these Greeks a proper burial,' he said severely; 'their shades must have haunted the place.'

'You're quite right,' Aunt Culni went on, 'for the people of Caisra then felt that they must expiate their misdeed and they sent to Delphi to enquire of the oracle how best to do it. The person chosen from amongst the noblemen of the city to lead this sacred mission to Greece was Sethre, the elder brother of Laris Matunas, to whom I was then betrothed.' Pride rung in her voice and Marce looked at her with surprise.

Trust him not to know that his kinswoman was the bride of my uncle, Larthi thought, tempted once again to upbraid Marce for his ignorance. Meanwhile Aunt Culni went on, 'Sethre was the head of this family, but he fell ill on his return from Delphi and died shortly afterwards. When my sister Seianthi married Sethre's younger brother Laris, I moved with her from Tarchuna to live in her house. We were the last of our ancient line there.'

'I see,' Marce said, 'I wondered why you settled in Caisra, when our common forbears had always lived at Tarchuna. My mother never mentioned that side of the family to me, and I suppose my father thought I knew all about it.'

Larthi again felt shocked by Marce's lack of interest in his own descent, but she managed to keep quiet, while her aunt continued to enlighten him about the family history.

'It is difficult for you, I can imagine. However, let me tell you what message Sethre Matunas brought back from the oracle. The gods advised us to erect this funeral mound for the dead Phocaeans and to honour them with magnificent games, both gymnastic and equestrian; and to this day we observe the customs that were then instituted.'

'I see,' Marce said again; 'and is that the stadium for the games over there?'

'Yes,' Aunt Culni answered, 'but I'm afraid we must get down now and walk. Look how crowded the road is.'

She climbed from the carriage with difficulty, and told Teitu to wait for Cupe to relieve him of the mules. Slowly the three of them then wound their way through the throng of people, animals and carts towards the raised wooden stands which had been erected on the earth-banks surrounding the stadium. Larthi remembered how hard the benches on these temporary wooden structures were, and had brought the cushions on which they had sat in the carriage. Aunt Culni supported herself on Marce's shoulder, carefully avoiding the jostling crowd. It worried Larthi to see her moving as if in pain; she suddenly felt intensely fond of her aunt and resolved to try and behave in a manner pleasing to her.

Marce seemed impressed by the deference with which they were greeted by everyone, as they entered the confines of the stadium and made for the part reserved for the Lauchume and the great families. Almost all the seats were already occupied. Many spectators had to be content with the grass-covered verge in front

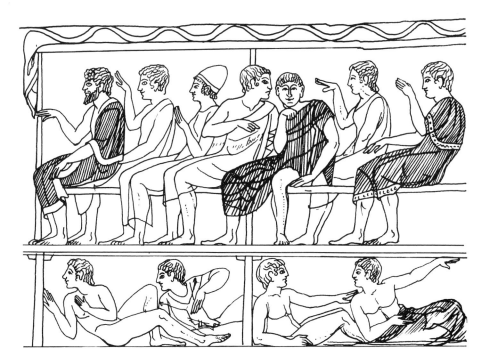

Spectators watching games from a tribune. Drawing after a fresco in the Tomba delle Bighe. Tarquinia, Museo Nazionale

of the stands, while the slaves crouched or lay in the confined space underneath them, in the hope of catching a glimpse of the events to come.

Some of the slaves cleared away stones and weeds from the arena with mattocks, while others sprinkled the ground with fine white sand.

Laris Matunas in his priest's garments was standing next to his cousin Velthur, surrounded by the most important of the noblemen and by a number of other haruspices and a scribe with tablets and stylus. They were talking together and appeared to Larthi to be unduly serious. As his family approached, Laris Matunas led them to their seats on the left of the royal box. Larthi followed him with her eyes as he returned to his place beside the king; she felt proud of her tall and dignified father.

A coloured awning had been spread on top of the stands to protect the spectators from the burning sun. Aunt Culni sat down on a cushion and closed her eyes, while Marce looked about him with more alertness than usual and Larthi reminded herself not to tease him for the rest of the day. He noticed the Lauchume's purple mantle with the embroidered border, the gold wreath on his head and his sceptre, surmounted by an eagle.

'Your king's signs of sovereignty are much the same as ours,' he said to her, 'and I see he's got a lictor with a bundle of rods and the axe standing behind him, too. Is that folding chair of his made of ivory, as ours is?'

'Of course, it is!' Larthi remonstrated; 'you don't seem to realize that all these symbols of royal power were invented by us Rasenna; you in Ruma have only got them because the first Tarquin brought them over there.'

At that moment Larthi noticed Ramtha and her parents on a stand further along; her friend had been waving, trying to attract Larthi's attention. She waved back and pointed her out to Marce.

'Can you see that fair-haired girl in an embroidered white mantle, over there? She's my best friend, Ramtha Vestiricinai, I'll introduce you when there's a break.'

Marce's only reply was a churlish grunt.

Suddenly there came the sound of trumpets, announcing the beginning of the events. As the sacrifices and the solemn procession of all the competitors had already taken place the previous day, the foot-races started immediately. As usual, they began with the short distance races, followed by the longer ones. Grouped according to age, the boys ran first, the men next. Larthi watched with keen interest when Ramtha's brothers were competing. To her delight Rasce, the elder of the two, won the event for his age-group. But Arnza, the youngest, was over-excited and broke away

Footrace. Limestone relief from a funerary monument. From Chiusi. Palermo, Museo Nazionale

from the starting-line too early. He was flogged by the trainer for causing delay and slunk away looking miserable. Each time another group of runners started off, there was a great deal of shouting from friends and supporters to encourage the athletes. Larthi felt sorry for the men competing in the race for fully armed warriors, the weight of their heavy, bronze-clad shields made it a particularly strenuous feat. But the sun flashing on the bright golden bronze helmets with their streaming crests was a marvellous sight to see, it reminded her of the story of Achilles pursuing Hector round the walls of Troy.

When the races were over, Larthi signalled to Ramtha to come and join her, but Ramtha was busy congratulating and com-

29

forting her brothers and did not notice her friend's signs. People had got up and were discussing the runners' individual performances. Larthi looked at the neighbouring tribune, where her father and the royal party sat, again engaged in serious conversation which, she suspected, had nothing to do with the games. Vaguely wondering what could be preoccupying them, she gazed around.

The confined, shady space below the wooden floor of the royal box was now almost deserted; the slaves who had been watching the races from there had gone to stretch their limbs. Only two men had remained behind lying on the grass, their backs turned towards her. They seemed to think themselves unobserved, but Larthi realized that they were making love.

The trumpets sounded again and as she turned away, she saw the two lovers separate and suddenly recognized them as Elachsantre and one of the Lauchume's Greek slaves. Marce, who was seated beside her, had been following her gaze.

'What an effeminate creature your father's slave is,' he said disdainfully.

Larthi was so upset that she could think of no reply. She turned abruptly on her heel and sat down next to her aunt pretending not to have heard his scathing remark. With her eyes fixed on the arena, she tried to fight down a turmoil of feelings which she could not understand. Why should a mere slave amusing himself have the power to make her angry and hurt? It was humiliating! She decided not to waste any more thoughts on Elachsantre, whom she had, in any case, determined never to speak to again. He would simply cease to exist for her. This resolution helped her regain her composure. Nevertheless, she was grateful that Marce was no longer looking at her.

It was now the turn of the heavyweights. To most of the spectators the boxing and the wrestling-matches were the favourite part of the games and Marce, too, watched the centre of the stadium with growing excitement. The competitors were large, muscular men with close-cropped hair, they wore nothing but cloth belts and leather thongs strapped round their hands and wrists. Referees in short mantles wielded their curved staffs and saw to it that the rules were obeyed, while flute-players, as usual, stood by to accompany each bout. Naked boy attendants, carrying small, globular oil-flasks, bronze scrapers and sponges soaked in vinegar, were ready to minister to their masters in case of injury.

Larthi cared for neither boxing, nor wrestling. Although many of the fighters came from good old families, their appearance struck her as uncouth; and all the thumping and groaning and the delight of the crowd when one of them had been badly hit or thrown, disgusted her. Marce, however, was completely absorbed by the fights and kept punching the air in sympathy and once even hit his knuckles on the wooden balustrade in front of him with a resounding noise. It made Aunt Culni sit up with a start. Throughout the break she had leaned against a pillar with her eyes closed. Larthi had hoped that she was asleep and that the shrill sound of the flutes beginning again would not disturb her. She peered anxiously at her aunt's face and was reassured a little when Culni, smiling wanly, gave her a slight wink.

At last the judges announced the winners, reading their names off the tablets on which they had been noted down by the scribe, and the prizes were handed out. Each victor received one of the splendid large bronze cauldrons which had been exhibited at the foot of the judges' tribune throughout the events. All the spectators now crowded out of the stadium to get some food and fresh air. It was well after the start of the new day, which had begun

Spectators on part of a tribune. Limestone relief from Chiusi. Palermo, Museo Nazionale

when the sun was at its highest point, and the heat under the awning was oppressive. Larthi's father had told his slaves to spread blankets and cushions in the shade of a group of pine-trees on a hillock beyond the stadium. They were busy setting out a meal there on a bed of fresh leaves. Most people had brought provisions in baskets and were jostling for space on the sparse grass, so that the family of Laris Matunas had to pick their way carefully. Attendants cleared a path for the king to an airy tent put up for the occasion. Larthi caught a glimpse of his young wife, Veilia Hapisnai, whom he had married recently, having been a widower for many years. She was resting inside the tent, propped up on a soft bolster, idly picking a few grapes from a silver dish by her side. Larthi noticed that she was pregnant.

'Where is Elachsantre?' Laris Matunas asked Teitu, when they had settled down on mattresses placed on the dry ground. 'Why is he not ready for us with the wine?'

Larthi felt stifled, despite the sea-breeze that rustled in the spreading branches above.

'I have not seen him for some time, master,' Teitu replied and sent Thresu, the household slave, to search for the cupbearer, while he himself fetched wine and water from the large amphorae kept cool in a packing of leaves at the foot of the pine-trunks. Larthi had long looked forward to this meal in the open air, but for some reason she now did not feel like eating. Neither did her father and aunt eat with much relish; only Marce fell upon the food in his usual way. Feeling parched, Larthi drank some water

Banquet. Low relief on a limestone cinerary urn from Chiusi. Chiusi, Museo Nazionale

32

and listened absent-mindedly to her father telling Aunt Culni what he had been discussing with the king and the other noblemen. It appeared that the destruction of Sybaris was already having dire effects on the trade of Caisra. Larthi seemed unable to absorb what he was saying as she suddenly made out Elachsantre and Thresu approaching in the distance. Her mouth still felt dry and she hastily drank another cup of water.

'Elachsantre,' her father said sternly, 'you have neglected your duty. If it happens again, I shall have to have you flogged.'

Reaching for a fruit, Larthi tried vainly not to look at the slave. Elachsantre made no reply but just stood with a sullen face until Teitu shoved him in the direction of the wine-cooler. Marce had been filling his cup there and now watched Elachsantre with a contemptuous smile. Larthi could see that he was saying something as Elachsantre stumbled towards him. Elachsantre controlled himself for a second and then attacked Marce furiously battering him with his fists. Her heart leapt into her mouth when Marce raised the bronze ladle which he was still holding. Before Teitu could intervene, Marce had lashed out with it and hit Elachsantre on the side of the head. Blood spurted from a gash on his temple and he fell to the ground with a moan. Larthi and her father started up in dismay, while Aunt Culni covered her eyes with her hands and sank back on her cushion. They were all appalled by the sacrilege - a fight and bloodshed during the sacred ceremony of the games!

People sitting nearby began to notice what had happened and got up with exclamations of horror and disapproval at such impious breaking of the truce. Marce dropped the blood-stained ladle and stared down at Elachsantre in bovine astonishment. Larthi did not know where to turn first. Aunt Culni seemed to have fainted and Elachsantre, pale and bleeding heavily, lay unconscious on the grass. Feeling stunned, she thought Marce must have killed him. But happily Teitu splashed some water on Elachsantre's face and he turned his head with a sigh. Larthi knelt down beside her aunt and tried to revive her by rubbing her wrists and temples with wine and putting a few drops on her lips. Laris Matunas meanwhile had succeeded in calming the crowd and went to inform the king and the other haruspices of the imperative need to interrupt the games with a ceremony of purification.

Teitu ran to fetch the mule-carriage. When he and Cupe returned with it, Thresu helped them lift Aunt Culni into the seat, while Larthi got in beside her to support her. She was reluctant to leave however, since Elachsantre had still not opened his eyes. But her father came back accompanied by the other priests and told her to let Teitu drive them home. As the carriage slowly moved through the mass of agitated people, Larthi managed to glance back and caught a glimpse of Marce kneeling on the ground with Elachsantre's head cradled in his lap. He had torn a strip of linen from the cloth on which the dishes had been set out and began to bandage the wound.

5

Three days later, the gods had signified their approval of the continuation of the games. A purification ceremony had been performed and Marce, having undergone lustration, was advised to remain in isolation for a while. Elachsantre had been taken to the house of the freedman Teitu to ensure his recovery away from the ceaseless noise in the slaves' quarters. He was being tended by a Greek physician, Sombrotidas, the son of Chrysos from Cos. Aunt Culni remained in bed, weakened by shock.

Larthi sat in the royal box to watch the second part of the games and felt heartily relieved that Marce was not there. Though she was still worried about her aunt and the fight between Marce and Elachsantre, her spirits began to rise gradually. The royal box was spacious and comfortably furnished with cushions and precious woven rugs. Larthi was the only female in the party as Veilia, the king's wife, whose confinement was near, had thought it safer not to leave the city. None of the men took the slightest notice of Larthi and she felt free to watch the preparations still being made in the centre of the stadium.

A jumping-pit had been dug and filled with soft sand. The competitors were rubbing themselves with oil and swung the bronze jumping-weights in their hands to warm up, while the flute-players, whose tunes set the rhythm for the event, began to take up their positions. When the judges and the attendants with the measuring-rods had arrived, the trumpets sounded and the athletes lined up at a certain distance behind the starting-sill.

Larthi found this part of the games by far the most interesting, since skill rather than mere strength was involved. It was exhilarating to watch the jumpers run up to the take-off point, project themselves into the air, thrusting their hands with the weights forward at first, then moving them backwards and finally land, their arms having swung back to the rear. The judges, after closely supervising the measuring from the starting-sill to the imprint of the jumpers' feet in the sand, marked the distances achieved by scratching lines. Next came the discus-throwing, another event which appealed to Larthi because of the disciplined beauty of the performers' movements. The thrower, standing in a rectangular space behind the starting-sill, first swung the heavy bronze disc up in his left hand while steadying it with his right, then moved it down and backwards in his right hand only and finally hurled it up into the air, uncoiling his tensed body like a spring. The disc flashed in the sun, rose and descended in an arc and hit the ground with a thud, throwing up little fountains of sand. Again, the point of impact was marked, this time with a small wooden stake, so that the judges could easily compare the results.

The javelin-throwing which followed proved an equally satisfying spectacle of exactly measured movements: the athlete running up to the mark, first carrying the elder-shaft level with his shoulder, then taking the right arm back, extending the other arm forward to balance the action and finally throwing the javelin without overstepping the line. Two of the competitors, however, twice failed to do so and had to be disqualified. Others suffered from having tied the leather loop of their javelin-thong badly so that it came off the shaft just before the throw. And in one incident the javelin toppled to the ground like an injured bird, its thong having become entangled with the athlete's fingers instead of slipping off smoothly. Only those throws were counted in which the javelin stuck in the ground or left an easily identifiable mark. Larthi remembered her first visit to the games some years back when she thought that the point of javelin-throwing was to hit the turning-post at the far end of the stadium, which had been left in position there from previous races. She had felt so disappointed on discovering that it was a question of achieving distance rather than accuracy of aiming.

Once more the winners were honoured with handsome bronze cauldrons which had been stacked in front of the judges' tribune and were much admired throughout the contests. The final events of the day, the horse- and chariot-races, were to be held on the race-course after a break, during which a meal was being served in the royal box.

There was no need to search out a shady spot under the trees, as the day was much cooler now; a sea-breeze made the awning above the stand flap pleasantly. Larthi listened to the Lauchume and the other noblemen's talk while she ate. She had always been in slight awe of Cousin Velthur; the king was tall, powerfully built and wore his black hair and beard long. His deep voice sounded like a growl, and on the rare occasions when he had spoken to her directly, she had been overcome by a shyness which she did not feel in the presence of other people. Recently he had seemed more approachable, and she wondered if this was due to the influence of his beautiful young wife.

At the moment, however, the king appeared somewhat agitated by the events of the past week. Larthi heard him ask her father if the sacrilegious bloodshed which had occurred portended further misfortune. Laris Matunas explained that a fight between a Greek and someone of Rasenna blood presaged danger and that in conjunction with the recent unseasonably heavy rains from the south, it might indicate that foreign nations in that quarter were inimical towards Caisra. As if uncertain of his interpretation of the ominous happenings, he said that he would consult the ritual books after the games to discover if rites of expiation were advisable in addition to the purification ceremony already performed. He warned that further sacrifices might be necessary. Larthi felt uneasy at her father's evident uncertainty in the face of the portents. The king, too, looked worried.

'We are already troubled enough by other nations,' he said. 'I have just had a message from Aranth that he has had difficulties obtaining provisions for his ships in Laos. The Phocaeans of Elea have been emboldened by the destruction of Sybaris to menace her colonies on the Tyrrhenian coast - and you know that they are absolutely vital points of supply for us.'

'Certainly, Laos and Skidros are more important than ever, now that the land-route to the Ionian Sea is lost,' Laris Matunas agreed in a subdued voice.

'Much the best policy for us would be to take the island of Lipara and so secure our undisturbed passage through the Straits,' said Larce Alvethna, one of the great mine-owners. 'If we had a stronghold there, we could keep both the Phocaeans and the Chalcidians in check.'

The king nodded gravely.

'Aranth already suggested that to me some time ago - long before Sybaris fell.'

Larthi had little recollection of her cousin Aranth, the king's son by his first marriage, though she often thought enviously of the exciting life he led. He was away from Caisra most of the year with his father's ships, trading between the metal-producing harbours in the North and the Greek cities of Kyme and Pithekoussai. Occasionally he would sail through the Straits, sometimes as far as the coast of Asia Minor, when he would be absent for several years. If ever he were to come home for a winter, she would try to get him to tell her about all the foreign parts he had visited and alien peoples he had seen.

'The Phocaeans of Elea worry me less than all the Greek cities of the Straits and our so-called allies,' Larthi heard Nerie Peipnas, an ancient nobleman sitting behind her, say hoarsely.

'I don't trust the Carthaginians at all. They are always trying to compete in our markets, and the way they are infiltrating our spheres of influence is really sinister - I'm thinking of Sardinia and Corsica in particular.'

The others agreed gloomily, and the old man went on in his tetchy voice: 'Of course, I wouldn't put up with it for one moment, if I were young again. I told my grandsons only recently not to set out for Corsica like sheep, unarmed and trusting to luck. If you are seen to be collecting the annual contribution of resin, wax and honey from there, you might well be tempting some impudent pirate these days. Times are not what they used to be - we are no longer undisputed masters of the Tyrrhenian Sea.'

The lauchume rose with a frown. 'Let us concentrate on the games now,' he said irritably. 'The sun has moved on and we must go over to the hippodrome.'

Larthi followed the men to the race-course. A vaster place than the stadium, it was devoid of stands for spectators. People sat on the rising ground surrounding a level stretch of sand, which was marked by wooden starting-boxes at one short end and by the turning-post near the other. The riders were already exercising and warming up their horses, while the crowd excitedly discussed their chances.

Larthi felt lost. Her father was talking to the haruspices Larth Repesunas and Piana Velavesnas about consulting the ritual books on the following day; she knew that she must not disturb him. The king and the other noblemen had gone to inspect the horses bred from their stables and already mounted by their sons and kinsmen. She began to stroll about aimlessly, looking for Ramtha or some other familiar face. A wind had sprung up and blew gustily across the course, driving clouds of dust from its sandy centre onto the banks. Larthi rubbed her smarting eyes. It was useless; she could find nobody to keep her company. As she walked on, it struck her that the majority of people around her were slaves. The sheer mass of them suddenly frightened her. They must outnumber us greatly, she thought, and there are all these foreigners from the harbour-towns up here as well for the games. Usually Larthi enjoyed identifying their origins from the differences in their dress and their speech. But today this throng of strange human beings seemed menacing - the wild-looking Sardinians in their short, rectangular cloaks, as much as the Carthaginians in their smooth, clinging tunics. Larthi could not help remembering with a shudder the stories of how they used to sacrifice their first-born children.

A sudden burst of clapping and laughter in the distance attracted her attention. From the height of the earth-bank where she was standing, she could make out a tall pole erected on the level ground between the side of the hippodrome and the coastal dunes. The top of the pole, surmounted by a little wooden platform, served as a perch for a monkey. A cloth bag which appeared to contain food, was suspended below it. Shinning up the pole, a young boy had repeatedly tried to reach the bag but as the wood

Terracotta cinerary urn painted with figures of youths and horses. Tarquinia, Museo Nazionale

seemed to have been covered with grease, he never managed to get higher than a couple of feet, before sliding to the ground again. Derisive applause came from the circle of bystanders after each futile attempt. When the boy had finally given up and stood fingering his sore limbs, a tall negro pushed his way through the crowds. He picked up a handful of sand, rubbed his arms and legs with it and swarmed up the pole in a flash. While the monkey threw nutshells at him, he snatched the bag and slid down, holding it out triumphantly. Everyone pressed round the negro, who had crouched down to inspect the contents of his prize.

The owner of the sideshow now tried to drive back the onlookers to make room for another attaction. He invited volunteers to jump over a dangerous obstacle, constructed of three spiky tree-trunks which formed a pyramid of shoulder height. Nobody seemed prepared to try his luck. With a flourish the showman now turned and pointed to a squat youth, dressed in brightly coloured trunks, who strutted forward confidently. While Larthi still wondered whether he would manage to clear the top of the pyramid without coming to harm, he had already projected himself into the air like a ball and vaulted over the tallest of the three spikes. Shouting with amazement, the spectators saw him land on his feet again. The next moment the youth was walking on his hands all round the circle, accompanied by the clapping of the crowd. The applause reminded Larthi of the races and she hurriedly turned away from the popular entertainment to return to her father's side. In the centre of the long southern slope of the embankment the king's ivory folding-chair had been put up by the slave responsible for it, and the Lauchume was just sitting down, surrounded by the most distinguished members of the great families. Larthi joined the group and gazed with admiration at the horses lined up for the first race. They were beautiful creatures, perfectly groomed and decked out with shiny bronze trappings. The trumpet now sounded and the horses were off. They thundered past the royal party, down the length of the course, round the turning-post, and up along the far side; the field was already well drawn out and two of the horses riderless. It was the boys' race and Larthi noticed that during the last lap the son of Larce Alvethna moved into the lead. At this point his father, who had been sitting next to the king, did not manage to remain calm and dignified. He got up, shouted encouragement to the boy and in a great finishing burst the horse gained another length and won the race. To the cheers and congratulations of his family and supporters, Larce Alvethna walked over to the starting-line to speak to his son and pat and praise the horse.

A series of other races had followed, when the weather began to change. A thin veil of cloud covered the sun and the wind from the south was getting stronger. It looked like rain again, and Larthi hoped that they could see the events through before it started. At last the moment for the chariot-races arrived. The light, two-wheeled vehicles had already been assembled. In front their high, curved parapets were covered with leather or wickerwork, while

40

the lower sides consisted of arched bronze bars only. Teams of horses were being harnessed to them, two abreast under a yoke. The charioteers, dressed in short tunics of diverse colours and wearing protective helmets, now mounted the vehicles and tied the reins round their waists. The excitement of the crowd grew and Larthi noticed that certain groups amongst the spectators chanted messages to individual charioteers, as they drove up to the starting-boxes.

Chariot-race. Low relief on the base of a limestone funerary monument. From Chiusi. Palermo, Museo Nazionale

With the sound of the trumpets they were off, in a volley of small stones and clouds of dust, followed by the roar of their supporters. Larthi bent forward, trying to make out what was happening near the far end of the course. As a great number of chariots were participating, the confusion was considerable as everyone was trying to gain the advantage by hugging the turning-post as closely as possible. Despite much dangerous side-skidding at this point, all but three seemed to round the bend without mishap. During the following turns the remaining charioteers manoeuvred with greater caution. But when the trumpets sounded again announcing the last lap, they all urged their teams into a frenzied final effort. The second chariot, whose driver had been goading his horses furiously to draw ahead of the leading vehicle, suddenly seemed to disintegrate.

41

Larthi could not quite see what was happening, but a great shout of horror went up from the spectators nearer the scene. The charioteer in a red tunic hurtled through the air and the two teams collided in a tangle of kicking and rolling horses and pieces of broken chariots. A third chariot, which had been moving up from behind, only just managed to avoid this obstacle. Tearing past the accident, the driver looked back anxiously to see if any of the surviving competitors in the race were trying to catch up with him. Luckily they were all far enough behind to steer clear of the injured men and horses and they raced on, though without a chance of victory.

While the onlookers near the collision-spot surged onto the course to help the wounded, the winner was welcomed with wild enthusiasm by a group of people Larthi had never seen before. Nor had she ever set eyes on the victor himself, a handsome young man, though somewhat thick-set, with short brown curls. As she turned to ask her father who this charioteer might be, she heard him reply to a similar question of the king:

'I don't know his name either, but I'll find out.'

He walked over to where the victorious driver was being hoisted onto the shoulders of two of his jubilant supporters. The king meanwhile told one of his attendants to discover what injuries the victims of the accident had suffered. It turned out that both men had broken limbs but the one in the red tunic had serious head wounds. The near-side wheel of his chariot had come off while overtaking and the driver had been pitched, head first, onto the ground. His frightened team had collided with the horses of the leading chariot, which had also shied and thrown their driver. One horse had been killed outright by the sharp, splintered end of a broken chariot-pole and two others with damaged legs had to be put down. It was a depressing story.

Larthi began to hate it all - the noise, the wind-blown dust, the confusion and the jostling crowd. Now she wished passionately that her father would take her home quickly. It was some time, however, before he managed to get back to them. He looked puzzled while reporting back to the king:

'The man's name is Thefarie Velianas. Not much seems to be known about his family, except that his father is a wealthy trader.

They moved here from the Phoenician harbour recently and have settled in the commercial quarter.' Casting a glance over his shoulder, he added 'Those rather noisy supporters of his are apparently mostly artisans and slaves and, oddly enough, Carthaginians from the port.'

Larthi saw Cousin Velthur frown at this news and furrow his beard in a preoccupied way. Large, isolated drops of rain suddenly fell and the king got up, while his attendants cleared a way towards the place where their horses and mule-carriages were waiting. Larthi hurried after the men, pulling her mantle over her hair against the buffeting wind and threatening rain. Her father kept looking upwards intently, where heavy clouds of a curious russet colour raced across the sky, whipped along by an angry southerly gale. Before the royal party could reach shelter, dusty red drops began to bespatter them. Teitu and Cupe tried to calm the mules, who laid back their ears and showed the white of their eyes, while shifting their feet uneasily. As Larthi and her father hastily got up into the cart, the heavens opened and sheets of water poured down blotting out everything visible.

6

Marce bent over his wax-tablet, laboriously scratching letters on its surface with a bronze stylus. He pressed his lips together tightly in an effort to copy as correctly as possible, some lines previously written out for him by Larthi. When at last he had finished his task, he raised his head, screwed up his eyes and surveyed the result critically.

'What do you think of this?' he said, showing his tablet to Ramtha, who sat on a stool next to him in the shade of the porch of Laris Matunas' house.

'You are getting better,' she said encouragingly, I can now recognize the letters you've written - but they should really be in a straight line, not all crooked like this.'

Marce leant towards her to cast an eye on her writing-tablet. It was covered with even rows of well-shaped letters running from right to left.

'It's all right for you with your small hands,' he grumbled, 'I'm just not used to holding anything as thin as this.' He put down the stylus with a grimace.

'I know it must be hard for you but you would find it much easier, if you didn't hold it in your fist as if it were a spear - more like this.' She poised her own stylus, a beautiful object with a handle in the form of a boy holding a tablet, between her thumb and two fingers and started another line.

Marce watched with admiration. Everything about her was so neat and attractive. She quickly finished her row and said, 'Of course, it helps to have the model alphabet carved on the frame of my tablet. That's even better than copying Larthi's writing. Would you like to borrow my tablet until you are quite familiar with the letters?' Smoothing back her fair curls from her forehead, she offered it to him. Marce took it absent-mindedly.

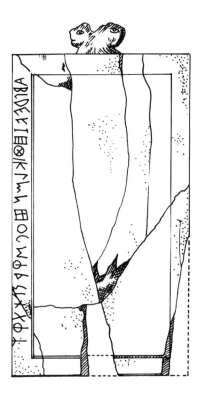

Ivory writing tablet with a model alphabet engraved on the frame. From Marsigliana Albegna. Florence, Museo Archeologico

44

'Thank you,' he said, gazing at her friendly face and wondering why it was so pleasant to accept help and advice from this girl.

Laris Matunas had delegated the task of teaching Marce to read and write to his daughter. Marce had hated his first lessons alone with Larthi because she always made him feel clumsy and inferior. Her teasing, impatient ways were exasperating and he resented a mere girl being put in authority over him. As their personalities grated on each other, his progress had been painfully slow. During one of these unprofitable lessons Ramtha had unexpectedly appeared and asked to be allowed to take part. Larthi was surprised by her friend's sudden interest in scholarly pursuits but had agreed readily for she was only too glad to be relieved of Marce's tedious company. From then on she would set them a task, and then leave her two pupils alone together. Marce began to look forward to the hour when Ramtha came over to settle down next to him with her tablet.

Marce suddenly realized that he could not take his eyes off her. Ramtha flushed, while he, wishing to distract himself, picked up his stylus, stabbing nervously with its point at the ivory frame of the tablet on his knees.

'Don't,' Ramtha said in a low voice, 'you might ruin it. It belonged to my great-grandfather. He had it made for his own use, shortly after our people had learnt to employ the letters of the Greeks of Kyme; so it's quite old.'

Marce looked contrite and fingered the tablet uneasily. After a little while Ramtha went on, 'I meant to ask you about the gold bulla you're wearing round your neck. Here children are given such lockets with charms in them to protect them from evil spirits but our young men don't often wear them.' She touched the lentil-shaped gold pendant hanging on his chest and turned it round. 'I like yours, although it hasn't got any figures embossed on it like ours do.'

Marce felt the warmth of her fingers through his tunic. He looked down at his bulla and awkwardly put his hand over hers. Some unknown force, at once sweet and disturbing, swept through him and filled him with a desire to do something outstanding, to distinguish himself before all others. As Ramtha's hand slipped away, he said, 'I shan't wear it much longer. Next year, when I reach manhood, I'll take it off for good and my toga praetexta, too.'

Bronze stylus crowned with the figure of
a boy holding writing implements.
Berlin-Charlottenburg, Antikensammlungen

46

He pulled at the woven edge of purple bordering his semi-circular mantle.

'And what will happen then?' Ramtha asked.

'I'll dedicate them both to the Lares, our household deities, when I assume the full toga of the citizen.'

'By then you'll also be an expert at writing,' Ramtha smiled, smoothing the wax on her tablet and putting it on his lap again; 'All you need is a little more practice.'

Marce seized the stylus with a will and within a short while had engraved on the waxen surface a recognizable copy of the letters and syllables carved on the tablet's frame. Proudly he presented it to Larthi, who had come across the glaring courtyard from the slaves' quarter. Such sudden progress seemed incredible to Larthi and for a moment she suspected Ramtha of having done Marce's work for him. But her pupils indignantly denied cheating, and Larthi quickly tried to make amends. Taking up the stylus, she added a line at the bottom of the column and read it out to them:

'Marce zichunce - Marce wrote this.'

Ramtha and Marce turned towards each other, exchanging a glance and a smile which made Larthi feel suddenly excluded.

Larthi's life had been busy recently. Although Teitu had taken Elachsantre into his house and his wife was nursing the patient as best she could, Teitu often had to call in Larthi. The wound on Elachsantre's temple was healing cleanly, but he still seemed to be suffering from headaches and giddiness and on the few occasions when he had attempted to get up, he began to act and talk so oddly that Teitu was at a loss to understand him. When asked to help, Larthi found that Elachsantre had relapsed into a mumbling Greek, which she only understood imperfectly. Though on the whole she managed to guess what his needs were, the visits of the Greek physician Sombrotidas proved a great relief to her. Not only could she relinquish the task of interpreting to him, but Elachsantre appeared to be soothed by his presence.

Sombrotidas was a sturdily-built man with greying hair and beard and a wide forehead. Larthi was impressed by his quiet, yet firm manner. She knew him to be a native of Cos, who had travelled widely before settling in Agylla, where he had established a practice amongst the Greek merchants and artisans. Rumour had it that he was exiled from his island many years ago for some infringement of the law. To sit and listen to Sombrotidas while he was gently reasoning with Elachsantre in his more querulous moods, imperceptibly improved her knowledge of Greek; and to hear him talk about the many lands and cities he had seen during his wanderings before he came to Caisra, was a source of delight and instruction to her. She almost came to dread the moment when Elachsantre's state would no longer require the regular visits of Sombrotidas.

Elachsantre improved physically but continued to behave so strangely that Larthi began to feel deeply afraid of him. He took to walking about aimlessly with a fixed expression in his eyes, occasionally bursting from low murmurs into unintelligible shrieks. After many weeks of witnessing such distressing scenes, Sombrotidas confessed to Larthi that he feared that Elachsantre's sanity had been permanently affected by the blow on his brain. He could do nothing to restore the balance of his mind. Larthi made the sign to avert evil. A presentiment that divine retribution might befall their house chilled her to the bone.

7

Aunt Culni, at last, seemed to be getting better. One morning, when Larthi had finished her lessons, Aunt Culni asked her if she would accompany her to the metalworkers' quarter. It occurred to Larthi that a new set of bronze cauldrons for the kitchen might be needed. She liked watching artisans at work and as her aunt was already dressed and stood waiting in the doorway expectantly with Peci holding her parasol and fan behind her, Larthi hurried to tie on her sandals.

'I'm going to order a bronze mirror for you,' Aunt Culni said while hugging the shady side of the street on their way to the eastern part of the city. Larthi was so overcome by excitement that she stood still for a moment.

'Oh, Aunt Culni, how did you guess?' was all she was able to say.

48

Bronze mirror with relief decoration of Hercle abducting Mlacuch. Probably from Vulci. London, British Museum

She had secretly longed for a mirror, as it was difficult and frustrating to try and catch a reflection of her face in a bowl of water. Occasionally she had therefore borrowed her aunt's polished bronze mirror, which was decorated with a relief and silver inlay on the back and had a handle of turned ivory. Culni kept this treasure suspended by a cord from a nail in the wall above her bed.

The metalworkers' quarter overlooked the wide torrent-bed to the north-east of the town. It was a noisy and smelly neighbourhood and lacked proper paving and drainage. The artisans' mean houses and workshops were crowded round small yards, heaped with ingots and lumps of scrap metal and piles of wood and charcoal. The air rang with the constant din of hammering; workmen beating sheet metal into shape to make bronze vessels, straightening out dented ones or joining handles to them with rivets. Acrid smoke rose from the furnaces and the dusty lanes were busy with slaves driving heavily burdened donkeys along, which jostled with each other in the narrow cracks between the houses. The plaster of their mud-brick walls had been scraped off by the projecting loads of constantly passing packed animals.

Larthi was fascinated by all the bustle but her aunt looked with distaste at the fly-blown rubbish encumbering the paths. The sweaty bodies of the grimy workmen gave out a sour smell, and the deafening clangour of their hammering made her close her eyes as if in pain. Larthi realized that it was something of a sacrifice for her aunt to have brought her to this part of the town. With relief they stepped into the shady entrance of one of the larger workshops. Its owner hastened to meet them, deferentially showing them the way into a room which gave onto a courtyard. As he beckoned to a slave to bring in some seats, Aunt Culni said, 'I want you to show us some mirrors, Ranazu.'

Her voice sounded tired. The heat in the low, windowless shed was stifling. Peci, who stood behind her mistress, began waving the long-handled fan. Ranazu went to fetch some finished mirrors while they waited in the semi-darkness. Every so often the room was lit up brightly by the flare of the furnace in the yard, where a slave was working the bellows. Larthi's eyes were getting used to the subdued light. She began to make out a workbench, a table and, hanging from the walls, tools and some whitewashed wooden plaques, covered with charcoal line-drawings. Ranazu returned with a selection of mirrors, which he displayed on a table by the door. Their highly polished reflecting-surfaces shone like gold, while the backs of the bronze discs were engraved with figures framed by ornamental designs. Aunt Culni inspected each one closely before passing it on to Larthi. The choice was difficult. Although Larthi thought that the mirrors were rather small, she liked their designs and could not make up her mind as to which was the most pleasing.

50

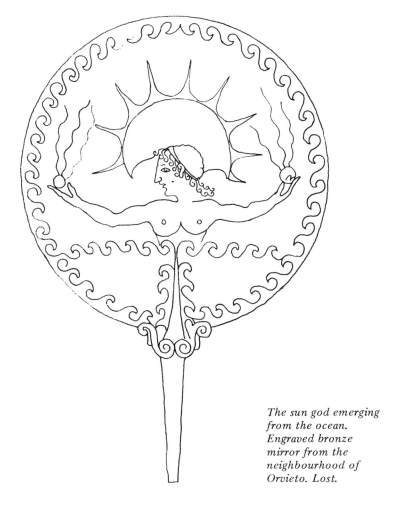

The sun god emerging from the ocean. Engraved bronze mirror from the neighbourhood of Orvieto. Lost.

'Are there no bigger ones?' Aunt Culni now asked Ranazu, as if she had read Larthi's mind. 'I find these too small to be of much use.'

'I've just recently finished casting a batch of larger ones, but they still need polishing and engraving.'

'Let's see one of them for size.'

Ranazu brought in a mirror with a bigger disc, the surface of which was still rough and dull, as it had come from the mould. Larthi seized it by its tang and held it up. Despite its weight she could handle it well. Aunt Culni nodded approvingly.

*Engraved bronze mirror
with a winged goddess
between two boys.
From Praeneste. London,
British Museum*

   'We'll have it fitted with an ivory handle,' she said. 'And now
about the design. Show us some of your patterns, Ranazu.'

   He took down a number of the wooden plaques from the
wall. Each bore a scene with figures drawn in outline and adapted
to a circle. There was the head of Usil, the sun-god, surrounded by

*Engraved bronze mirror
with a dancing maenad and
satyr. From near Viterbo.
Brussels, Musées Royaux
d'Art et d'Histoire*

rays, one of the goddess Turan with two boy attendants, another
of a girl dancing between two satyrs, a goat being led to an altar, a
banquet and finally one which Larthi recognized as the Greek
story of Eos and Kephalos: the winged goddess of dawn in a flow-
ing chiton carrying off the beautiful mortal youth she loved. The
design was framed by a tendril of flowering ivy.

53

Engraved bronze mirror with Eos and Kephalos. Berlin-Charlottenburg-Antikenabteilung

'May I have this one?' she asked, irresistibly attracted by the theme.

'You have chosen well,' Aunt Culni said with a smile, and Larthi felt that she was pleased by her choice of a Greek subject.

Ranazu promised to have the engraving done by one of his most skilled men and to deliver the finished mirror as soon as possible.

As they made their way out, Larthi heard him call to the slaves to stand by for the casting; the bronze in the crucible on the furnace was beginning to melt. She would have loved to have stayed on and watched this exciting process but Aunt Culni seemed anxious to get away from the noise and discomfort of the place, so Larthi just made the sign of good luck and hoped that Sethlans, the god of metalworkers, would favour the enterprise.

It was pleasant to reach again the western end of the town where all the great families resided. The rectangular houses here were large and set well apart, so that the slightest breeze from the sea could circulate freely. But even here the heat was oppressive and a stench rose from the drain below the cobbles. The road reflected the sun with a merciless glare. Dogs lay panting in the narrow strip of shade at the foot of the wall of their house, and even Krankru barely raised his head as they reached home.

8

Laris Matunas and his fellow-priests consulted the sacred linen books to discover which of the gods had sent the portents so disquietening to the king, what their meaning was and what measures should be taken to appease the divine powers. Their findings were ominous. They revealed that three divinities in particular had been offended by the pollution of the ancient rites and that their wrath threatened the safety of the city. Enemies both from within and without were plotting against the existing order. This danger could be averted only by the founding of a new temple, dedicated to the supreme ruler of the sky, Tinia, and to the goddesses Menerva and Uni. It was to stand in an elevated place, surveying the whole of the large territory of Caisra. The precise spot on which the foundations were to be laid out had been determined by augury, three eagles having been observed circling above it on three successive days.

The location thus designated by divine will was near a small hill-settlement, inland from the harbour of Pyrgoi. All the practical preparations for the inauguration had already been made by the local inhabitants under the supervision of the nobleman Venel Leinies, whose properties lay in the neighbourhood. The auspicious day for the ceremony was fixed and Laris Matunas, attended by his colleagues Piana Velavesnas and Larth Repesunas, was to perform the rites as representative of the king. Velthur Velchanas himself would in due course dedicate the finished building to the gods. As the place was remote from the city, the priests and their families and assistants had to allow three days for the enterprise, a complete day being devoted to the ceremony itself.

Laris Matunas with Larthi and Marce, accompanied by Teitu, Thresu and Cupe, started well before sunrise. They left Caisra by the seaward gate and soon turned north into olive-groves, passing below the rocky ridge on which the main cemetery lay. Larthi's father touched his lips devoutly with his right hand and raised it to salute the heroized dead; they all followed his example. In the pallid light of dawn the countless funerary mounds loomed eerily above their path.

'Why are your tombs so much larger than ours?' Marce asked. 'Do you bury all your freedmen and clients in them as well as members of the family?'

Laris Matunas explained that the tombs were built for the great families only, and that such size was necessary because the mound contained complete houses for the dead with chambers, pillars, doorways, windows and beds, all carved from the rock, so that in the afterlife the dead would be assured of having every necessity provided for.

'I see,' Marce said; 'but what happens to the slaves when they die?'

'They are simply buried outside,' Laris Matunas answered; 'but my freedman here might well find his place in the entrance of our tomb.' He turned with a smile to Teitu, who, despite his age, was walking sturdily beside the slave driving the packed ass.

'I hope there will be room for Peci, too,' Larthi said quickly, for she was fond of her aunt's slave.

They had left the cemetery behind and were crossing harvested fields, when the sun rose above the hills in the east. Its slanting rays made the wide expanse of stubble ahead of them shine like burnished bronze. The soil of this coastal plain was rich and yielded the best crops in the whole of the territory, much of it the property of the king.

Marce was now curious to know why low-lying land so close to the sea was not water-logged. Laris Matunas pointed to the entrance-shaft of an underground channel, cut in the porous, brownish rock beside their path, and said, 'My grandfather directed the ritual of the drainage of this area and laid out the whole network of culverts that are still in use.'

Heaps of dark soil, dumped near the mouth of the man-hole, indicated that slaves had recently cleared out the subterranean passage accessible through it.

'You see how we have to pay constant attention to keeping these drainage channels cleaned and the emissaries on the coast free of sand, so that our land does not turn marshy again.'

'Our Forum at Roma was drained by King Tarquin,' Marce said, 'and all our water-diviners are Etruscan.'

For the first time, Larthi thought that she could detect a note of pride in Marce's voice at being partly of their blood.

Stroking his short beard, her father said, 'We Rasenna have been renowned for our knowledge in this field from time imme-morial.'

'And for measuring and apportioning the land,' Marce added, much to Larthi's surprise.

As they were passing an upright boundary-stone marking the *tular*, the border, of the king's property, she stopped and told Marce to spell out the inscription on it. The rough surface made it difficult to read the uneven letters.

'Tinia has conferred sacredness on this stone . . .' he faltered, and Larthi quickly deciphered the rest for him - a malediction on those attempting to remove the boundary-stone.

'The prophetess Vecui told our ancestors that it was Tinia, who first decreed the demarcation of the land, since he knew human greed coveted its possession,' Laris Matunas explained, mindful of his duty to teach Marce the origin and meaning of the revelations in the sacred books.

They had reached the foot of the hills now and their path wound up through an open forest of oaks, chestnuts and pines. Climbing slowly, they caught occasional glimpses of the sea in the distance. Some bright specks studded the clear blue surface, the sails of ships coasting north towards Pyrgoi. Larthi was thankful for the shade. It had turned hot and, now that she possessed a mirror, she realized that a white skin would suit her better than one bronzed by the sun. She used not to care whether she got tanned or not, but recently she had begun to wish for a milky skin like Veilia, the king's wife, who never left her house without a slave holding a sunshade over her. Since she had given birth to a son, Veilia seemed even more beautiful and Larthi secretly longed to look like her.

At the start of the new day, when the sun had reached its zenith, they halted in a clearing to rest and refresh themselves. At its far end charcoal-burners had built their turf-covered kiln and were about to light it. Thresu was then able to cook a meal on their fire, while Cupe tethered the animals and Teitu spread blankets under a gnarled old oak-tree. Large trunks of felled chestnuts and pines, already stripped of their bark, were lying at the edge of the clearing, ready to be transported to the plain. Their size amazed Marce. He had never set foot in such a large forest before, though he well remembered the awe with which those people in Roma, who had ventured to travel a great distance from the city, spoke of impenetrable woods covering the Ciminian mountains. But this sun-lit, open forest surrounding him, did not seem in the least menacing.

'What do you use all that timber for?' he asked Laris Matunas, who was settling down against the trunk of the oak, having made sure that no ill-omened bird was perched in it.

'We need it mainly for building and for ships, but also for mine-props and smelting.'

'Where are the mines?'

Larthi waved her hand in a north-westerly direction, 'In the hills over there,' she said vaguely.

'And who works in them?' Marce persisted.

'Our slaves,' Laris Matunas replied.

Larthi hoped that Marce would not ask any further questions about the mines. As recalcitrant domestic slaves were sometimes sent there for punishment, they were bound to be dark and horrible places and she preferred not to think of them.

58

The appearance of Teitu and Thresu with their meal now diverted Marce's attention and he devoted himself to the business of eating with his usual vigour. Drowsy with food, heat and the humming of insects, they were about to fall asleep, when the sound of a horn suddenly came from the woods beyond the kiln. A rough-looking man in a pointed felt cap and dressed in a goat's skin, pushed his way into the clearing holding a trumpet. Behind him trotted a large herd of swine, snuffling and hunting for acorns and chestnuts under the dead leaves. Larthi burst out laughing at the sight, but Marce was amazed.

'How unusual for pigs to run after a herdsman with a trumpet. Our pigs always have to be driven along with a stick.'

'Surely you must have noticed by now that we use the horn and the flute far more than any other people,' Laris Matunas remarked, rousing himself slowly; 'our domestic animals recognize the sound and follow it.'

'Oh, but wild animals do too!' Larthi exclaimed; 'Uncle Caile told me that once, while he was out hunting, he managed to lure deer into the nets simply by playing softly on his flute.'

Ivory plaque from a small casket carved with a stag hunt. From Orvieto. Florence, Museo Archeologico

Her father did not reply, but from his derisive smile she knew what he thought of this story. The swineherd and his charges disappeared into the distance and while Larthi listened to the fading rustle in the undergrowth, she wondered why it should not be true. Was not Orpheus in the Greek tale said to have played his lyre so marvellously that not only men but beasts followed the enchanting sound?'

When Thresu and Cupe had packed their belongings they resumed their journey. After a while their path descended over rough boulders into a valley-bottom and they were forced to dismount from their mules. Reaching a stream which cascaded in smooth, glassy curves over dark stone slabs bordered by ferns, they followed its course uphill. The trees here were sparser and soon two scrub-covered, rocky outcrops came into sight, towering high above them on the left.

'The site of the new temple is just beyond that saddle,' Laris Matunas said encouragingly, as he had noticed that Larthi was flagging a little.

'I'm sure it will take us till nightfall to clamber up there,' she moaned when her father silenced her suddenly by holding out his arm. Following his eyes, she saw a woodpecker on the trunk of a fir ahead on the right; they had disturbed it in its hammering. The bird spread its wings and disappeared noiselessly between the treetops.

'A good omen,' Laris Matunas breathed, 'Had it flown towards us or crossed our path to the left, it would have been most inauspicious.'

Larthi began to feel tired. She had slipped several times on the moss-covered stones and the bronze hinge of one of her sturdy wooden sandals had worked loose, causing a sore on the sole of her right foot. Only the thought that her father might regret having asked her to accompany him, stopped her from complaining.

As they toiled slowly uphill, Laris Matunas tried to distract her with stories about the place they were going to visit.

'We're going to a very old settlement,' he said, 'people lived there even in the days before the Rasenna became masters of the land. There are many caves in the rocks around here which served as houses and tombs for these early men; and even now herdsmen,

60

who use the caves as shelters, sometimes find stone tools and weapons in them that belonged to those ancient people.' Emerging from the woods, they saw above them a great cone of rock dominating some houses on a grass-covered col. The pasture was dotted with countless sheep, whose faint bleating could be heard from time to time.

'That's where we shall be spending the night,' said Laris Matunas pointing ahead and Larthi took heart again. But it was almost evening before they reached the first cottages. They were approached by fiercely barking dogs who came running towards them and soon they were surrounded by children and country-folk who gazed at the strangers in wonder. Laris Matunas sent Teitu ahead to inform Venel Leinies of their arrival. He was the chief landowner, whose large house stood at the foot of the pinnacle of rock. When they had recovered their breath, Larthi and Marce turned to look back over the steep hillside which they had just climbed. The forests and the coastal plain were plunged into shadow and in the distance the sea began to turn the colour of fading roses with the sinking sun.

'I can just make out our harbour Pyrgoi there,' Larthi said; 'and on the shore this side of that shallow promontory lies the sanctuary of the goddess Uni.'

'The territory of Caisra is much larger than I imagined,' said Marce, surprised. 'Compared with Roma, your city is quite small but I didn't realize that so much arable land and pasture belonged to it, as well as all these woods.'

'The people up here are mainly shepherds, who make the big cheeses you like so much.' Laris Matunas smiled at him. 'Venel Leinies is sure to have a good supply of them.'

Even Larthi began to feel hungry and she was glad to see Teitu return with several slaves, led by a very large nobleman, whose progress was made slow by his obesity. Venel Leinies was as friendly as he was fat. His face shone with sweat and he apologized for keeping them waiting and for the simplicity of their reception. Larthi sensed that their host regarded her father, the representative of the king, with great awe.

When the travellers had washed and refreshed themselves, they lay down to a large dinner of country food, together with the family of Venel Leinies and the two haruspices, colleagues of Laris Matunas from Caisra, who had come up with their slaves by a different route. Thana, the youngest of their host's seven daughters, had taken a fancy to Larthi and ran up to her couch several times to bring her a wreath of flowers she had made and tit-bits of food. When they had finished eating and Larthi had played with the child for a while, Thana suddenly whispered that she was going to give Larthi a present. She tripped out to fetch it. Her tiny fist was tightly closed when she returned and she held it behind her back teasingly:

'What do you think it is?'

'A flower?' Larthi guessed, deliberately wrongly.

Thana shook her head delightedly.

'A stone?'

The little girl looked uncertain. 'I don't know,' she faltered and hesitantly opened her fist.

Larthi saw what looked like an arrow-head, fashioned from a light-coloured stone.

'Lathite, our head-shepherd, gave it to me. He found it in the big cave and father says it's very old. Would you like it?'

'I would love it.' Larthi took the gift from the child's hot little hand. It felt crisp and sharp as if it had been made yesterday.

'It's beautiful; thank you very much for it!'

When Larthi showed it to her father later on, he said that he had never seen anything so finely wrought from stone and suggested that she have it set in gold as an amulet to hang from her necklace.

9

The family of Venel Leinies as well as the local landowners and all the villagers who were not needed as labourers, had assembled on a grassy knoll overlooking the spot where the inauguration ceremony was to take place. Larthi and Marce stood in front so that they could follow the ritual closely.

A sacrifice was performed first, accompanied by flute-music. The victims were a pig, a sheep and a bull of flawless beauty and adorned with fillets. Sacrificial attendants killed them on an altar built of turf squares, while Laris Matunas pronounced the appropriate prayers. When the sheep's entrails had been taken out, he stepped towards the altar to inspect the liver, intoning the ritual formula. Placing his left foot on a low rock, he held the liver in his left hand and aligned it with the north-south axis of the sky. Beginning in the north and moving east and thence onwards, he

Sacrifice at an altar. Low relief on a limestone sarcophagus from Chiusi. Paris, Louvre

carefully traced with his right hand the individual parts of the liver, corresponding to the seats of the gods in their sixteen heavenly regions. Soon he was able to announce that the liver was perfectly formed and that the divinities had entered into their respective places. It augured well.

Marce had been following every movement and word of Laris Matunas during this vital part of the ceremony. He, too, held a liver in his left hand, but a model one, made of bronze. Engraved on its surface were forty individual compartments with the names of the divinities in the proper sequence according to their regions in the heavens. It was a teaching-model of a liver which Laris Matunas had handed to Marce, so that he could familiarize himself with the practice of relating its parts to the divisions of the sky ruled by the different gods - microcosm mirroring macrocosm.

Larthi observed her father with intense pride. Taller than his two colleagues, he moved with innate dignity and authority. Over his short-sleeved linen tunic he wore a sheepskin with the fleece

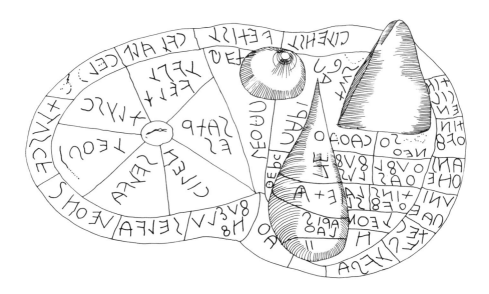

Bronze model of a sheep's liver engraved with the names of Etruscan, divinities. Piacenza, Museo Civico

inwards, pinned at the chest with a large bronze fibula of old-fashioned shape. His dark brown hair was covered by a cap with a tall conical top and tied by two straps under the chin. The other two priests wore the same traditional clothes of the *netśvis*.

The whole area of the future temple was marked off by woollen fillets and wreaths. Boys and girls, whose parents were both still alive, held branches of fruit-bearing trees and, having dipped them into buckets of fresh spring-water, sprinkled the ground freely. After the pertinent parts of the sacrificial victims due to the gods had been offered on the altar, Laris Matunas implored Tinia, Uni and Menerva to lend their assistance to the work about to begin and to view its completion with favour. He then stepped into the centre of the sacred area and stood with his back to the north, holding his augural staff with its spiral crook in his right hand. With the point of this lituus he drew a circle, dividing the visible space in front of him - sky and earth - into four parts by tracing from the cardinal points two lines at right angles, which crossed each other where he stood. Following the lines with his eyes, he defined and named the front and the back, the left and the right.

64

As he did so, Larthi heard Marce murmur *'pars antica, pars postica, pars familiaris, pars hostilis.'* Turning towards her, he said excitedly, 'Our augurs divide the templum in exactly the same way, only it's a square they start with.'

Bronze votive statuette, of a haruspex.
Vatican, Museo Gregoriano Etrusco

'Hush,' Larthi whispered, putting her index-finger against her lips. 'You mustn't disturb the ceremony - father is still observing the regions of the sky.' She gazed apprehensively into the distance, where a swarm of crows were circling the rocks towering above the house of Venel Leinies. Their raucous screeching alarmed her - what if these ill-omened birds were to fly towards the sacred site?

While they waited in absolute silence - with only Laris Matunas moving his lips - a large eagle suddenly appeared in the north-eastern quarter of the sky and sailed slowly and majestically over the watching crowd. Laris Matunas' two fellow-priests turned to look at him in amazement. Exalted by his success in obtaining this extraordinary omen, he consulted briefly with them and announced that this most favourable sign had been granted by Tinia himself, emanating, as it did, from the auspicious first region of the heavens. A murmur of pleasure and satisfaction came from the assembled people.

With the help of his colleagues and attendants Laris Matunas now proceeded to mark out the plan of the temple on the ground, using the sun to get the bearings and the groma for measuring. The building was to contain one chamber each for the cult-figures of the three divinities, to be set side by side against a blank back wall. The larger central chamber would be reserved for Tinia, the smaller, flanking chambers being assigned to the goddesses. A deep porch with columns was to form the façade of the temple. It was to be approached by a flight of steps, and a spacious enclosure with an altar was to be laid out in front of it. A sacrificial pit had been dug, in which Laris Matunas now deposited the remains of the slaughtered animals together with votive offerings of gold, silver and bronze. After that, the large foundation-stone, wound round with woollen fillets, was pulled into place above the pit and the priests pronounced the ritual words, touching the fillets as they did so. This marked the end of the inauguration ceremony. Once Laris Matunas had rejoined them, Marce enquired why a temple with a triple cella was being built in such a small and unimportant village.

'Surely,' he said, 'only proper cities should have a capitolium, dedicated to Jupiter, Juno and Minerva. We in Roma are just finishing a big new temple for the Capitoline Triad.'

66

Model of an archaic Etruscan temple

Laris Matunas suppressed a smile and replied, 'However small this settlement, it is part of the great city of Caisra. But above all, there is no doubt about the expressed will of the gods. Do not forget that Tinia himself decreed the nature of the sanctuary to be built here.'

Venel Leinies now showed them the newly cut stones from a nearby quarry to be used for the foundations of the temple, as well as large stacks of seasoned timber for the superstructure already lying on a level site close at hand. The master-builder, a man from Caisra, was to live in Venel Leinies' house, while the actual work would be carried out by local labourers under his supervision. Once the building was finished, craftsmen were going to face the wooden parts of the temple with coloured terracotta plaques, tiles and decorative figures, moulded and fired in workshops of Caisra.

'King Tarquin brought the Etruscan sculptor Vulca from Veii to Roma to make a clay statue of Jupiter for our new temple on the Capitol,' Marce said proudly.

Laris Matunas smiled at him and then at his daughter. From the little wink he gave her, Larthi knew that by now it was no longer necessary for her to remind Marce that Ruma depended on them for all its more civilized needs.

10

Larthi felt unsettled and depressed; once again one of her headaches seemed imminent. However, she could not refuse to accompany Aunt Culni on a walk in the orchard when asked, as she had
just got up after spending several days in bed again. Although
weak and somewhat unsteady on her feet, Aunt Culni insisted that
she needed nothing but fresh air. As Larthi led her out into the
autumn sunshine, she was struck by her aunt's sickly pallor. So far
Culni had not allowed Sombrotidas to examine her, despite his
regular visits to their house to see Elachsantre. Whenever Larthi
suggested that they ask the doctor's advice, Aunt Culni protested
that she felt no pain. It was obvious, however, that she was getting
weaker every day, and her beautiful chestnut-coloured hair had
lost its sheen and even showed some strands of grey.

Larthi made an effort to chat gaily, despite her alarm at her
aunt's state, while Culni clung to her arm as they walked slowly
into the shade of the fruit-trees. Over the years Peci and Fasti had
helped their mistress to make the garden a particularly fine and
productive one. The sight of flowers and ripening fruit used to give
her great pleasure and satisfaction, but now she only had disparag-
ing comments to make.

'They have let it all go to seed,' she said shaking her head
mournfully. Look at the herbs here, they are being strangled by
weeds.'

'Fasti had to pick all the apples and pears and store them,'
Larthi said apologetically, 'and Peci, as you know, has been looking after you, so there wasn't much time for them to do the weed-
ing.'

'Fasti should have got one of the male slaves from the fields
to help her, if she couldn't keep the garden tidy by herself. These
apple-trees will need pruning soon.'

'Do you know,' Larthi said in an attempt to distract her, 'I
believe Elachsantre has come here several times recently. Sombrotidas told me he's seen him wandering about under the trees. He

was pleased because he felt the visit might have soothed Elachsantre's mind.'

They had reached the far end of the garden, where the rocky plateau of the town dropped precipitously into the valley below. The place was a natural look-out and Larthi loved leaning on the wall here to enjoy the fine view of the sea and of the busy road leading south into the coastal plain. Hundreds of swallows were wheeling and diving at the edge of the honey-coloured cliff.

Aunt Culni, who hardly ever ventured as far, stepped back from the parapet and said, 'Let's go back. Looking down into that valley makes me feel quite giddy. I wish people wouldn't throw all their rubbish here,' she added petulantly. Even Larthi had to admit that this end of their garden was somewhat neglected, with broken tools and stakes lying about and roses and bindweed forming a thicket which was slowly invading the path. Suddenly Aunt Culni gripped her arm and said in an agitated voice, 'I believe there is a black fig-tree growing over there.'

Larthi glanced at the shadowy corner to which she was pointing and made out the twisted dark shape of the tree amongst a tangle of ivy. 'You are right,' she said, at the same time clutching her head as a stab of pain pierced her left temple.

'How they could have overlooked such an ill-omened tree, I cannot understand, Aunt Culni said, full of misgiving. 'We must have it removed and burnt at once. Go and get Fasti and two of the men to bring axes and a saw.'

Larthi urged her aunt to go and rest meanwhile, but she would not hear of it. Upset and weakened, she sat down on a nearby well-head, while Larthi hurried back to the house to call the slaves. When they returned, Aunt Culni ordered the men to cut down the tree and dig out its roots, 'No trace of it must be left, lest it attract disaster. I will see myself that this is carried out properly.'

The screeching noise of the saw set Larthi's teeth on edge. When the slaves had almost cut through the thickness of the trunk, it suddenly keeled over with a moaning sound and crashed to the ground, narrowly missing them. They were just beginning to hack at the roots when Fasti, who had been squatting beside them, called out, 'Mistress! The soil here's been disturbed. It looks if someone's been digging at the bottom of this tree and it certainly wasn't me.'

'Go and see what it is,' Aunt Culni said to Larthi; 'I'm not up to it.' Pressing her hand against her throbbing forehead, Larthi went over to the tree-stump and crouched down to inspect the soil beneath it. There was no doubt about it, the earth looked as if it had been freshly turned over - dark and loose.

'Take the spade and dig carefully,' she said to Fasti, 'we had better find out what's been going on.'

Fasti had lifted only two shovels of soil, when Larthi saw a metallic gleam amongst the roots of the fig-tree. She stopped her maid and pulled from the hole a strip of lead, rolled up and transfixed by a nail. She opened it out and wiped it clean on a clump of grass. It was an elongated tablet with writing scratched on it. When Larthi stepped into a sunny spot to read the inscription, she was surprised to find it was Greek.

'Tell me what it is,' Aunt Culni said anxiously, struggling up from her seat.

'It's a curse,' Larthi answered, once she had deciphered it; she felt sick with her headache and for a moment pondered whether to keep the truth from her aunt, but decided that she could not - it was far too serious. 'I have put a curse on the hateful Marce and the Spurinna family and the whole family of Laris Matunas and I have consecrated them all to the powers of the underworld,' she translated hesitantly.

Aunt Culni sank back with a gasp and the slaves dropped their tools and shrieked with horror.

'Be quiet!' said Larthi sternly to them, pulling herself together. 'This is the senseless deed of a madman. It has no significance. Dig up these roots at once and burn them and every bit of the tree.'

She went over to the well-head and scratched through the inscription on the lead with the nail before throwing the tablet into the depth of the disused shaft and making over it the sign to avert evil.

'Come on, Fasti,' she said, 'help me take your mistress back to the house.'

The slaves returned to their work reluctantly, while Larthi and the maid supported Aunt Culni, who kept clutching at her throat. They had barely managed to lead her a few steps, when someone could be heard rushing towards them and calling Aunt Culni's name.

'What is it?' Larthi shouted back, dreading some fresh disaster. She was relieved to see Marce appearing between the trees. 'Come and help us,' she begged. He was panting and looked distracted.

'Don't be alarmed,' Larthi tried to reassure him, although at that moment she suddenly knew that misfortune must have struck him as well; 'It is just that Aunt Culni has overdone it,' she went on mechanically; 'she is not strong enough to walk so far and must lie down now. I don't feel all that strong myself, so would you mind carrying her back to the house with Fasti?'

Marce pressed his lips together grimly and nodded. He lifted up Aunt Culni who leaned limply against his shoulder with her eyes closed. With great care he carried her to her bed and put her down gently. Fasti went to fetch Peci first and then hurried to get Sombrotidas.

As Larthi bent over her aunt's bed to cover her with a blanket, Marce muttered, 'A messenger has just come from my father. He is on his way here accompanying King Tarquin and his relations. There has been a revolution in Roma and the royal family has been expelled.'

11

The past two weeks had been so full of unexpected events and the coming and going of kings, councillors and messengers, that even Larthi felt that life could be too exciting. All existing order seemed upset and complete uncertainty reigned as to the future. Larthi saw little of her father, whose advice was constantly sought by the king. Avile Spurinna had left on a mission on behalf of the exiled Tarquins, taking Marce with him. Now that he had gone, Larthi began to miss Marce; for just recently he had changed from being a burden into a trusted helper. Now that her father was frequently absent from home and Aunt Culni completely bedridden, much of the running of the household rested on Larthi's shoulders. Elach-santre's alarming and unpredictable behaviour had added to her worries, so that Marce's sturdy presence was reassuring.

She was not alone in wishing him back. Ramtha had turned up once or twice with her writing-tablet, as if the continuation of their lessons were her main concern; but in fact she was anxious for news.

'Marce has gone to Tarchuna with his father and I don't know when he'll be back,' Larthi told her, surmising the reason for her latest visit. Ramtha looked upset and said, 'Oh, I had hoped that now that his father and the King of Ruma have come to Caisra, Marce might have stayed here for ever.'

'Nobody can know what the gods have decreed. Meanwhile King Tarquin is sending two of his sons to Veii to ask for help and troops and Marce's father is trying to get assistance from Tarchuna. Later he may even go to plead with King Porsenna of Clevsina.'

'Does King Tarquin want to go back to Ruma then?' Ramtha asked incredulously. 'I would be frightened to return after what had happened there.'

'Of course, he wants to be restored to power! But it may be difficult because he has so many enemies in Ruma.'

'But who are they and why don't they want him to be their king any more?'

'I'm afraid it isn't easy for us to understand. Father told me there were many different factions in Ruma, who were conspiring to get rid of the Tarquins, each for their own reason. They finally succeeded when the king was away from the city on a campaign. His eldest son fled to Gabii, but was killed there. The other sons managed to escape, however, and join their father.'

'It must be awful to be so disliked by one's own people,' Ramtha said pensively.

'The people of Ruma are by no means all Rasenna,' Larthi reminded her; 'on the contrary. And all those others, who are not of our blood, are likely to want to free themselves of what they think of as foreign tyrants. You know that the Tarquins made the people do a lot of slaves' work for them, like draining the Forum and building a huge new temple on the citadel. They may well have resented that.'

72

'But I've heard a rumour that the Tarquins were opposed even by some of their own countrymen who had settled in Ruma, and I simply cannot understand that,' Ramtha went on.

'I think there are quite a number of Rasenna families in Ruma, not related to the Tarquins, who envy them their power. Father mentioned that King Porsenna of Clevsina had partisans living there, too, who would like him to become king. Ruma, you see, controls the river and therefore the passage of all the goods down to the coast, whereas Clevsina has no port of its own and needs one badly.'

'I wish all the Rasenna cities were friendly with each other,' Ramtha said with a sigh.

'So do I,' Larthi agreed, 'but there is envy and unrest everywhere in the world. I believe there is another faction in Ruma, who have become rich through commerce, who want to have good relations with the Carthaginians, so that they can trade without hindrance along the coast to the south. These people resent the friendship between the Tarquins and the Greeks of Kyme, who are enemies of the Carthaginians.'

Ramtha raised her hand to her forehead. 'It's all too confusing. I still don't quite understand it. Marce told me how much the Tarquins did for Ruma and for the Rasenna there. They gave Marce's father a splendid house on a street they call the Vicus Tuscus. I would be proud to be ruled by such a family.'

Larthi could not help smiling. Ramtha was so touching in her loyalty to Marce and everyone related to him.

'I've been thinking about it a lot,' she then said, turning serious again, 'I'm afraid that something like that might happen here, too, one day.'

'Oh, no!' Ramtha exclaimed, gazing at Larthi, terrified. 'Surely everyone in Caisra likes the Lauchume and his family. Nobody would ever want to overthrow our king!'

'I hope not,' Larthi raised her fingers to ward off evil, 'but we don't know what the gods hold in store for us.' Putting her arm round Ramtha's shoulder, she added affectionately 'I'll let you know as soon as we've heard anything from Marce.'

12

Larthi stood in front of the house by the mule-cart piled high with linen to be washed in the stream which rose below the small sanctuary of Selvans outside the city. She was giving instructions to Cupe and the maids, telling them to make good speed, as the days were getting shorter, when Ramtha came up the street. She was carrying a basket full of apples.

'My mother has sent me,' she said. 'These are for your aunt. How is she?'

'Would you like to come in and see her?' Larthi replied, motioning Cupe to move off with the cart. 'I've got to give her her medicine.'

'I hope she doesn't mind visitors,' Ramtha said as they went indoors.

'No, but you'll find her changed,' Larthi warned her, fetching the small jar that Sombrotidas had brought some days before. 'Don't let her see that you've noticed any change in her.'

Aunt Culni was propped up high on her bed, supported on large, tasselled cushions. She had been coughing and was visibly out of breath. Larthi pulled up the striped woollen blankets, which had slipped down, and tucked them round her aunt's thin shoulders. The sick woman could only smile at Ramtha who prattled away, attempting to hide her shock at such wasted looks.

'Don't you want the brazier a bit closer to you?' Larthi asked, wheeling the open bronze box nearer to the bed; 'it's quite cold in here.'

'Don't bother, please,' Aunt Culni whispered, as Larthi poked the smouldering charcoal pieces with the fire-rake, shaped like a human hand, blowing on them at the same time. 'I'm warm enough; all I want is more air. I have asked Peci to take the hangings from the window, but it doesn't seem to make any difference.'

'Sombrotidas' medicine will ease your breathing,' Larthi said soothingly and poured some of the liquid into a cup of water.

Bronze torch-holder. Switzerland.
Private collection

'I want to talk to him,' Aunt Culni gasped after drinking it and getting over another bout of coughing. 'Send one of the slaves to fetch him, please. It concerns Elachsantre. I have thought a lot about him: I might get better if we did the right thing . . .' She leant back into her cushions exhausted and closed her eyes.

'Can you stay here while I call Peci?' Larthi asked Ramtha, who watched Aunt Culni's pale face apprehensively.

'Do be quick,' she said in a low voice. 'I couldn't bear to be alone with your aunt if anything were to happen to her.'

As Larthi hurried out to send for the doctor, she wondered what Aunt Culni had in mind. Laris Matunas had refused to punish Elachsantre for his curse on the Spurinna family and his own, as it might have made matters worse. So Elachsantre had continued to haunt their house and the garden like a ghost, murmuring to himself and shunned by everyone. He seemed to Larthi to belong to another world, and the sight of his scarred, gaunt face filled her with fear and pity.

When she got back to Aunt Culni's bedside, Ramtha jumped up from her stool with obvious relief.

'Your aunt's asleep,' she whispered; 'I think I'd better go home now. Shall I come back again tomorrow to see how she's getting on?'

'Do,' Larthi said, 'and perhaps there will be some news from Tarchuna by then.'

Dusk was falling when Sombrotidas arrived. Peci brought in two bronze candelabra, stuck candles to their spikes and lit them with a taper. The flickering light lit up the small bronze figures forming the candelabras' finials, making them appear alive. The physician looked at them intrigued.

'Your bronze utensils are beautiful and useful,' he said, 'and I've got accustomed to the candlelight of the Tyrrhenians now; in Greece we light our rooms with oil-lamps.' Bending forward in his chair, which was covered with a sheepskin, he warmed his hands over the charcoal-brazier, caressing one of the small bronze horses that decorated its four corners. 'I like this as well,' he added, full of admiration. As Larthi had always assumed that all Greek things were finer than any others, she was surprised and pleased by his appreciation of Etruscan utensils.

'I'm glad that you like our bronze-work. From the way Elachsantre always spoke, I got the impression that the Greeks looked upon us as barbarians and despised the way we lived and the things we produced.'

'You're entirely wrong. Tyrrhenian bronzes are famous in Greece and as for your gold and silver tableware, it is without compare.'

Aunt Culni stirred on hearing these words and opened her eyes. 'Peci,' she said slowly, 'get me the golden cup that belonged to my grandmother from the chest in the corner; it is wrapped in a linen cloth.'

Gold cup decorated with granulation. From Praeneste. London, Victoria and Albert Museum

Larthi was surprised. With the exception of her Greek vases, this cup was Aunt Culni's most treasured possession. She never used it and had shown it to Larthi only twice. What could she possibly want to do with it now? Peci carefully placed the linen bundle on Aunt Culni's lap.

'Larthi, unwrap my cup and show it to the Greek physician,' Aunt Culni said.

The girl stepped forward to do as she was told. When she held out the cup to Sombrotidas, the candlelight illuminated the innumerable little gold granules which patterned the fluted surface, making it glitter like wind-ruffled sea in the sun. Sombrotidas gasped at the sight of it and took the cup in both his hands, admiring it as he swung it backwards and forwards.

'This is the finest piece of workmanship I have ever come across,' he exclaimed; 'I remember once seeing some old jewellery in Kameiros on Rhodes, decorated with small granules of gold like this, but it was nothing compared to the scale and perfection of this.'

'I am grateful for your kindness in coming to see me and I'm glad that you like my cup,' said Aunt Culni addressing herself to Sombrotidas.

'I have learnt to appreciate many things in this city and in this house and I come here with pleasure,' he replied.

'May I ask your advice on a matter that has much concerned me of late?'

'The Lady Larthi has told me that it's something to do with Alexandros, the son of Timachidas.'

Aunt Culni nodded and went on 'The gods have willed that this youth should come to harm while in our service and though it was through no fault of ours, I feel that we should make amends.'

Sombrotidas agreed sadly.

'I would not wish to add any further injury to those already done to Greeks by residents of this town, but such things happen and we must atone for them. Many years ago when we repented of our treatment of the Phocaeans, we dedicated many valuable gifts to Apulu at Delphi that are are still kept in our treasury there. As you are familiar with the sanctuary you will know if this cup would be an acceptable offering for the god.'

Sombrotidas rose from his chair and held up the cup considering it before answering, 'It is more than worthy of such an honour and will surely give joy to Pythian Apollo.'

Aunt Culni smiled wanly and continued: 'I have given much thought to who should take this gift to Delphi. At first I had

78

hoped to do it myself, but now I am certain that I'm nearing the end of my allotted life-span.'

It had never occurred to Larthi that her aunt might die. Overcome with grief, she crouched down by the bedside and burst into tears. Aunt Culni stretched out her thin, white hand and laid it on the girl's shoulder.

'Don't cry, Larthi,' she said gently; 'it is our destiny. We all have the duration of our life apportioned to us individually, just as that of the whole nation is immutably fixed by the gods . . .' She was interrupted by an attack of coughing. But Peci, who always had an infusion of herbs sweetened with honey ready for her mistress in the evening, raised her up and gave her some of this soothing drink.

Sombrotidas meanwhile had become strangely silent, listening intently and watching the candlelight with an abstracted expression.

Aunt Culni, restored after the drink, continued, 'My next thought was to send Elachsantre to Delphi instead, but I fear his condition would not allow it. He would have to be accompanied by someone to look after him and see him safely through the hazards of the long journey.'

Delphi - Larthi suddenly saw in front of her mind's eye a mountainous, deeply indented coast and, under rocky peaks, encircled by eagles, a sanctuary whose shining temples was surrounded by countless statues of marble and bronze. Absorbed by this vision, she only half listened to what Aunt Culni said, 'I have talked to my brother-in-law about my intentions and he has suggested that we should arrange for Elachsantre to be accompanied not only to Delphi, but back to his native island and to the house of his father.'

Larthi was momentarily taken aback, struck by how little she knew what was in her father's mind. He was prepared to give a slave his freedom and return him home, despite his having put a deadly curse on the whole family! This was not the usual way to treat a rebellious slave; others would have had Elachsantre flogged or sent to the mines or to drain marshes.

At this point, Sombrotidas turned towards Aunt Culni with an enlightened expression. 'Some god must have put this thought into the mind of Laris Matunas,' he exclaimed; 'For months now I have been thinking of going to Delphi to consult the oracle about the chances of ending my exile. Nobody wants to eat his heart out far away from home when old age is approaching. The Pythia will not deny a speedy answer to one of the Asclepiades, when all the sacrifices have been duly offered. For the promanteia, the privilege to ask the god's advice before all the others, was granted to my family because my father Chrysos, the son of Nebros, died heroically fighting on the side of the Delphians in the Sacred War. If the god's reply from the tripod is favourable,' Sombrotidas raised his open palms in supplication, 'the priests of rocky Pytho will purify me with Apollo's laurel and the waters of the sacred spring. Then I shall no longer be sullied by the infringement of an ancient religious law, unwittingly committed in my youth. Once cleansed, I shall offer up your shining cup to Phoibos Apollon and take Alexandros with me to Cos. His father will surely come there in one of his ships to bring him back to Lindos.'

Aunt Culni's sunken eyes lit up as she understood what Sombrotidas had said. 'A great weight has been lifted off my mind.' She made the gesture of adoration. 'Let us implore the gods for their help.'

The others silently followed her example.

While Peci attended to a guttering candle and carefully wrapped up the gold cup again, Sombrotidas continued, 'I shall have to wait for the spring and the beginning of the sailing season before setting out. Meanwhile, would you like me to take Alexandros into my house, so that I can look after him better and prepare him for the journey?'

Aunt Culni looked at him with gratitude. 'His master will have to decide that, but I think Laris Matunas will not fail to see that your kind suggestion must have been prompted by the gods, who do not wish Elachsantre to remain in this house any longer.'

Larthi suddenly felt immensely relieved. Surely, now that her aunt had promised her beautiful cup to the Delphic god and her father was going to grant freedom to Elachsantre, his curse would be powerless and all the misfortune that had already begun to descend on their families might be stemmed. Larthi saw Sombrotidas out of the house, but in the general relief and excitement of the moment she only thanked him and totally forgot to ask him what he thought of his patient's condition.

13

Aunt Culni's strength slowly ebbed away. Larthi tried desperately to think of how she might prevail on the gods to relent and prolong the life-span they had allotted to her aunt. On a sudden impulse she asked Peci to come with her to the bronze-workers' quarter where she had chosen a figurine representing a noble lady from one of the workshops for votive bronzes. It was about a hand high, exquisitely modelled and finely engraved. Larthi had deliberately selected a statuette which resembled Aunt Culni as closely as possible. She felt convinced that if she were to dedicate this lovely figure to Hera in the Greek goddess's sanctuary in the town, Hera would be pleased and inclined to grant her prayer to extend Aunt Culni's life. Ramtha offered to accompany Larthi to the temple and was waiting for her as she came from the sick-room.

'I must just tell Peci to heat some water for my aunt and then we can go,' Larthi said.

It had turned cold and misty; Larthi had shivered while sitting by Aunt Culni's bedside, who had wanted the window open all the time and complained that the fumes from the brazier made her cough. In trying to think of some way of keeping her warm under her blankets, it had occurred to Larthi to fill a goat's skin, normally used for wine, with hot water instead.

Ramtha wore a thick woollen cloak and Larthi, too, wrapped her own tightly around her. After Larthi had picked up the bronze figurine, the two girls set out in the direction of the market-place. Larthi did not say one word about her intentions to Aunt Culni herself, but Peci knew of her plan and encouraged her to carry it out. Both of them could not bear waiting inactively for spring to come, when Sombrotidas would take the gold cup to Delphi. The god Apulu might chose to make Aunt Culni better, but by then it might well be too late; she was wasting away fast.

'I can't understand why you don't take your offering to the temple of Uni or Thanur, our own goddesses,' Ramtha said in a tone of censure; 'I think that might be more helpful.'

Bronze votive statuette of a woman walking. From Falterona. London, British Museum

'I don't know; but I have a feeling that Aunt Culni would prefer me to pray to Hera rather than Uni for her recovery. And you must remember, the curse was written in Greek and by a Greek.'

One could hear in the distance the melancholy cry of wild geese travelling south. Winter had come unusually early and in the bleak landscape which they overlooked from the plateau of the city, only the wooded ridges on the eastern horizon still retained some colour in the dry foliage of their oak-trees.

Approaching the road leading into the market, the girls noticed a mass of people milling about.

'How odd,' Ramtha said, 'the market must have finished hours ago. I can't think why there's still such a crowd here.'

'It is strange - and they are all foreigners and slaves. What can they be doing here? Oh, look! There's Uncle Caile!'

He ran past them in the direction of Cousin Velthur's house but failed to notice them. Larthi hurried after him and caught hold of his arm: 'Uncle Caile, can you tell me what's going on here?'

He turned round and retorted indignantly, 'It's scandalous! Seditious speeches in the market while the king is sitting in court. These people must have chosen this moment deliberately. I just happened to be passing when I overheard what was going on. I must report it to the Lauchume immediately.'

He hurried on. Larthi stood perplexed. Who could be trying to incite such a rabble while the members of all the respectable old families were attending the weekly dispensation of justice by the king?

Ramtha said tremulously, 'Do you think it is wise to go on? I don't like the look of these people.'

'I'm not going to be put off by a crowd like that,' Larthi retorted and made for the square, looking as haughty as possible.

Ramtha followed her reluctantly. Whatever had caused the excitement seemed to be over. Larthi could not make out a single prominent person who might have addressed the crowd. People were still arguing and gesturing in little groups, but the meeting had clearly broken up. No one paid any attention to the girls, though they were jostled occasionally by men trying to get away quickly. They had almost reached the far end of the market-place, when a couple of ruffians, who had been shouting to the bystanders, turned upon them with insulting remarks. Larthi, indignant as much as frightened, chose to walk on ignoring them.

Man seizing a woman. Low relief on a limestone funerary monument from Chiusi. Copenhagen, Ny Carlsberg Glyptotek

'Ah, the lady's too grand to notice a mere slave,' jeered the bigger of the two. 'I'll teach you who's going to be master here soon!' He seized the tasselled corner of Larthi's mantle to pull her round so that she had to look at him.

'Let go of my mantle at once, or I'll have you flogged,' she said, staring into his scarred face, barely able to keep her voice steady.

Ramtha, cowering behind her, whispered anxiously, 'Please, be quiet and come away.'

'You just wait and see what I'll do to you!' the slave hissed, gripping Larthi's arm and squeezing it painfully. 'The days are numbered when you can trample us under.'

A group of people had quickly collected around them. They were shouting and egging on the bully. He began to twist Larthi's arm, trying to force her down to her knees. She almost fainted with pain. However, she managed to summon up what strength remained and hit out at him with the bronze figurine which she had been clutching in her right hand. It struck the man's collar-bone and with a howl he let go of her arm to reach for the bruise. There was an uproar amongst the bystanders - then sudden silence. Before her attacker could assault Larthi again, a carefully dressed young man, whose face seemed vaguely familiar to her, pushed him aside and a number of retainers armed with sticks came running up. Her rescuer shouted at the mob to get out of the way and had the two slaves seized by his followers. To Larthi's intense relief the crowd meekly obeyed; they seemed to accept the authority of this person. He ordered them to leave the square and they dispersed with hardly a murmur.

Now that the danger had passed, Larthi felt near to collapse; but Ramtha was sobbing so hysterically that she felt obliged to pull herself together to comfort her. When she had become a little calmer, Larthi turned to the young man gratefully and said, 'Thank you for your help. It must have been the goddess to whom I was on my way, who sent you. I must go now and make my offering to her.'

'Surely, Larthi' Ramtha said plaintively while drying her eyes, 'you can't be thinking of going to the temple of Hera now! Some more of these brutes might be lurking about still - I just couldn't bear you to come to any harm!'

Herakles protecting a goddess. Decorative group from a bronze tripod. Copenhagen, Ny Carlsberg Glyptotek

'The daughter of Laris Matunas is quite safe to continue on her way - I myself will accompany her,' their rescuer said, gazing intently at Larthi.

'There's no need for that,' she replied. 'I'm not afraid to go by myself. The goddess has already shown me her protection.'

As she spoke, it occurred to her that this young man looked not unlike Hercle, the hero who saved Hera when she was attacked by satyrs; his sturdy build and curly hair reminded her strongly of statues of the hero and his stout, knotty stick might almost have passed for Hercle's club.

'I would feel safe to come, too, if you would only let . . .' Ramtha turned towards the young man appealing for his name - 'Thefarie Velianas accompany us.'

Larthi immediately recognized his name as that of the victor in the chariot-race during the games earlier in the year. He was now giving orders to his attendants who were standing guard over the two slaves and they led away the two subdued and miserable looking figures. Larthi was in two minds about his offer to escort them but tried not to appear ungrateful. Shaking back her hair, dishevelled in the struggle, she adjusted her mantle and said to

Ramtha, 'Let's go, then. If Thefarie Velianas wishes to accompany us as far as the temple-enclosure, I'm not going to prevent him. But once we are inside, nobody can harm us.'

'Oh, I am relieved,' Ramtha said and thus they set out together, soon reaching the street at the end of which they could see the broad roof of the temple with its coloured end-tiles rising into the leaden sky.

Larthi was surprised to hear her friend chatting so freely with Thefarie Velianas, when only a moment before she had been sobbing in an uncontrolled way. Feeling worn out and weak now, she was in no mood to talk herself, but she could not help noticing that Thefarie Velianas kept giving her sidelong glances, when not answering Ramtha's nervous questions. Though he never addressed Larthi directly, she sensed that he was more interested in her than in Ramtha. She was flattered and almost tempted to join in the conversation, but exhaustion and a reticence which she could not explain, kept her silent. She tried to concentrate on the task awaiting her in the temple. Yet, since they had left home so much had happened that it appeared to her that within the last hour she had undergone a profound change: she felt no longer a child. But for the moment she banished from her mind the nagging question of who had incited the rebellious crowd in the market-place and by what authority Thefarie Velianas had managed to make them obey his orders and began to think of what to say to the priestess of Hera.

When they reached the precinct which enclosed the temple, she stopped and said to Thefarie Velianas, 'Please, don't trouble to come any further. Thank you once more for your help. I shall tell my father how indebted we are to you.'

'I did nothing worth talking about,' he said quickly. 'I'm sorry you were molested and I hope that you will find your way to forgetting it all.' He now seemed rather anxious to leave them; bidding farewell to Ramtha only briefly, he quickly turned down one of the deserted side-streets. Ramtha continued to chatter excitedly as she looked after him until Larthi reminded her that they were about to enter the sacred precinct and must guard their thoughts and tongues. With a guilty face Ramtha put her finger against her lips and followed Larthi to the water-basin at the entrance for the ritual ablution. Both girls cleansed their hands and Larthi also washed the bronze figurine, defiled in the struggle with the slave. They stepped into the sanctuary saluting the goddess by kissing the fingers of their right hands and raising them. Neither girl had ever been there before as the temple was frequented mainly by the inhabitants of the Greek quarter.

Four Greek ladies, accompanied by an old man, were at that moment preparing for sacrifice by the burning altar in the open air. Larthi beckoned on Ramtha, who was hanging back shyly; she was anxious to watch the ceremony from close to. They approached the altar and stopped a little behind the other women, passing a number of ritual pits, a well and a frozen pool into which a water-conduit led.

It was true then, what Elachsantre had said, Larthi thought: Greek ladies are obviously never allowed out by themselves. Even here in the temple-precinct, they have to be watched over by a male relation. The only other man present was a sacrificial attendant, who stood at one side with a heifer which was wreathed and decked with woollen fillets. The priestess of Hera, a tall woman of Aunt Culni's age, held a flat basket on which lay the sacrificial knife, covered by a garland of evergreen and a small pile of barley. She walked round the altar to the right, stopped in front of it, took a burning twig from the fire and dipped it into a basin of water, which a girl attendant had been carrying after her. With this she sprinkled first the blood-bespattered altar and the animal and then the worshippers. Next she made them take a handful of barley from the basket and then she turned to the altar again to pray. Larthi managed to follow most of what the priestess said. Now she felt suddenly moved to whisper her own prayer to the goddess, entreating her to restore Aunt Culni's health. During the prayer all the participants scattered the barley towards the altar and then raised their right hands. When the priestess had finished her invocation, the Greek women responded with a long drawn out ritual chant.

After that the priestess cut a tuft of hair from the heifer's head and cast it into the flames. Handing the knife to the attendant, she stood by while he forced the animal down by kneeling on its back. He seized it by the muzzle, pulled back its head and cut its throat. Crouching beside him, the girl attendant caught the steaming blood in a bowl. Some time passed during which the victim was skinned, its inner organs taken out and the parts destined for the goddess cut up and wrapped in fat. Meanwhile the priestess had sprinkled the altar with the blood and roasted on a skewer the heart and the other internal parts for the sacrificial meal. Flute-music accompanied the whole proceedings and the burning of the meat for the goddess. Finally, the portions due to the priestess were laid on the offering-table whilst the Greek family collected the remaining meat from the attendant and prepared to return home.

As the priestess bade them farewell and was about to enter a small neighbouring building, Larthi felt emboldened to step forward and tell her about her concern for her aunt's health and her hope to propitiate the goddess by dedicating a votive figure to her. The priestess listened patiently to the girl's halting Greek.

'My child,' she said, 'I've seen you and your friend participating in our sacrifice and I am sure the goddess will accept your prayer and your gift.' Taking the bronze figurine from Larthi's hand, she exclaimed, 'You feel cold! You shouldn't linger out of doors any longer, the winter is early and severe this year.'

'I'm frozen,' Ramtha murmured, holding her bluish hands in front of her mouth and breathing on them. 'We have had such a terrible time on our way here, that I'm afraid of going back.'

'What happened to you, my children?'

'Shush,' Larthi interposed quickly, 'it's not worth talking about; we got here safely, thanks to the goddess.'

'Perhaps you had better hurry home before dusk falls,' the priestess said. 'I will offer up your figure to the Lady Hera and add my prayer to yours.'

As Larthi thanked her in her awkward Greek, the priestess smiled and sent them on their way with an invocation for their safety.

The girls left the sanctuary with a lighter heart.

14

Keening round the bier had gone on all night. The wailing women had ceaselessly beaten their breasts, torn at their hair and lacerated their cheeks as a sign of mourning, and left exhausted.

When Aunt Culni died the previous day, Larthi had laid her out with the help of Peci and Fasti. They had washed and anointed her with scented oil from an alabaster flask, dressed her in her most precious clothes and jewellery and wrapped her in an embroidered mantle, covering her hair with a veil. She rested on a thick mattress now with her head raised by a high support on a bed which had turned legs and an elaborately painted frame. A small servant-girl stood beside it with a fan to keep the flies away, and incense was burnt to purify the air.

Throughout the day the members of the other great families of Caisra came to call and pay their last respects, touching the corpse and raising their hands to their heads in lament. When they left again, they all stopped by the large broken clay vessel filled with

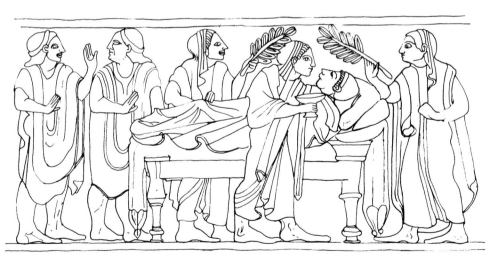

Mourning over a dead woman laid out on a bed. Low relief on a limestone funerary monument. From Chiusi. London, British Museum

89

spring water, that Larthi had had brought from a neighbouring house and placed by the door in accordance with ancient usage. Dipping laurel branches into the water, they sprinkled themselves as a token cleansing from contact with the dead woman, her abode and her mourning relatives.

Laris Matunas had been busy with the preparations for the funeral. Aunt Culni was to be buried in the family-tomb beside her betrothed, Sethre Matunas. The great mound in the northern cemetery that Larthi's grandfather had had erected some fifty years earlier, covered four separate groups of tombs, all belonging to ancestors, whose burial chambers had been carved from the rock generations ago. The stone slabs blocking up the stepped entrance-corridor leading down into the most recent tomb had to be removed and the interior of the chambers fumigated and cleared up. Avile Spurinna, Aunt Culni's kinsman, who had returned with Marce from Tarchuna a few days earlier, helped to direct the arrangements.

Larthi sat in her mourning clothes waiting for the carriage that would take Aunt Culni's body in solemn procession to the cemetery. Peci brought her a bowl of hot milk sweetened with honey and said, 'Drink this, mistress, it will do you good.'

Too tired to protest against suddenly being called mistress, Larthi told the maid to get a hot drink for herself. Neither of them had had much rest or food recently. As she warmed her hands on the steaming bowl, Larthi stared vacantly ahead, overwhelmed by grief. Why did Aunt Culni have to die, despite all their prayers and the offering to Hera? She had not been old and was always kind and patient with her and the slaves. Was it Elachsantre's curse which had brought about her death, or had it long since been decreed by the inexorable gods?

Deep fear of the coming burial ceremony and of the heavy new responsibilities awaiting her made Larthi shiver - there was nobody now to whom she could turn for help and advice on the duties and difficulties of a woman's life. The bier on which Aunt Culni lay had been lifted onto the two-wheeled ancient wagon kept exclusively for funerary processions. The dead woman's most cherished belongings were placed around the body. Peci and Fasti had taken particular care to wrap up her beloved Greek amphorae, signed by the potter Nikosthenes, in sheepskins, so that their fragile handles would not come to any harm during the passage to the tomb.

When everything had been loaded, Teitu seized the bridle of the leading mule and the cortège set out, preceded by musicians. The wagon was followed by the family, their friends, funerary priests and slaves who carried baskets of food, vessels containing liquids and offerings for the sacrifices to be performed during the ceremony.

It was a bright, clear morning. The bare branches of the trees lining the road stood out sharply against a pale blue sky and the distant streak of the sea on the horizon. In the wintry olive-groves slaves, who had been busy beating down and collecting the ripe fruit, stopped work and stood reverently while the procession passed. Having reached the tufa plateau on which the cemetery stretched towards the hills, the carriage turned and, with creaking wheels, followed a deeply rutted road, worn by centuries of use between funerary mounds and underground tomb-chambers.

The family's huge, grass-covered tumulus lay on the edge of the sepulchral road. Its circular base, crowned by a moulding of five horizontal bands, was carved entirely from the brownish rock. An altar constructed of large blocks of tufa stood facing onto the road and abutting against the base of the tumulus. Larthi saw that preparations for the sacrifice had been made on it.

To the right of the altar the entrance to the tomb appeared like a gaping dark hole above the top of the moulding. A temporary wooden ramp had been built up to it from the ground for easier passage into the corridor leading down to the rock-cut chambers. Larthi had never been inside the tomb before, nor had she ever participated in a funerary ceremony. No member of the family had been buried since her mother's death fourteen years earlier and the recurring sacrifices to the dead were always offered up by Laris Matunas. She hoped that it would all be over quickly, for she was exhausted with grief and lack of sleep.

When the bier had been taken down from the wagon and placed beside the altar-platform, the funerary priests and their attendants began their prayers to the gods of the underworld and performed the rites to the sound of the flute. Offering animal-sacrifices, bread, libations and incense in accordance with the sacred books of Acherun, they called upon each of the divinities in turn. Vanth, the winged female spirit of death, who hurries the soul on its journey to the nether regions, was invoked first. Next Calu, the terrible Lord of the Dead with his wolf-skin cap, and his mighty consort were implored to look mercifully upon the newcomer to their realm, haunted by the hammer-wielding demons Charu and Tuchulcha of the vulture-beak and snake-wreathed hair. Finally, the great benevolent mother was entreated to receive the soul kindly and ensure her passage into a new and higher existence.

To enable Culni's soul to attain this exalted new life, it was necessary for the women mourners to perform a slow, circular dance round her bier, every step and gesture of which was hallowed by tradition.

When the ritual outside the tomb was complete, Laris Matunas and Avile Spurinna lifted up the bier and carried it over the ramp into the tomb, preceded by the priests. Larthi and Marce followed. The air inside was dank and heavy with clouds of incense. When

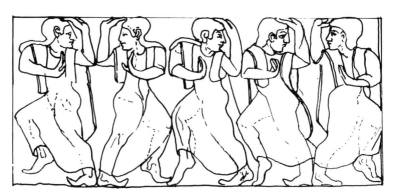

Dancing women. Low relief on a limestone cinerary urn. From Chiusi. Florence, Museo Archeologico

they had carefully descended a steep flight of stairs, flanked on either side by a cubicle, each containing a rock-cut bed for a man on the left side and a woman on the right, they reached a rectangular, atrium-like chamber. Its plan reminded Larthi of the hall of their own house, but everything was on a smaller scale and carved entirely from the living rock. Couches of differing shape for

92

men and women lined the long entrance-wall on either side of the door and on the two short side-walls; the long wall opposite the entrance was broken by three doorways leading into three dark alcoves set side-by-side, with pairs of couches joined at the head-end by a low platform for offerings.

The atrium, in the centre of which Aunt Culni's bier had been put down, was lit by the fitful, flickering light of candelabra. While the final rites were being performed by the priests, their shadows, eerily enlarged, moved restlessly over the painted walls and ceiling. Larthi hardly dared to look at the dark cubicles in front of her in which she knew the skeletons of her ancestors were lying. Two bronze censers full of smouldering grains of incense stood between the three inner doorways. Their frames, decorated by a raised moulding, had battered jambs with heavy, projecting lintels at the top. She stared at them, trying to overcome her fear.

While Larthi mused on the brevity of life, she noticed that the lower part of the door-frame opposite her had been roughly hacked at in order to widen the passage for a particularly broad bier. She remembered Aunt Culni telling her that Uncle Sethre had been an exceptionally tall and broad-shouldered man.

None of the rock-cut couches in the atrium were as yet occupied, but a quantity of funerary gifts, bronze vessels, black local pottery and finely painted Greek vases had been deposited on them during the earlier burials. Larthi caught sight of a Greek wine-jug painted with a chariot; an inscription scratched on the foot of the vase informed her that it had belonged to her mother. She was unable to contain herself any longer, and burst into tears for the first time since Aunt Culni had died. As she tried to suppress her sobs, she felt Marce's hand suddenly seize hers and hold it comfortingly. Overcome by gratitude, she did not let go of him until their fathers had taken up the bier again and carried it into the same alcove in which Sethre Matunas had been laid. Here they placed the body on the bed on the right, which was enclosed by a house-shaped outer casing, the traditional indication of the last resting-place of a woman.

The priests, who had been burning food on a portable clay hearth, now placed the blackened remains into little plates on an offering-tray. It was believed the smell of it would reach the soul in the other world, while the charred relics served as token of an everlasting supply of nourishment. Small cups containing wine, milk and honey were also put on the tray beside a bowl with eggs, the symbol of eternal renewal of life.

These everyday things offered to Aunt Culni seemed to Larthi to make her death more bearable; they would not only sustain the dead woman in her new existence, but they were something familiar, a link with the past and with those who had remained behind. Another profound thought began to comfort Larthi: there would be continuity. The blood of her mother and her aunt flowed in her own veins and through her they would go on living.

The rites were completed. They all stood in the atrium, facing the inner burial-chambers and saluted their dead for the last time before leaving the tomb which would now be sealed up again.

The mourners returned home, where a dinner had been prepared for all who had participated in the funeral. Reconciled as she was to Aunt Culni's death, Larthi now felt overcome by a need for sleep. She decided to slip away to bed, when the main dishes had been served. As she left, she heard Avile Spurinna tell her father that the Tarquins had found only half-hearted support at Veii and Tarchuna for their plans to regain power at Ruma by force of arms. Before risking a battle, the king thought of appealing to Laris Porsenna of Clevsina to cease fomenting the rebellion in the city. He expected Avile and Marce to accompany him on this difficult mission. Larthi thought of Ramtha and pitied her.

Part II

1

The mule-carts creaked as they lumbered up the steep incline of the narrow road. On either side of it, brownish walls of volcanic rock rose to twice the height of man. Oaks and chestnuts, matted with ivy, almost touched each other overhead transforming the road into a green tunnel. Only a few shafts of sunlight pierced the luxuriant cover of foliage, whilst the smell of damp earth and mouldering leaves pervaded the air.

Larthi felt strangely oppressed. In contemplating the brooding cliffs which hemmed in the road, it occurred to her that this defile provided the perfect place for an ambush. There had been so much fighting and unrest lately - the countryside was no longer peaceful as it used to be when she was a child.

'How easily one could be trapped here by one's enemies,' she said to her father who was dozing next to her, swaying with the slow movement of the carriage. Aroused by her fears, he rubbed his eyes and looked at the train of vehicles following their own.

'We are at peace with our neighbours,' he said reassuringly; 'the heralds have proclaimed the truce and not even Laris Porsenna would dare to cause the wrath of the gods by breaking it while the Rasenna assemble for their federal meeting.'

On hearing that Larthi shook off her sudden, unreasonable anxiety. For the first time her long-cherished wish had come true: she was accompanying her father to the annual reunion of all the Etruscan cities at the sanctuary of Voltumna. Never before had she been so far from home and, although it was a tiring journey, she was greatly enjoying it. Pushing aside some dew-covered fern-fronds which had brushed against her temple, Larthi reflected on the curious fact that for some years now she had not suffered from any attacks of headache which used to presage her vision of things to come. Perhaps she had outgrown these visitations - or had been too busy keeping house for her father during the five troubled years since Aunt Culni's death to feel anxious over forthcoming events as she tended to do in the past?

At the point where the road had been driven over the very brow of the hill, the tufa walls on either side towered even higher and curved towards each other in an arch which almost excluded the daylight. Larthi noticed that near the bottom a groove had been scraped into the soft stone by the hubs of passing cart-wheels. She pointed it out to her father who inspected the side of their vehicle, saying full of pride, 'Look what skilful road-building this is. See how deeply they have had to cut into the hill to ensure that draught-animals with heavily loaded carts can negotiate the ascent without too much strain. And have you seen the drainage-channel along one side here, which prevents flooding in heavy rain?'

Larthi's admiration grew as she caught sight of the structure of a wooden bridge, boldly spanning a deep torrent-bed, which they reached shortly after emerging from the gloom of the cutting in the hillside. Massive abutments of tufa blocks supported the wooden bridge with its parapet of tree-trunks. At the bottom of the gorge a river gushed between large boulders.

Larthi was continually struck by unusual aspects of landscape and buildings and her ceaseless questions kept Laris Matunas from dropping off to sleep again. The ravine they were just crossing served as a cemetery for a small town situated on a promontory of rock on the opposite bank. One could glimpse rows of house-like tomb façades crowned with heavy moulding, partly hidden by overhanging trees and creepers carved into the precipitous cliff-face. Their framed doorways were hewn from the natural rock, while the passages below them leading into the subterranean tomb-chambers were sealed by closely-fitting slabs of tufa.

The next day, they reached partly cultivated, rolling uplands. Larthi noticed that even the few lonely hamlets in these parts looked different to the villages she was used to, where the dwellings were rectangular in shape. Here small groups of oval wattle-and-daub huts clustered together haphazardly. On the long sides of their roofs the thatch was weighted down by ridge-logs, the projecting tops of which crossed each other and were carved to resem-

Baked clay hut urn decorated with geometric patterns. From Vulci. Rome, Villa Giulia

ble pairs of birds perched back to back. Quaint faded figures of horses, waterbirds and foliage were painted on the flaking clay which covered the interwoven twigs of the walls. Whisps of smoke from the hearths in the cottages escaped through roof-vents below the ends of the ridge-poles; the peasants were cooking their meals. Beside the porches stood large earthenware storage-jars and the pestles and mortars used for pounding roasted spelt. A scattered flock of goats was cropping the grass between the huts.

'How very old these cottages look!' Larthi exclaimed.

'You're right,' Laris Matunas said, 'they remind me very much of a small black pottery urn which looked just like a model of these huts here. Years ago, the slaves found it in an old tomb which they had ploughed up by chance. When they brought me the urn, I discovered the burnt bones and ashes of the dead in it. I believe that in former days most houses looked like that and that it was the custom of our ancestors to bury their dead in tombs which, regardless of how small they were, resembled the houses of the living.'

'What happened to that little hut-urn?' Larthi asked. 'I should love to see it. Do you keep it somewhere at home?'

'No, I do not!' Laris Matunas looked at his daughter disapprovingly. 'It does not do to disturb the rest of the dead. After I had performed the proper rites of expiation, the urn was buried again with the usual offerings.'

Larthi stopped questioning her father. She turned to Peci, who was sitting behind them on a bundle, her legs swinging over the open back of the carriage. It was noon and getting hot on the treeless road.

'Could you pull my sunshade from under the seat?'

Peci managed to extract the tasselled parasol wedged between baskets of provisions and rolls of bedding and handed it over to her mistress. Well shaded and feeling cooler, Larthi was now able to admire the herds of white cattle with their long horns curved like lyres, roam the upland pastures. The soil was less fertile here than that of the coastal plain. Millet and barley were grown rather than the usual wheat, olives and vines. Scrub and sparse woods covered the distant hills, where one could see columns of smoke from charcoal-burners' kilns rise into the still air.

They now passed a dell from which hot springs bubbled up in several natural pools, rimmed by whitish incrustations; the water gave off a curious, pungent smell. Larthi wrinkled her nose and looked at her father enquiringly. He pointed to some of the children and slaves, covered by sores, who were bathing there and explained that these springs had healing qualities. A small rustic shrine stood nearby, where Larthi noticed a number of fillets hung up on bushes to propitiate or thank Śuri, the divinity of the waters.

As their small convoy of wagons progressed northwards, it met with an ever increasing crowd of travellers converging on the

Ladies riding in a cart shaded by an umbrella. Terracotta frieze from Murlo, near Siena

road to Velsena. Many rode in mule-carts or on asses, but the majority were on foot, accompanied only by a slave, who carried bundles suspended from a stick on his shoulder. Above the din of wheels, clattering hooves and voices calling out greetings, there rose occasional shouts of warning and cursing when vehicles overtook too closely or forced pedestrians off the road. In several places the local people had put up stalls by the wayside offering provisions.

Tempted by the smell of freshly baked bread, Larthi made Cupe stop and sent Teitu out for some from a nearby oven. While they were waiting for the old man to return, there was a sudden screeching of wheels and the crash of a collision which made them all turn round. Someone screamed and angry voices could now be distinguished above the general hubbub. But as the air was thick with dust, Larthi could not make out what had happened. Soon Teitu hurried back from the baker's stall, his arms full of loaves and reported, 'I think master Caile has come to harm. I saw his carriage run into another one.'

Laris Matunas frowned and climbed down to go to his brother's assistance; Teitu followed once Peci had relieved him of the bread. After a few moments they returned with the reassuring news that the accident had not been serious, though it had cost Caile a tooth. Impatient to overtake a wagon and catch up with the rest of the family, Caile had struck a stationary peasant-cart, cutting his lip and breaking a tooth in the process. Larthi felt sorry for her uncle but, at the same time, could not help smiling: as usual, he had been both hasty and clumsy. She suspected that the loss of a conspicuous tooth would upset him far more than a flesh-wound, since he was extremely proud of his looks. As a doctor was sure to be amongst those assembling at Velsena, they decided to do no more at present than let Peci and Caile's Greek slave-boy clean up the cut lip.

The mules now began trudging up a long, steady incline leading to what Larthi thought was the summit of a peaked mountain. There were fewer people up here, as most of the other travellers had taken the easier route which led further east through undulating pastures. The sun was already sinking when they reached the crest. Larthi caught her breath as she gazed in wonder at the unexpected sight spread out below them: cradled by the wooded slopes of an ancient crater, lay a large lake, the calm waters of which seemed like a silver mirror in the glowing light of the sunset.

'The Lake of Velsena,' Laris Matunas said with solemnity. 'I came this way in order to show it to you.'

Cupe halted to give the mules a rest and allow the others to catch up with them. Stretching her arms wide, Larthi breathed in the fresh evening air with delight. It struck her that this was the most beautiful spot she had ever set eyes on. She was just about to ask her father if anyone lived on the two islands in the lake, when he pointed to the darkening forests ahead and said, 'In a clearing beyond that hill lies the sanctuary of Nortia.'

Something like a shadow fell over Larthi's spirit. She knew that the shrine of the goddess of destiny was inextricably bound up with the fate of the twelve cities of the Rasenna. For every year, in accordance with an ancient rite, the chief priest of the federation had to drive a nail into the wall of the temple, each nail representing one year in the span of life allotted to the nation. Thus the inexorable shrinking of the remaining years, whose total number had been fixed by divine decree, was made manifest by the priest's symbolic action. And each new year could bring the dreaded portent heralding the beginning of a new saeculum, the duration of which was unknown to mere mortals.

A shudder of religious awe ran through Larthi as her father went on, 'This lake in the heart of our land has always been connected with the destiny of our nation. The gods who decide our fate have used it more than once to express their will and anger.

100

The waters look still enough now, but they can be roused to wild and destructive fury. In the distant past there were flourishing fishing-villages beside the shore down there, but tradition has it that in a great flood they were submerged under the lake and every human being was destroyed by the decree of Tinia and the council of the consenting deities.'

Larthi involuntarily raised her hands in a silent prayer for protection. How dark the past was and how impenetrable the future seemed!

The sensuous beauty of the landscape now bathed in the light of the full moon reflected at that moment so little of the fateful events it had once witnessed, that Larthi's spirits soon soared again. The road ahead was clearly visible now as a silvery band following for a while the rim of the crater. She knew that by morning they would have reached their destination - the sanctuary of Voltumna near the city of Velsena. She suddenly felt overwhelmed by a feeling of anticipation and joy when a nightingale began singing in the bushes by the wayside.

2

The plain below the rocky plateau of Velsena looked like a vast and bustling camp. Hundreds of covered wagons and open carts now served as temporary shelters for those who had arrived in them. Like all the other noble families that of Laris Matunas had had their tents put up a little apart from the mass of the people and their tethered draught-animals.

Patterned with chequers and stripes, the tents made brilliant splashes of colour under the trees. The road leading towards the russet cliff of the city was lined with wooden stalls set up by local shopkeepers and itinerant traders; all kinds of wares were displayed and haggled over there. Amongst these shops Teitu discovered the hut of a doctor who claimed to be able to set bones and mend teeth. Once Peci had washed the blood off Caile's face, which had made the injury to his mouth look more serious than it was, Larthi found that the damaged tooth was merely loose. Nevertheless, her uncle insisted that a physician be found to attend to it.

'It's a great shame that Sombrotidas left Caisra for good,' he now said to Larthi, as they were following Teitu through the crowd. 'He was the only doctor I had any confidence in. I wonder what became of him and that Greek slave of yours - wretch that he was - whom he took to Delphi?'

'We've had no news at all of him. But I shall always be grateful to Sombrotidas for having relieved us of Elachsantre.' Larthi made the gesture to avert evil. The passage of five years had done nothing to lessen her dread of his curse on their entire family, for Marce, who had provoked it, continued to suffer its consequences: he and his father were homeless, obliged to travel from town to town with the exiled king who still hoped to return to power at Ruma. Larthi now believed this to be a vain hope, but she never confessed her doubts to Ramtha, for whose sake Marce occasionally came to Caisra. On his last fleeting visit he had told her that he was now following the Tarquins south to Tusculum.

'Here's the doctor's place,' Teitu said, stopping by a hut, in the dusty shade of which a group of common people with crutches and bandaged limbs were waiting.

'Make room for your masters,' shouted Teitu, pushing a scowling youth with a festering sore on his arm out of the way. Subdued grumbling followed them into the hut. The doctor was in the process of bleeding a patient with a bronze cupping-vessel. A sickening smell of blood filled the close little shack, overheated by a charcoal-brazier on which further cupping-vessels stood. When a fat, red-faced man lying on a camp-bed began to groan under the treatment, Larthi quickly retreated, whispering to her uncle as she did, 'I'm sure Teitu would be more help to you here than I would. I'll wait for you outside.'

Having glanced around the hut fastidiously, Caile nodded in a preoccupied way and Larthi escaped into the open air.

Earlier that day, when strolling about the shops with Peci, she had noticed a stall where some particularly fine linen was for sale. She now attempted to find her way back to it, as her father was in need of some new linen tunics. Aunt Culni had always impressed on her that the flax of Tarchuna was superior to all others and Larthi was determined to make sure that this linen did, in fact, come from. there and was not of the coarser kind produced in the

Faliscan land. In Caisra itself no flax worth having was grown. Standing on tiptoes and craning her neck, she could just make out the stall in the distance, when a man's voice behind her said, 'Has the daughter of Laris Matunas lost her way?'

Larthi turned round and recognized none other than Thefarie Velianas, whom she had not thought of for a long time; he looked a little stouter than before, and was surrounded by attendants with hefty sticks.

'No,' she answered, 'I was only looking for a shop and I have just this minute found it. These crowds are so confusing,' she added with some irritation, as she found the way he looked at her embarrassing.

Without taking his eyes off her, he said, 'It is many years since I had the good fortune of escorting you in a crowd. May I do so again now?'

Larthi was somewhat overcome at seeing him again so unexpectedly but could not very well refuse his offer without appearing offensive. While they were walking up the road towards the stall, his men officiously made a way for them. It struck her as a little presumptuous that someone of such obscure descent as Thefarie Velianas should behave as if he was a member of the aristocracy, and go about with a lot of attendants. True, his father was said to have become immensely rich by trade, but that was not the same as being of good blood. In fact, the heads of the great families and all those who counted, were at that moment assembled in the sanctuary of Voltumna to witness the annual election of one of the kings of the twelve cities as federal leader. While Larthi absent-mindedly inspected the length of linen displayed by the merchant, she pondered on where Thefarie Velianas could have been all the time since their first meeting during a riot at Caisra. He seemed to guess what she was thinking about for he said, 'I've only recently returned to this country. Business has kept me abroad for many years. Time has passed so quickly, and meanwhile you have turned from child to woman.'

Again Larthi could feel his eyes resting on her body; it made her feel uneasy. Fingering a piece of linen, she asked the shopkeeper where it was made.

'It's the best quality from Tarchuna,' he answered deferentially.

While she tried to work out how much would be needed for making four long tunics, Thefarie Velianas whispered into her ear, 'The linen of Egypt is much finer than this. I happen to have brought a quantity with me when I came back from Carthage to Caisra. Would you accept some of it from me?'

Offended by his lack of manners, Larthi said with reserve, 'I was not seriously thinking of getting any material,' and turning on her heel moved away, aware of the shopkeeper's disappointed face.

Thefarie Velianas followed her, sensing that she disapproved of his behaviour. He suddenly stopped and dismissed his attendants. When he had caught up with Larthi again, he pleaded with her, 'Forgive me if I have upset you. I only meant to please you. Won't you let me show you some of the beautiful things which I brought from abroad thanks to the protection of Uni.'

Larthi was appeased by his humble expression and by his piety and felt inclined to treat him less severely. 'Perhaps sometime when I am not so busy, but now I must see how my uncle is getting on.' With that she made her way once more towards the doctor's hut, having bid him farewell rather coolly.

Thefarie Velianas remained on the spot where she had left him, but Larthi felt his eyes on her until she was out of sight.

'I hope you've brought your mirror with you,' Uncle Caile repeated to Larthi as they were returning to their tents. 'I really must see what my tooth looks like now. It feels most odd.'

Larthi assured him again that her mirror was amongst her belongings in the tent and that his loose tooth now appeared to be firmly attached to its neighbour by a thin strip of sheet-gold.

'You'll find that it looks very neat,' she said and could not help adding, 'It will give a special radiance to your smile.'

Uncle Caile however kept touching the unaccustomed addition to reassure himself.

When Larthi got out her mirror, he seized it eagerly and inspected his reflection for some time, making all sorts of grimaces.

'What do you think of it?' he asked Peci, who had stifled her giggling while watching him.

'A skilful man must have done it, Master.'

'Yes, I know, but how do I look?'

*Bronze mirror engraved
with a running youth
by the sea. London,
British Museum*

At that moment Laris Matunas and his two fellow-haruspices came up and Caile at once bared his teeth and asked their opinion on his appearance.

'It's remarkably well done,' Laris Matunas said perfunctorily. 'Let me tell you, though, what happened at the kings' assembly just now - it was a most extraordinary scene,' he went on in a pre-occupied way, while Larth Repesunas pulled his grey beard and shook his head, mumbling to himself.

'Has Cousin Velthur been re-elected?' Larthi asked eagerly. Caile put down the mirror and turned to his brother questioningly.

'No, he was not,' Laris Matunas answered emphatically and before he could elaborate Piana Velavesnas broke in indignantly, 'It would have been much the best solution to have left the office in the hands of our Lauchume, since the other kings could not come to any agreement amongst themselves on who should succeed.'

'Yes, of course,' Laris Matunas resumed. 'In these troubled times the elected head of the federation would certainly have been the most experienced ruler amongst the kings of the twelve cities.'

Piana Velavesnas nodded repeatedly, while Caile said in a petulant voice 'Why don't you tell us what happened?'

'Well, in the beginning the kings of Tarchuna and Pupluna joined together with the Lauchume of Vetluna to suggest that Cousin Velthur be re-elected, since he had proved his great ability and wisdom during the recent unrest. Then, while the others were deliberating, Laris Porsenna of Clevsina rose suddenly and made a most violent attack on Cousin Velthur, accusing him of plotting with the enemies of the Rasenna for the sake of an incompetent and feckless family of runaways.'

'It was the most disgraceful outburst I have ever witnessed in my long life,' Larth Repesunas remarked, wiping his bloodshot, watering eyes and motioning Thresu to bring him a camp-stool.

'Do you mean to say that he referred to King Tarquin and his sons in this way?' Larthi asked incredulously.

'One can hardly believe it,' Caile exclaimed.

'Indeed,' Laris Matunas went on; 'he continued to abuse the Tarquins in the most intemperate language, blaming them for creating popular discontent in Ruma by their oppressive rule and showing themselves incapable of dealing with an uprising. He then proceeded to exonerate his own intervention and usurpation of power in the city, saying that he had merely filled a dangerous vacuum in the interest of all the Rasenna. As was to be expected, the Lauchume of Velsena applauded this disingenuous speech.'

106

'What impertinence,' Caile interposed, 'when everyone knows that Laris Porsenna's only interest is that of Clevsina. What he's after, is access to the sea and by controlling the territory of Ruma and the mouth of the Tiber, he can transport all his surplus grain cheaply by water and he gets the salt-pans at the estuary of the river into the bargain.'

'The way he played on the anti-Greek feelings amongst the majority of the kings was rather skilful,' Piana Velavesnas observed; 'at first he managed to impress them favourably by representing himself as a national champion, holding recklessly abandoned territory against threatened attacks by Latins and Greeks. Furthermore, he claimed to uphold the sacred principle of monarchy in a city seething with republican agitation.'

'However,' Laris Matunas resumed, 'the spuriousness of his assertions was soon shown up by the king of Veii, who takes a keen interest in what happens just across the river in Ruma. He has had ample opportunity to observe the machinations of Laris Porsenna from close quarters and he pointed out that, far from upholding the monarchy at Ruma, Porsenna had been forced to withdraw from the city after a while and agree to the election of two supreme magistrates there. Meanwhile he had contrived to get partisans of his elected to the new office of consul by denying grain supplies to the starving urban population. They were men like Spurius Larcius and Titus Herminius who, though of Rasenna blood, were unlikely to sympathize with the Tarquins and would be determined to keep the people and their republican ambitions firmly under control.'

'Did Cousin Velthur say anything?' Larthi asked.

'Not a word,' Piana Velavesnas said; 'he held himself aloof from the rather demeaning wrangle between the kings, not wishing to seem to push his claims - though he did at first rebut the charges made against the Tarquins, pointing out that they had gone to Tusculum only as a last resort, when none of the cities of the Rasenna had been willing to support them effectively.'

'Well, what happened then?' Caile enquired impatiently, so Laris Matunas went on, 'When Laris Porsenna realized that the king of Veii's speech had decisively swayed the meeting and that his ambition to be chosen as *zilath mechl rasnal*, leader of the Rasenna, had been foiled, he lost his temper so completely that he shouted furiously that he would withdraw his acrobats and actors from tomorrow's performance.'

'That really would be a great shame,' Caile exclaimed heatedly, 'his troupe is by far the best - I would hate to miss their act!'

Laris Matunas looked sternly at his brother and continued, 'This immoderate and childish behaviour turned the kings unanimously against Laris Porsenna. But, instead of inviting Cousin Velthur to continue in office, they decided to elect Karcuna Tulumnes, the King of Veii, for the coming year. He was chosen on the grounds that being nearest to the disputed and threatened territory, he would be best placed to direct combined operations from there if necessary. However, I feel sure that the real reason they did not re-elect Cousin Velthur was because of his connection with the Tarquins and their bias against both the Latins, with whom the Tarquins have now taken refuge, and the Greeks of Kyme, to whom they have also appealed.'

'The assembly made a most deplorable and unwise decision,' Piana Velavesnas exclaimed angrily.

Although Larthi completely agreed with him, she began to wonder what made him such a passionate supporter of Cousin Velthur's. She was naturally bitterly disappointed by the outcome of the meeting, for it was a blow to the pride of the family, but why should Piana Velavesnas be so concerned? Suddenly she remembered that he was, of course, a kinsman of Veilia, the Lauchume's wife.

'They will soon regret their folly,' Caile spluttered, 'particularly tomorrow!'

Laris Matunas interposed with the utmost seriousness, 'Let us pray to the gods that they do not prompt the kings' choice in order to hasten the end of the saeculum which saw the height of the power of Caisra.'

They all raised their hands in solemn supplication.

3

Larthi dressed with unusual care. She had chosen to wear one of Aunt Culni's gauzy chitons embroidered with rosettes and Peci now helped her to drape a light, semi-circular mantle, bordered with red, over her shoulder so that its two points fell in graceful folds in front and behind. Peci stepped back and eyed her mistress with approval. If only she could always persuade Larthi to take such an interest in her clothes, she thought, while handing her her mother's gold necklace, whose large, lentil-shaped pendants were embossed with evil-averting gorgons' masks. It was a striking neck-

Stamped gold necklace composed of hollow bullae decorated with gorgons' masks and lions' heads. The spacer-beads embellished with granulation and filigree. London, British Museum

lace with three central pendants slightly more bulbous than the rest containing small strips of linen drenched in scent. Larthi opened the stopper of one of them and held it to her nostrils.

'I haven't worn this for so long that the scent has all gone,' she said, closing it up disappointedly.

Peci knelt down and began to rummage about in Larthi's belongings in the tall wicker-basket which served as an improvised table in their tent.

'Wait, mistress, I know I packed a perfume-bottle with your dresses - here it is!'

She raised it triumphantly and between them they carefully poured a few drops of the precious essence from the alabaster phial into each of the three pendants. A sweet fragrance of flowers and herbs pervaded the tent. Having clasped the jewel round her neck, Larthi seized her mirror, shook back her curls and looked at herself critically.

'My face is too thin,' she moaned, 'and my cheek-bones are too high - and there is nothing I can do about it.' She dropped the mirror on her bed and added 'I don't like the colour of my hair either - do you think I should bleach it like Veilia?'

'No, mistress,' Peci said firmly, 'that wouldn't suit you at all. Your dark hair goes well with your dark eyes and to me you look lovely.'

Larthi embraced her with a rueful smile. 'What would I do without you?' she exclaimed, feeling strangely excited.

Laris Matunas, his brother and Larthi, followed by Peci and Teitu, set out for the assembly-green while the household slaves ran ahead to make way for them through the crowd. A stench of refuse and smoke hung over the camping-ground which they had to cross and Larthi clutched her necklace gratefully and breathed in the delicious scent exuding from it. Most of the encamped men had already joined the gathering at the foot of the hill on the summit of which stood the temple of Voltumna with its broad projecting roof. Everywhere one could see women with wailing infants clasped to their breasts crouched over portable clay stoves to cook gruel for their families.

Tethered horses and mules were cropping the few remaining blades of grass on the dusty soil and dogs scavenged amongst heaps of rubbish. In refreshing contrast, the water-meadows below the temple precinct were cool and shaded by poplars and elms, between which one could glimpse vines trailing in generous garlands. The curved slope of the sacred hill provided a natural seating-area for the most privileged of the spectators. Folding chairs for the kings had been placed in the front row and behind these ample space was reserved for their families and other grandees. The common people found room wherever they could on the slope and on the level ground beside the hill, while a number of boys had taken to perches in the trees, from where they could enjoy an unobstructed view of the whole site.

'There they come!' Larthi heard one of them shout and shortly afterwards the sound of approaching music could be discerned in the distance. Preceded by men with large, curved trumpets, the solemn procession of the kings of the Etruscan league now entered the assembly-green, having descended from the federal sanctuary where they had offered up sacrifices of thanksgiving for the plentiful harvest Voltumna had granted to them all. Only Laris Porsenna of Clevsina was missing. He had made good his threat to withdraw from the meeting with all his attendants and a specially trained troupe of entertainers.

The ruler of Veii led the group, surrounded by eleven bearers of the emblem of royal power, the double-axe, strapped up with a bundle of rods. Each of the other ten kings had released his own attendant for the occasion to symbolize his recognition of the temporary supremacy of the elected head of the federation. The priests of Voltumna and Maris and other local dignitaries followed behind the kings dressed in their splendidly embroidered robes of purple, while the rear was brought up by further musicians. And every participant in the procession wore a wreath.

All the assembled rose and received the cortège of the rulers with acclamation and awe. An overwhelming consciousness of the supernatural authority invested in them pervaded everyone. As mediators who interceded on behalf of the mass of the twelve peoples of the Rasenna with the inscrutable divinities presiding over the nation's fate, the kings' religious importance matched their temporal power. For the safety and prosperity of all could only be guaranteed through the minute observance of hallowed formulae and rites, a vast and complex tradition, which from time immemorial had been the sole preserve of the sovereigns and their priests, capable of interpreting the signs from heaven.

Familiar though Larthi was with Cousin Velthur's imposing appearance, she was struck by the aura of heightened dignity surrounding him on this occasion, as if his office and sacrosanct duties had raised him to a sphere of sublimity not accessible to ordinary mortals. With bated breath she watched him and his fellow-kings take their seats and it seemed to her that she was gazing on an assembly of gods enthroned in stately splendour. When the priests, lictors and other dignitaries had found their appointed places, the chief priest of Maris stepped forward into the open space where the altar stood. Raising his hands in solemn prayer, he invoked the god, calling him to witness that the assembled peoples of the Rasenna had agreed to close the period of warfare for the year, in token of which the traditional war-dance would now be performed.

The silence which fell after this appeal was sudddenly broken by the noise of a woodpecker hammering on a nearby trunk. A tremor of awe ran through the congregation - the god was present! The priest signalled to the trumpeters to sound the beginning of the ritual and flute-players stationed themselves on either side of the altar. While they started up a tune with a curious triple beat, a group of twelve priests of Maris appeared from behind a grove of elms in the middle distance. They wore short, brightly coloured tunics and tall, crested helmets. Each carried strapped to his left forearm, a studded bronze shield of oval shape with semi-circular indentations at top and bottom. Brandishing their spears, the brotherhood of priests capered forward in three time rhythm, clashing their weapons against their shields at regular intervals. The file of dancers was headed by a leader who indicated the direction and the steps to be executed, while behind him a singer chanted the words of a venerable hymn to which the dancers responded sonorously by beating on their shields. Twelve times they circled the altar of Maris in this way and ended their dance by leaping into the air with a piercing shout of triumph and clashing their shields together. The chief priest of Maris then performed the sacrifice, after which the dancers suspended their shields from a pair of spears carried horizontally on the shoulders of two of the brotherhood. They took them back to the sanctuary to be stored there until the next performance of the dance in the spring which marked the reopening of the season of warfare.

Larthi followed the ritual with eager interest, recalling the tradition stemming from the days of King Tarchon when one of these shields had fallen from heaven as a talisman for the ruler and the people of Tarchuna. To preserve the divine gift from theft and

112

perdition, Tarchon had eleven replicas made of the shield which were kept together with it, so that no-one could tell which was the original. In time the twelve shields came to symbolize the twelve peoples of the Rasenna and were used each year for the sacred performance she had just witnessed. Listening to the deep clangour of bronze ringing through the grove, Larthi had been pervaded by a sense of power emanating from the magic shield. All those assembled, swaying in time with the rhythm of the dance, had experienced the same sensation - the place was alive with divine potency.

Slowly the spell was broken and the kings stood up and began talking amongst themselves. Larthi's father, too, rose and said, 'Let's join Cousin Velthur for a while. There is just enough time before the ritual of the Truia begins.'

He beckoned to Caile to accompany them. Larthi looked across at the group of kings, who were now mingling with their families. She suddenly noticed that a tall, dark-haired young man stood opposite Cousin Velthur with his back towards them. As they came up, he turned round and smilingly stretched out his hand in greeting.

'Aranth has returned to us for good,' Cousin Velthur said, putting his arm round his son's shoulder as if presenting him to Larthi; 'He arrived at Caisra after we'd left and so followed us on up here. Did you recognize your cousin?' he teasingly asked Larthi, whose hand Aranth was still clasping.

She lowered her eyes abashed by the intensity of Aranth's gaze. 'He has your stature and features . . .' she murmured, her voice trailing away inaudibly.

'When I last saw you - ,' Larthi responded eagerly to Aranth's deep, warm voice - 'you were a wild little girl, who wanted to see my ship and hear some old Greek tales of monsters that swallow up sailors down south near the Straits.'

Larthi looked up with a smile to face again the quizzical expression in Aranth's eyes, brown like Cousin Velthur's, but flecked with gold, as if laughter lit them up perpetually.

'I still want to see your ship,' she said gaily, 'and you must tell me whether you ever met such creatures as Scylla and Charybdis. You've been away for so long that I really thought you had ended up in the Land of the Lotus-eaters and forgotten us all.'

*Woman between two
men. Engraved bronze
mirror. From Tarquinia.
London, British Museum*

'Other things have kept me far from home. One day I will tell
you about my life amongst strangers.'

'I can't wait,' she said, light-headed with elation.

'We have decided to celebrate Aranth's return with a feast this evening,' Cousin Velthur broke in, 'and we would like you all to come. But now let us take our seats again, for I see that the riders are ready.'

Absent-mindedly Larthi followed her father and uncle back to their places.

'Do you think it's the growing pressure from the Greeks in the South which has put Aranth out of business?' Caile asked Laris Matunas.

'Yes, I do. Time is not on our side down there,' he answered gloomily.

Larthi paid no attention to their conversation. She was overwhelmed by feelings of excitement which swept away her habitual concern with political events and the future of her people. Would Aranth remain in Caisra from now on? And if he did . . .

The sound of trumpets and subdued thunder of hooves on the turf woke her from her day-dreams. Three squadrons of young horsemen were galloping across the green to line up in separate groups of twelve riders, each with a leader in front. Amongst them Larthi recognized the sons, aged between six and seventeen, of some of the noblest families of Caisra and Tarchuna who, with their peers from other cities, had been carefully trained to perform the sacred game of Truia.

'It must be the last year for Larce Alvethna's boy to be eligible,' she said to her father, pointing out the young man, who in the past had impressed her with his feats of horsemanship.

'Yes, he will reach manhood next year,' Laris Matunas replied, following the youth with his eyes as he took charge of the squadron which opened the game.

Like the rest of the riders he wore a pointed cap, very reminiscent of a dolphin's head. Larthi noticed that while the young men forming the squadrons all carried round bronze shields and lances, their leaders remained unarmed. Having saluted the sanctuary on the hill and the seated kings, the first group of twelve horsemen rode forward in pairs and on command separated to the left and the right. With their lances at the ready they proceeded to ride at each other as if to attack, an exercise repeated several times with complicated convolutions suggesting that the riders were following the paths of a labyrinth. Finally they paired up again and galloped off after their leader, while the next squadron took over to perform a similar manoeuvre which varied only in the intricate form of movement and counter-movement.

Larthi mused over the meaning of this ancient rite and its name 'Truia'. Did it recall that of Troy, the city besieged by the Greeks during ten long years for the sake of one woman? How beautiful Helen must have been to arouse such fatal passion in so many men. Passion - what was love like? An apprehensive longing filled her to discover its secrets and delights. But who was there to guide her? She recalled overhearing snatches of talk between giggling slave-girls by the fountain and feeling too proud to ask Peci for an explanation.

She turned towards her father who sat gazing at the spectacle before them, totally absorbed. It seemed to her that for the first time she saw him as a person separate from herself and unreachably distant, despite all familiarity. She knew then that although he had initiated her in the proper form of so many rites and had explained their significance, he was incapable of being her guide in the new world she was about to enter. A wave of tenderness mingled with pity flooded through her as she watched him, aware that his dark hair was now streaked with silver and that his tall figure had begun to stoop a little. She stretched out her hand to lay it on his shoulder affectionately, when he started up in dismay. She withdrew, only to realize that he was upset by some event on the green and had not even noticed her caress.

'An evil omen,' he murmured, while all around them the spectators stirred and whispered despondently.

Larthi quickly surveyed the scene and realized why there was such general consternation. A fair-haired young man from Veii, the leader of the last squadron to perform, had lost his cap while executing a pirouette-like movement with his horse; the head-dress lay on the ground, trampled underfoot by many horses. In a daring manoeuvre the young commander snatched a lance from one of his troops, dashed to the spot where the cap was beaten down into the grass and picked it up with the point of the weapon. Swinging it through the air triumphantly for a moment, he took it off the lance and replaced it on his head.

116

The king of Veii had risen from his seat in a state of alarm, but sank back with an expression of relief at the outcome of the ominous happening. The majority of the spectators began to cheer the young rider, but Laris Matunas pondered the event for some time dejected and overwhelmed by a sense of impending doom.

'This presages disaster for Veii, though the gods may delay it for some time,' he said finally.

Larthi shivered apprehensively, despite the heat of the midday sun.

4

The lengthening shadows of the tall elms streaked the saffron-coloured fabric of the royal dining-tent with bars of dusky blue. Through the tent's wide open front the slanting sunlight fell onto the gleaming bronze candelabra and incense-burners placed amongst the couches in preparation for the feast. A crowd of slaves in short loin-cloths bustled over charcoal-stoves. Three-legged tables covered with banqueting vessels and baskets of provisions stood beside the tent. The scent of herbs and broiling meat pervaded the warm evening air. The king's large hunting-dog which had been observing the preparations for dinner with seemingly undivided interest, suddenly bounded into the neighbouring grove with furious barks. Aranth stepped out from his own tent and followed the dog under the trees.

'Come here, Aefla!' he called out as he heard the voices of approaching guests.

He managed to restrain the dog by its bronze-studded collar as he welcomed Laris Matunas and his family who emerged from the copse accompanied by their retainers. Larthi's heart began to race when Aranth touched her hand and greeted her with a smile. She noticed with pleasure that Aranth's short, semi-circular mantle was of the same light blue colour as her own fine linen dress. Her attire had occupied her for a long time and she ardently hoped that Lasa, the nymph of beauty, had invested her with special grace. As they reached the tent, servants began lighting the

Bronze incense burner
supported by the
figure of a boy acrobat.
Rome, Villa Giulia

candelabra and Velthur Velchanas and Veilia came forward to receive their guests.

Larthi was so distracted by Aranth's presence that she did not notice the king's magnificently embroidered purple cloak. Her eyes kept wandering back to Aranth almost against her will, though she was aware that Veilia was dressed in a new white chiton, spangled with tiny figures of walking lions and secured on the shoulder by golden buttons. Despite her beautiful clothes Veilia looked sullen and seemed disinclined to talk. When Laris Matunas asked after her son, she replied only briefly that young Mamarce was unwell.

'What a shame that he won't be able to celebrate his elder brother's homecoming with us,' Caile remarked, as Veilia turned away.

Piana Velavesnas who had just joined the party with a number of other guests, quickly remarked, 'The boy complained of pains in his stomach this afternoon while we were watching the games together. This unseasonable heat is most unhealthy.'

'What a poor performance the jugglers gave,' Caile grumbled; 'not a single new trick and the same old tattered clothes as last time. I heard that Laris Porsenna's acrobats rehearsed some outstanding acts and that he had all his mimes fitted out with splendid new costumes. It's very disappointing that he deprived us of a good show by withdrawing them at the last moment!'

Servant-girls had meanwhile handed wreaths to all the diners and when the king had shown everyone to his place, he began to prepare the sacrifice, assisted by the priests. Larthi, much to her delight, found herself occupying the same couch as Aranth on the right hand side of Cousin Velthur's. As she settled down next to Aranth on the soft mattress supporting her left elbow on two bolsters, she struggled against a strong impulse to lean back against his bare brown shoulder. She attempted to concentrate on the familiar ritual which preceded every feast, wondering at the potent feelings, at once pleasurable and disturbing, which flooded through her being and threatened her self-command. Anxious to appear calm and natural, she joined in a toast to Aranth which his father proposed after duly thanking the gods for his protection and safe return home.

'They tell me your ship was groaning with treasures when you anchored at Pyrgoi,' Caile said. 'How many Greek merchantmen did you capture this time?'

Aranth smiled wryly. 'What I carried in the hold was not loot but the rewards of years of trading abroad. Mind you, I had to defend my property against pirates who attacked while we were passing Lipara. Thanks to Nethuns, who sent a squall which drove one of their fast ships onto a rock, I was able to deal with the other. I had had the prow of my ship resheathed with bronze only a short time before and in the rough seas that we encountered that light vessel of theirs was no match for my sturdy and well-loaded craft.'

Larthi shuddered inwardly at the thought of the dangers through which Aranth had passed. She herself had never set foot on a ship. Although the sea was always visible on the horizon, it was unfamiliar to her and she knew little about the actual hazards to which those who sailed and fought on it were exposed. The vast expanse of water that bordered the west side of the land they were living in, reminded her of age-old beliefs in the abode of the dead that lay beyond and the journey thence of the departed. Silently she repeated the prayer of thanks which Cousin Velthur had pronounced at the beginning of the meal and, as if under a spell, continued to dwell obsessively on Aranth.

She watched him divide a fowl. Leaning over the serving-table in front of their couch, he deftly severed the legs and wings and carved a slice of the breast which he offered to her. As he did so, he bent forward and their bodies touched for a moment. A flame of desire leaped up in Larthi, so consuming in its sweetness that it took her breath away. She sensed the working of an overwhelming new power in herself which she was both tempted and frightened to explore further. With an effort she steadied herself and tried to join in the general conversation. Veilia still appeared gloomily preoccupied by the illness of Mamarce. In an attempt to distract her, Larthi complimented her on her dress.

'Aranth gave it to me with a lot of other things he brought back. it's Ionian work, I believe,' Veilia answered without smiling.

Larthi experienced a sharp pang of jealousy. She suddenly realized that although Veilia was Aranth's stepmother, she was two years younger than he was and still very beautiful - no wonder

120

Aranth admired her and showered her with presents. She felt unable to talk to Aranth without revealing her distress, and was relieved when Cousin Velthur began to question him on the advisability of sending a squadron of ships south to raid pirate-infested Lipara.

'This doesn't seem to me the right moment,' Aranth replied, 'the situation nearer home is so confused. We must watch what is happening in Latium, now that the Tarquins have gone there. I've also noticed an unusual amount of naval activity off Kyme.'

'You're probably right. In any case, at present we cannot do without our entire fleet being to hand. Laris Porsenna is quite capable of trying to force the issue of Ruma now, which might well give the Latin cities the chance they have been waiting for. Our land-route to Campania is therefore in grave danger and we must retain control of the sea-communication at all cost.'

'I wonder if we are not going to have to pay too high a price for our old loyalty to the Tarquins?' Larthi heard Aranth murmur.

'I need hardly tell you, Aranth, that the king has brought the troops to a state of readiness unequalled in living memory,' Laris Matunas said; 'their equipment and training are superb and they've been organized in separate units now.'

'I caught a glimpse of it as I came through Caisra,' Aranth replied and, turning to his father, he added, 'the guards there were most impressive, but I noticed a high proportion of commoners.'

'The developments of the last years have made that inevitable. It's no longer possible to rely only on the aristocratic families and their dependants for service; there are simply not enough of them. The richer commoners are eager to play their part now and they are well able to provide their own armour and weapons.'

'Certainly we need more heavily armed troops,' Aranth agreed; 'we have relied far too much on the fleet in the past few decades. But there is a danger in recruiting outside the aristocracy and their retainers. It will give access to power to a class whose aspirations are eventually going to be directed against us - one can never be certain of their loyalty. Just look at what has happened at Ruma since Servius Tullius reorganized the army a generation ago.'

Larthi meanwhile had forgotten her preoccupation with Veilia as she gazed at Aranth in mute admiration. He had voiced unequivocally all the ill-defined thoughts which had been troubling her for some time. But Cousin Velthur replied sharply, 'You have been away from home far too long to have a clear understanding of the situation. Such fears are groundless.'

'We'll keep those fellows in their places!' Caile exclaimed, raising his cup. 'Velthur may not have been re-elected *zilath mechl rasnal*, but he still remains the lauchume of Caisra, the greatest city amongst all the Rasenna.'

He has had too much to drink already, Larthi thought, deeply upset by her uncle's tactless toast. The others looked at each other in silent embarrassment until the king himself drank to Aranth, saying in conciliatory tones, 'I am happy to have you back at my side, my son. I shall need all your help and advice in these difficult times.'

'Count on me, father,' Aranth replied with a smile. 'My thanks to you and Veilia for the warm welcome you've given me.'

'We are all extremely glad to see you amongst us again,' Laris Matunas said, applauded by the other guests.

As Larthi turned to throw her father a grateful look, she caught a glance of secret understanding passing between Veilia and Piana Velavesnas, which puzzled her.

While the remains of the meal were being removed and the slaves brought water and towels, the king called for more wine and beckoned to the entertainers who stood waiting in the gloaming outside. A magnificent large mixing-bowl for wine and water was carried in and placed in the centre of the tent. The two tall handles of this bronze krater were attached to its body by intricately wrought figures of gorgons clutching snakes, while round the neck of the vessel ran a relief-frieze of warriors and chariots. The workmanship was greatly admired by all and, as the royal cupbearer began to fill the cups, Velthur Velchanas first poured a libation and then said proudly, 'Let us taste this Chian Aranth has brought back with him. It's the only wine worthy to be mixed in this splendid krater which was his present to me.'

'Where did you find such a superb piece of work?' Caile asked. 'And what did you give for it?'

'I acquired it from a Tarentine merchant in exchange for a shipload of crude metal,' Aranth said modestly, but Larthi could see that he was pleased by the impression his gift had made.

'A marvellous bargain, I'd call it.'

'A wonderful wine as well,' Laris Matunas said, quaffing it appreciatively. 'The Chians are justly famous for it.'

Larthi sipped carefully from her own cup as she watched two young slaves - not a hair disfigured their smooth bodies - perform astonishing feats of dexterity, circling the big mixing-bowl to the tunes of double-flute and cithara. They advanced and retreated in the re-enactment of a mock-battle, rapidly whirling long-handled bronze axes which flashed in the candlelight. Next appeared a slave-girl wearing a transparent garment girdled at the waist; the loose upper part of the dress was held in place by crossed shoulder-straps decorated with large metal discs. Her hair was coiled up in a tutulus and she carried castanets with which she began to accompany herself as she danced gracefully round the tent. Passing a serving-table, she suddenly put down her castanets, picked up a bronze censer full of smouldering grains of incense and placed it on top of her head. Having steadied it for a moment, she started to spin around with her arms akimbo. As the rhythm of the music increased in speed, she rotated faster and faster until her light skirt billowed out from her legs and the draught caused by her rapid movement made the incense glow, wafting its heavy scent into every corner of the tent. The performance was greeted with ex-clamations of delight by the onlookers.

'This is much more exciting than those poor fellows juggling with balls this afternoon. Let's see more!' Caile clamoured, but the dancer had already slipped away.

Larthi felt her pulse throbbing with the heat and the effect of the wine. She smiled at Aranth, who had reached out to the neigh-bouring couch to take an alabaster scent-bottle which Veilia had handed him. Clasping his arm round Larthi's shoulder, he asked her to open her palms so that he could shake a few drops of the perfumed oil onto her hands. She obeyed in a haze of happiness, breathing in the heady mixture of the scent and smell of his warm brown skin.

Meanwhile a young girl acrobat had stepped into the circle of candlelight. She wore nothing but brief, colourfully embroidered trunks and wide bracelets on her upper arms; her long curls were caught up in a golden net. With wonderful agility she began turning somersaults and cartwheels amongst the couches. Then she planted three short swords, points up, in the turf close to each other; standing on her head one moment and arching over the swords in a slow backbend next, she flicked herself up like a whip-lash into a standing position again, much to Larthi's relief, who hated the thought of that beautiful white body being grazed.

The girl next asked for an empty silver cup which she placed on the floor beside the big mixing-bowl. She first balanced herself on her hands in front of it, legs in the air, then carefully lowered her forearms onto the ground, flexing her knees while she did so, until her feet touched the bronze wine-ladle suspended from one handle of the krater. With finger-like nimbleness her toes grasped the hooked end of the ladle, lifted it over the rim of the vessel and plunged it into its depth. Gasps of amazement burst from everyone as she slowly raised the filled dipper and, twisting her tautly arched body slightly to one side, managed to pour the wine into the cup without spilling one drop of it. When she had replaced the ladle again with her toes, she swung her legs back until she was kneeling on the floor. On getting up she seized the cup and stepped onto the serving-table. With one leg raised horizontally backwards and her right arm stretched forward in perfect counterpoise, she offered Aranth the cup. There was a roar of applause as Aranth accepted it and threw her his wreath in exchange. All eyes were spellbound when she posed with the garland for one moment before alighting from the table and tripping from the tent, holding it high above her head.

'Father!' Aranth exclaimed gratefully, 'your acrobats are as superbly trained as your troops. Thank you for the great pleasure you have given us!'

He raised the cup and drank his father's health, which was echoed by the company. Before draining the rest of the wine, Aranth suddenly called for the kottabos game to be placed next to the mixing-bowl. The slave responsible for the dining-utensils carried into the centre of the tent a tall bronze stand with a project-

124

Dancing couple.
Engraved bronze
mirror. Berlin,
Ehemals Staatliche
Museen

ing bronze disc fastened half way up its slender shaft. He carefully balanced a separate smaller disc on the pointed top of the stand and stepped back as lightly as possible, so as not to bring the precariously poised disc crashing down prematurely. Before Larthi knew what was happening, Aranth had raised himself on his left arm and threw the dregs of his wine cup at the top of the cottabosstand, dislodging the bronze disc on top of it. It fell onto the projecting lower one with a resounding clangour.

'May my love look upon me with favour!' Aranth called out excitedly, while everyone cheered his skilful hit.

Larthi turned towards him in a turmoil of feelings, gazing at him in silent but eloquent appeal. 'Who is she?' her eyes were asking, but she could discover nothing but laughter in his.

Now the musicians' rhythmic tunes made the feet and limbs of everyone present move in time and the dancing began in earnest, sweeping the banqueters into a whirl of ecstatic movement - a pure expression of the joy of living and a gesture of worship of the gods, the bountiful providers of wine, food and love.

5

'Mistress,' Peci exclaimed, bursting into the tent where Larthi was still asleep; 'here's a present for you, but whom from I couldn't possibly tell you.'

Larthi rubbed her eyes and sat up, not yet fully awake. 'What is it?' she mumbled. 'Where's the fire?' She pointed to the glowing light which shone through the fabric of the tent.

'The fire?' Peci teased laughingly. 'Don't you recognize the sun?'

'Oh, I must have dreamt it all then - ' Larthi said slowly. 'There were these two torches which Teitu and Thresu were carrying last night when we returned from the feast - they suddenly seemed to merge into one and became an immense fire which threatened to consume everything . . . it was terrifying!'

'Don't think of it any more, mistress; I'm sure it means nothing. It may just have been the sunlight and the heat in here which caused you to dream. Take a look at this and forget about fires.'

She held out a small box made of scented wood. Larthi took it and examined it closely. 'Is it for me?'

Peci nodded and while Larthi carefully opened the box, she informed her that it had been given to her for her mistress by an unknown slave, who simply said that his master wished to present it to her with his love. Larthi's hands trembled as she unwrapped the fine linen wound round the gift. There could be no doubt as to whom it was from. She glimpsed a necklace through the last clinging layer of the semi-transparent wrapping material. It was com-

126

posed of golden beads next to oddly shaped blue and greenish ones. Larthi lay back, overcome with happiness.

'I'm too excited,' she murmured. 'Do get it out for me.'

Peci freed the necklace from its wrappings and held it up for inspection. 'What lovely jewellery,' she said. 'Such pretty colours - but I can't quite make out these figures.' She stepped to the entrance of the tent and peered at the necklace holding it up into the light. 'They must be demons, mistress. I don't think I like this thing. What do you make of it?'

She handed the necklace back to Larthi who had sat up again saying gaily, 'Oh, don't be silly.'

She examined the figured beads closely. They were moulded from an opaque, glassy substance and coloured a vivid turquoise and green. Some represented strange composite creatures. there were dwarfish leonine figures with feathered crowns, rearing serpents and beetles bearing discs on their heads and tiny human figures with animals' heads. Curious beads, certainly, but beautifully fashioned by some eastern craftsman. Larthi put on the necklace and gazed at her reflection in the mirror, wondering from what distant foreign harbour Aranth had acquired it.

'It suits you, mistress; but I don't really like those demons on it. What else can they be? Look, this one has a lion's head and that one with its wolf's head is just like the monster Olta, which had to be destroyed by lightning,' Peci said doubtfully.

'I don't know and I don't care,' Larthi replied, abandoning herself to a wonderful feeling of certainty that Aranth loved her. The knowledge suddenly gave a completely new purpose and meaning to her life and filled her with pulsating energy. Her habitual concept of human existence as the mere living out of a predestined and inescapable fate gave way to a burgeoning sense of freedom and the joyous possibilities of personal choice and fulfilment. Aranth now appeared to her to be the embodiment of all her newly discovered aspirations.

The air inside the tent suddenly seemed stifling so she got up quickly, leaving Peci to pack up their belongings for the journey home. An urge to get away from the noise and commotion of the camp breaking up drove her to walk some distance until she found herself amongst pine-trees on a hillside. Even here in the shade the heat was intense. A thick layer of dry pine-needles on the ground silenced her footfall and the only sounds in this lonely forest were the shrilling of the cicadas and occasional sharp cracks when a pine-cone, warped by the heat, burst open.

Larthi enjoyed treading on the springy carpet of shiny needles; it heightened her feeling of buoyancy. Though Aranth was not there beside her, she was filled with an elation she had never known before. He might have been with her, she felt so close to him and so sure that their future together would be happy and un-menaced by evil forces.

Which divinity was she to thank for this marvellous turn her life had taken? Lifting the necklace to her lips, she leant pensively against a tree to ponder this question. There was another cracking noise in the wood; a squirrel scurried past her and disappeared be-hind the skeleton of a fallen pine. Larthi felt moved to offer up grateful prayers to both Turan, the goddess of love, and to Uni, the great goddess who presides over marriage and the life of all women. She took a step forward and raised her hands, looking up at the sky which appeared whitish in the heat-haze.

As she began her invocation there was a sudden rustle behind her, she was seized round the waist and clasped violently to the body of a man. Such was her surprise and fright and so tight was the hold of her attacker, that she could only gasp. After a second's fight for breath, she shouted angrily, 'Let go of me at once! Who are you?'

'There's no need to be so spirited, my love,' came a voice she knew but could not identify, as she was lifted up and carried a few paces.

'Help!' she shrieked desperately, tearing at the man's hard hands and trying to kick him. 'Help!'

'You would have thought that I'd got a wildcat in my arms rather than the daughter of Laris Matunas,' he said, as he twisted her round and pinned her back against the broad, leaning trunk of a pine-tree. She stared into the smiling, sweat-covered face of The-farie Velianas.

For a moment she was speechless with shock and indignation. 'How dare you?' she exclaimed. 'Let go of me this instant!'

128

'But why, my beauty?' he said. 'Do I not deserve a word of thanks for the Phoenician collar you are wearing round your lovely neck? It suits you well. I've been observing you ever since you came out of your tent and I know that you like my gift.'

Larthi felt as if someone had struck her, her head and shoulders fell back defeated against the tree-trunk. The cruel truth dawned on her. She had completely deceived herself into believing that the necklace was a present from Aranth - that it was he who loved her. With despair she now realized that her future was not going to be as she had so exultingly imagined it only a few moments ago. Searing grief made her heart contract painfully and drained her of every vestige of strength. As her head drooped limply to one side, she could feel her hair being caught by the rough bark of the pine oozing with resin. It did not matter - nothing mattered any more. She did not know how long she had lain against the tree-trunk in a state of collapse when she became conscious of Thefarie Velianas' hands caressing her face, her shoulders, her body and of his voice urgently calling her name again and again. A feeling of utter revulsion revived her vigour and lent her unexpected strength. The languid, seemingly compliant body of the girl he had supported against the tree, tensed abruptly and her knee hit him sharply in the groin. Thefarie Velianas was completely taken by surprise. As he doubled up in pain and tottered back on the sloping ground, she hurled herself at him pushing him so violently that he fell, tripped by a gnarled root.

'I loathe you!' she panted. 'If I had known this necklace was yours I would never have touched it!'

Groaning, he attempted to stumble to his feet. In a frenzy of rage she ripped the collar from her neck and threw it at him. The string broke and the beads were scattered all over the ground. While she turned to run, certain that he would pursue her, Thefarie Velianas dropped to his knees again with a shriek of dismay groping for the gold beads which had disappeared amongst the pine-needles.

Her heart pounding wildly, Larthi sped through the forest until she reached the hot and glaring encampment. Here she was forced to thread her way through a mass of departing wagons and crowds of preoccupied people. Completely exhausted by the incident, her damp hair disarrayed, her clothes torn and soiled, she staggered into her tent and fell into the arms of Peci, who had been watching out for her mistress, full of growing concern.

'What's happened to you?' she exclaimed with alarm while supporting her to her bed, 'You look terrified as if all the ghosts of the nether regions had been chasing you.'

Larthi shivered and reached for her aching forehead. Her cracked lips moved, but she could not utter a word. Her breath came in short, painful gasps. Deeply distressed, Peci crouched beside her mistress, feeling for her pulse, never once averting her eyes from her face.

6

The fever had abated at last. Larthi lay with closed eyes, feeling for the first time since her illness began, that she might recover again. She was terribly weak still, but her head and limbs felt light and unburdened now. For days her temples had burnt like fire, her body had been racked by convulsions and frightening nightmares had made her scream in horror. From time to time she had recognized Peci or her father bending over her with concern, placing cool, wet bandages on her forehead and round her wrists, but during most of the past week she had been more or less unconscious, while her body battled with the demon of fever.

Slowly she gazed upward, her eyes wandering over the fabric of the tent until gradually she realized where she was lying. The painful memory of what had happened on the day after the feast celebrating Aranth's return flooded her mind. With a moan she let her head drop sideways. As she did so, she suddenly saw that some-one was sitting beside her bed. It was Aranth watching her intently.

He now placed his large, warm hand on her slight shoulder and murmured, 'How are you, my love?'

Larthi's eyes closed again. She felt that she was dreaming and did not want to wake up.

'My love' came his voice again, accompanied by a gentle insistent caress, 'At last, you do seem a little better, thanks to the gods. I long to talk to you! Will you listen?'

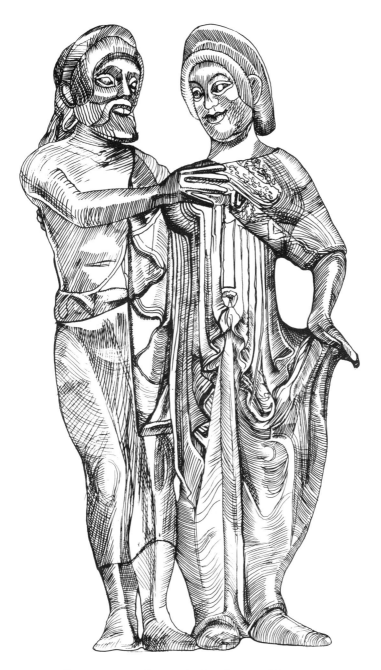

Bronze group of a couple. London, British Museum

Larthi looked at him incomprehendingly through her tears, but gave a slight nod.

'I now understand what's made you so ill.' His words tumbled out as if impatient to express what he had had to hold back for so long. 'I feel so distressed about all this - but I thought you knew all along. Oh, that scoundrel! How dare he raise his eyes to you! Peci told me what happened and you talked about it incessantly in your fever. If only I had known, I could have explained earlier!'

Larthi's eyes widened and her lips parted. She still did not understand why he was referring to her private sorrow in such an impassioned way.

'Why? What is it to you?' she whispered despondently.

'But Larthi!' he cried almost indignantly. 'Didn't you realize that I've always wanted to marry you ever since you were a little girl?'

She caught her breath sharply. Her mind refused to believe what she had just heard and she shook her head with a sad, incredulous smile.

'I've always loved you and I was certain you knew it. There was no point in saying anything about it on the few occasions I met you - you were still a mere child.'

Larthi felt as if carried away weightlessly by a stream. She gazed into Aranth's eager face and knew that he spoke the truth.

'But now I want you to promise me that you will marry me as soon as you are well enough.'

Emotion prevented her from answering at once.

Seizing her hand, he squeezed it gently between his palms. 'Promise!' he urged her again.

'I will,' she murmured, faint with joy. His eyes sparkled with happiness.

'You must go to sleep again now, so that you get better quickly,' he said and jumped up from the camp-stool beside her bed. Feebly she responded to the pressure of his hand and followed him with her eyes as he left the tent. The sudden surge of unexpected happiness had taxed her strength and she soon sank back into a deep and dreamless sleep.

The next day Aranth brought her a present. It was a little scent-jug of multi-coloured glass, supported in a ring-shaped stand of gold intricately decorated with patterns of filigree.

132

'It's beautiful,' she breathed, taking the vessel and letting a shaft of sunlight play on its subtle shades of opaque blue, aquamarine, turquoise and yellow. 'Thank you so much. The scent is lovely, too!' she added appreciatively when she had opened the stopper. Aranth looked down at her from his great height with a pleased and protective smile.

'It's only a small thing, but I'm glad that it gives you pleasure.'

'It does,' she said gratefully; 'but shall I tell you what would please me even more?'

He looked puzzled.

'I should love it if you could sit with me for a while and tell me about your life at sea and all the foreign places you have been to. You see - I know so very little about you.'

He laughed incredulously, doubtful that anyone could possibly be interested in what had happened to him in the past. Only the present seemed important to him. He did not care to recall past experiences or brood over things to come. But he sat down beside her indulgently enough and answered her many questions about strange phenomena such as the smoke-plumed mountains of the Aeolian islands and of Sicily, from whose interior the gods occasionally made flames and fiery rocks fly into the sky and about the sweet water of the fountain of Arethusa which rose mysteriously out of the briny harbour of Syracuse.

She wanted to know what Sybaris looked like before its destruction and about the coined silver and gold the Greeks used for trade instead of the cumbrous bronze bars which served as a means of exchange at home. His explanations were brief and concise and much that she had not understood in the past now made sense, looked at through his experienced eyes. Secretly however she longed for more. She would have loved to have known what he felt when faced with danger or an unfamiliar situation, or confronted by foreign men and women, or with signs sent by the gods. In her consuming love for him there was a deep desire to know his every thought, to understand him completely. It was not prompted by prying curiosity, but by an ardent wish to enter his mind so that she could make him happier than he had ever been before in his lonely, roving life.

133

While she slowly regained her strength, he came again and again and laughingly responded to all her questions, until finally he said, 'At this rate you'll soon know me better than I know myself.'

She wished it were true, but realized that his innermost being would always remain alien and remote from her. She also sensed that he was now anxious to return to Caisra. Inactivity and patient waiting were trying to his nature, and eventually she asked him to leave her behind in the care of her father and Peci until she was well enough to face the long journey home.

'If you want it that way, I'll certainly go,' he said, sounding somewhat relieved. 'There's so much to be done before our wedding and I don't seem to be of any use here.'

She smiled up at him with a mixture of joy and sadness. For a fleeting moment he had appeared vulnerable like a child.

7

Facing Aranth who was seated like her on a carved ivory stool, Larthi stretched out her right hand towards him. He seized it and gazed at her intently with shining eyes. She held a pomegranate, the symbol of fertility, in her lap and her hair was covered by the bridal veil. They both wore richly embroidered clothes with wide coloured borders. Aranth's red boots were of the softest leather, while Larthi's sandals were tied with straps of gold.

The various members of their families had assembled in a circle around them, all carrying laurel and myrtle branches, while the priests and youths with double-flutes and a cithara waited nearby. Accompanied by music throughout, Veilia and an elderly female cousin of Laris Matunas', who stood in for Larthi's dead mother, now approached the couple, bearing a large mantle with a rounded edge. Larthi's father and the priestess of Uni performed the sacrifice and intoned the ritual words of the marriage ceremonial, while the two ladies held up the newly woven mantle like a canopy over the heads of the seated pair. The heavy material hung down at the sides, partially hiding them from view. Aranth's mantle act-

Marriage ceremony (?) Low relief on a limestone funerary monument. From Chiusi. Rome, Museo Barracco

ing as a symbol of shelter and union emphasized their oneness as a wedded couple and their separateness from those outside.

Larthi was overcome by the solemnity of the occasion and with happiness. She felt her eyes fill with tears, but managed to smile at Aranth reassuringly. He squeezed her hand protectively and she recognized the familiar twinkle in his eyes. When the mantle had been lifted from their heads and folded up, they rose, laying their hands on each other's shoulders while keeping their right hands clasped together and then they spoke the hallowed formula which made them man and wife for ever.

The invited guests who had been watching the ceremony now approached to wish the young couple a long and fruitful life together, calling the blessings of the gods upon them. While the final preparations for a great out-of-doors banquet were being made, all the assembled company passed along, admiring the trousseau of the bride, which was on display under the pillared porch of the royal residence. A large number of presents had been given by the families' friends and by the heads of all the city's noble houses. The procession which conveyed Larthi's belongings to the home of her bridegroom had taken place the previous day. Preceded by musicians, several carts loaded with pieces of furniture and bronze utensils had been followed by a file of slave-girls, carrying on their heads chests and baskets containing Larthi's linen, clothes and jewellery and the vessel in which the spring-water for her bridal bath was to be fetched early on the morning of the wedding-day. Larthi's eyes now wandered over all the gifts as she listened a little absent-mindedly to the approving comments of the guests. She remembered once again the long weeks of the past autumn when she had lain at Velsena, slowly recovering from shock and fever. On the day of Aranth's departure he had brought her another present, a toilet-box, before which she now instinctively stopped while surveying the array of her possessions. It was made of bronze and shaped like a drum with a domed lid decorated with an engraved lozenge pattern. Inside it was divided into separate compartments for alabaster scent-bottles, dip-sticks, hair-pins, combs, pincers and a mirror. This cista had given her infinite pleasure during her long separation from Aranth, as it was elegant as well as useful. Now Larthi saw Ramtha admiring it as she approached.

She had come up together with her mother and threw her arms round Larthi. 'I'm so thankful the gods have granted you all this after your illness; may you be fortunate for ever!'

Larthi embraced her gratefully and showed her the toilet-box.

'Look what Marce gave to me when he last visited us three months ago,' responded Ramtha proudly, holding out her hand to show off a gold ring with an engraved seal-stone of carnelian in the shape of a scarab. 'And look at the other side,' she said. The gem's flat underside had been carved with the figure of a warrior.

Gold ring with scarab-shaped seal-stone of carnelian, carved with a figure of Achilles. Florence, Archaeological Museum

'He said it was to remind me of him while he is away fighting for his king - as if he was ever far from my thoughts!'

Larthi kissed her friend again, this time with a feeling of both pity for Ramtha and intense gratitude for her own good luck. How uncertain was Ramtha's future compared with her own settled fate! Unless the Tarquins were able to regain power at Ruma, there was no chance of Marce establishing a home and acquiring a position which would allow him to marry. Ramtha's simple faith in a propitious outcome struck Larthi as naive and touching.

'Our sons are on guard-duty this month,' Ramtha's mother said, 'but they send you both their best wishes for the blessings of the gods.'

Larthi thanked her and all the others who came invoking divine protection for her union with Aranth.

Scores of slaves had meanwhile arranged the dining-couches in an open rectangle amidst the flowering shrubs and trees of the garden, protected against lightning by a fence formed by white grape-vines. Wreaths of spring flowers awaited the guests and the persistent bird song added a joyous note to the royal wedding-feast. The king and Veilia presided over the banquet, dressed in magnificent garments. Rarely had Larthi seen Cousin Velthur in so benign and relaxed a mood. He teased Aranth, who was in truth, impatient to be alone with his bride and hardly tasted any of the delicious dishes served in seemingly endless succession. Aranth kept glancing at Larthi who also longed for quiet and privacy, but out of good manners responded politely to the many jesting remarks addressed to the young couple. Little Mamarce had been allowed to sit at the foot of his parent's couch, but soon felt neglected, as everyone seemed to pay exclusive attention to his stepbrother and Larthi. He began to fidget and whimper until his father turned on him in irritation, causing the boy to throw himself into his mother's arms wailing.

'Take him away,' said Velthur sternly to his wife; 'a wedding must not be disturbed by the ominous sound of weeping.'

Veilia rose in silence, clasped the crying child to her breast and went into the house with him. After some time she returned to her husband's side with a rigid, unsmiling face and refused to accept any further food and wine.

Having observed the sky and the position of the sun, Laris Matunas now announced that the moment was favourable for the newly-weds to retire for their union. Everyone rose, the musicians struck up again as Aranth seized his bride's hand. Larthi pulled her veil back over her hair and stood hesitant and blushing, while the traditional bawdy remarks were made by the guests to ward off malevolent spirits and ensure healthy offspring for the couple.

Flanked by the king and Laris Matunas on their right and by Veilia and the elderly cousin on their left, Aranth led Larthi towards the part of the garden where their marital bed stood hidden in a bower of laurel bushes decked with coloured fillets. As they approached the arbour, Veilia suddenly sneezed, but only Laris Matunas realized the significance of the omen and quickly made a sign to avert the evil it portended. Larthi heard the cooing of the doves courting amongst the foliage, a lovely sound indicating the auspicious presence of the goddess Turan. Shyly she responded to the passionate caress of Aranth's hand while they both acknowledged the blessings pronounced by their parents, who then rejoined their guests again.

Only the subdued strains of the dance-music from the feast reached the young couple as they entered the sun-dappled enclosure where their couch awaited them. Over its swelling mattress and bolsters Aranth's large mantle had been spread as a cover. The blood began to sing in Larthi's ears and her breath came fast as Aranth gently removed the clothes from her scented body and lifted her onto the bed. Trembling, she shut her eyes and succumbed to his caresses until his ardent hands and lips had taught her the ways of the goddess of love.

*Engraved bronze mirror
with a young couple beside
a bed. From Tarquinia.
Berlin-Charlottenburg,
Antikenabteilung*

8

The vintage was in progress. Larthi sat sewing with Peci in the shade of the palace porch from where she could hear the rhythmic treading of the grapes, punctuated by flute music. The air was redolent with the sweet juice and seemed heavy to her. She was three months pregnant and suffered from frequent sickness. It was becoming increasingly irksome for her to remain for long in one position and she got up impatiently. Peci's eyes followed her mistress with concern as she walked round the corner of the main body of the house towards the yard where the slaves were pressing the grapes.

In recent weeks Peci had sensed a growing restlessness in Larthi and, though she dared not enquire the reason for it, had her own ideas. She hardly felt at ease in her new surroundings herself. She had been born in the slaves' quarters of the household of Laris Matunas and had always looked upon that as her home. There she held a position of importance amongst her fellow-slaves, first as the trusted maid of Culni and then as an almost maternal friend of Larthi. Now that she was a part of the big and crowded royal establishment, she was just one of a vast body of servants to whom nobody paid any special respect. Larthi and her husband occupied handsome rooms and could have maintained a separate household from that of the king had they so wanted. In effect, however, they seemed to live the life of perpetual guests, with none of the independence and freedom of action that comes so naturally to the owner of a house of which he is the master. Aranth was often absent from the city, while Larthi's condition inevitably tied her more and more to her new abode. No wonder she felt unsettled and frustrated.

Against the walls of the courtyard which Larthi had entered, rows of tall conical baskets piled with grapes had been stacked by the pickers as they came in from the vineyards. In the centre a wide, flat-bottomed basket stood on a raised and slightly tilted stone trough with a shallow rim. The lowered side of the trough

140

was provided with a spout, underneath which a large clay jar had been placed to collect the grape-juice oozing from the bottom of the basket in which two slaves were treading a diminishing mass of grapes. The tune of a double-flute set the speed for their stamping which became gradually slower, eventually ceasing altogether. A slave who was supposed to replenish the supply from the full baskets waiting alongside the wall, unaccountably disappeared. Larthi stood gazing at this idle scene, lost in thought, when she was suddenly aware that the heat of the afternoon sun was giving her a headache. Massaging her temple in a long forgotten movement, she cast a worried look at the sky, where heavy clouds were threatening the north-west.

Just at that moment Veilia stepped into the courtyard. In the ordinary course of events Veilia would never have supervised the labours of the slaves, a task which was performed by Cae, the royal steward. As he was out on the slopes, assessing the amount of the harvesting still to be done, the domestic slaves had been left to work on their own. All the king's personal attendants had accompanied him on his annual hunting expedition in the coastal marshes. When Veilia saw the flautist crouching in the shade resting and the two slaves in the basket indolently eating the fruit instead of treading it, she called out sharply, 'Get on with it, you lazy lot!'

Without making any seeming distinction between the slaves she had reprimanded and Larthi, who had inactively stood by, she briefly glanced at her daughter-in-law with an expression of undisguised hatred. The slaves fell to work ostentatiously, while their mistress retired into her part of the house again. Larthi felt as if she had been hit by a whiplash and hastened from the yard. When she had reached the porch, she sat down heavily, supporting her aching head in her hands. Peci jumped up from her stool, alarmed by the distress in Larthi's face. Kneeling down beside her, she gazed at her mistress with pity and asked, 'Are you feeling sick again? Perhaps you'd better lie down in your room; it's really sweltering out here.'

Larthi shook her head. 'I will not go in there again,' she suddenly said vehemently; 'never again!'

'Mistress!' Peci exclaimed, deeply apprehensive, 'What do you mean? This is the house of your husband and it is your home.'

But Larthi went on, the words coming from her lips in strange and broken tones, 'There is evil lurking here - I mustn't stay.' She rose slowly and as if in a trance, began to walk away towards her father's house.

Peci glanced about her anxiously. Nobody was in sight whose help and advice she could have sought. The sky looked menacing now, thunder-clouds rapidly obscuring the sun completely. Snatching up the piece of material she had been hemming, she rushed after Larthi to protect her from the rain which had begun to fall heavily. Larthi appeared not to notice her servant as she slowly continued to cross the square in front of the royal residence on which she had turned her back. With fixed eyes and ignoring the ominous and prolonged rumbling of thunder, she wended her way through the rain-swept streets until she reached her former home. Hardly had she stepped under its projecting eaves, when a blinding flash of lightning, followed immediately by a terrifying thunder clap, made Peci cower at her feet and burst into gabbled prayers. Larthi turned silently and made the sign to avert evil.

Her father, who at that moment hurried from the house, instinctively echoed her movement.

'What has brought you from your home in such weather?' he asked her sternly, looking distractedly at her pale face and at the lowering clouds. 'You should take more care of yourself and the child you are carrying. Where is your husband?'

Larthi woke as if from a nightmare. 'He went to Pyrgoi two days ago to see about beaching the ships,' she answered slowly, moving her hand across her forehead. 'I'm afraid for him now - the storm came from the north-west.'

Laris Matunas peered into the distance and murmured, 'That quarter of the sky looks brighter now; do not be alarmed. The peril is elsewhere.'

He stepped into the street and turned in the direction from which Larthi had come.

'This awesome lightning must have struck somewhere close - I dread its import, as today is the hazardous seventh day of the week,' he mused.

From the neighbouring houses people began to emerge hesitantly, looking with apprehension towards that part of the town

142

where the thunderbolt appeared to have fallen. The rain had ceased. Laris Matunas called for Teitu and Thresu to accompany him and told Peci and Fasti to prepare a bed for Larthi in the meantime. She looked ashen and leant weakly against a pillar of the porch. Devoid of all strength, she was supported into her father's house by the maids.

Laris Matunas hastened through the wet streets which gleamed in the eerie light of the re-emerging sun. When he had almost reached the open space in front of the royal palace, he was met by two of Veilia's slaves who had been sent to fetch him. Talking and gesticulating incoherently, they told him how their mistress and her young son were beside themselves with fright, as the lightning had missed their house only narrowly, striking the paved part of the square directly in front of it.

Laris Matunas clapped his hand over his mouth, stifling an exclamation of alarm. According to the sacred books on the interpretation of lightnings, the lightning which hits a public place is a sign for the king himself, indicating imminent danger for his life and rule. Hurriedly dispatching Teitu and Thresu to ask Larth Repesunas and Piana Velavesnas to attend him in the execution of his religious duties, Laris Matunas now approached the inauspicious spot, which was already surrounded by large numbers of agitated people. He raised his augural staff and ordered everyone to stand back; the crowd obeyed awestruck.

Shattered and blackened remains of one of the large paving-slabs lay strewn about a gaping hole in the ground near the entrance of the abode of Velthur Velchanas. Some of the fragments had been thrown up against its façade and had damaged the terracotta decoration of the gable. These signs of the force and direction of the thunderbolt's impact left no doubt in Laris Matunas' mind: it was the third and most dangerous of the three lightnings which Tinia, the supreme god, was able to hurl. This ultimate lightning at his disposal could not have been cast by Tinia without first consulting the shrouded gods, eternally enveloped in mystery and known to be pitiless. The gravity of the portent was overwhelming.

In the absence of the king and his eldest son, the responsibility for performing immediately the proper rites of expiation fell on Laris Matunas as chief augur, haruspex and interpreter of light-

Bronze statuette of an
augur. From Gabii. Rome,
Soprintendenza archeologica

144

nings. He informed Veilia of his intentions through her servants and asked her to send messengers to her husband and Aranth without delay. Nerie Peipnas, one of the few noblemen who, on account of advanced age and infirmity, were not serving in rotation with the army, had joined Laris Matunas and now offered to summon the priesthood of Tinia. This enabled Laris Matunas to make the necessary arrangements for the burial of the lightning and the sacrifices of atonement. On arriving home again, he was informed by Teitu that he had not found Piana Velavesnas in his house. Nobody knew where he had gone when he left with Thefarie Velianas, some hours before the storm broke. This unexpected piece of information was perplexing. What business could a fellow-haruspex, closely related to the royal family, have with a man like Thefarie Velianas?

Laris Matunas' thoughts were interrupted by the appearance of Larth Repesunas, who had responded promptly to the call to join in the singular rite. But senility and over-excitement rendered him useless. In an agitated effort to assist, he dropped the sacrificial knife of iron, so that part of its ivory handle split off, and when attempting to fill the censer with the swinging handle, he spilt most of the incense grains. None of this boded well for the ensuing ceremony.

It took some considerable time before all the instruments and oblations had been collected into baskets and the two stone-masons had arrived with a cart containing all their necessary tools, as well as several stone slabs. Laris Matunas and Larth Repesunas, followed by slaves carrying the baskets and by the builders' cart, set out again for the ominous spot. The priests of Tinia with their sacrificial attendants and musicians had already assembled near it, while at a certain distance an ever increasing crowd was moving about uneasily.

The traditional expiatory slaughter of a sheep preceded the rite of the burial of the thunderbolt. All the blackened fragments of stone and tiles and the scattered lumps of soil were carefully gathered and placed in the hole made by the lightning, together with the prescribed offerings. Next, the tomb was filled up, the ground levelled and four slabs of stone erected above it in the shape of a small ridge-roof. The masons secured the slabs in position with metal clamps and finally constructed an enclosure around the spot. Henceforth this precinct was to be for ever inaccessible to human beings - a place both sacred and accursed!

When Laris Matunas had performed his duties, the priests of Tinia began to intone their prayers, interceding with the god on behalf of the threatened head of state. While they were engaged in propitiatory oblations, the tempest, to which nobody had had time to pay any attention, returned with renewed fury. A cloud-burst extinguished the sacrificial fire on the portable altar and diluted the offered liquids. In fear and dismay the priests snatched up the sacred utensils and fled for shelter to the temple of Tinia. The crowd, too, had scattered. Laris Matunas was seized by a terrible feeling of foreboding. A premature darkness enveloped the city as the storm-clouds blotted out the setting sun. It became increasingly clear to him that the gods had indicated that they were implacable - no further prayers or gifts could avert the fate they had decided upon. All that remained for mankind was to suffer what was decreed.

9

The king's body, covered by gold-embroidered robes, had been laid to rest beside that of his first wife in the royal grave-mound. Most of Velthur Velchanas' precious possessions - his splendid armour and weapons and the ceremonial chariot which had belonged to his father before him - were placed in the anteroom of the burial-chamber, together with the big bronze krater, Aranth's homecoming-gift. Gold and silver dishes, cups, jugs and wine-strainers were hung from nails driven into the tufa rock of the tomb's walls, which were carved with brightly painted, life-size reliefs of shields. A pair of rock-cut chairs with high, rounded backs and footstools flanked the door to the central alcove where the royal couple lay. These thrones symbolized the heightened existence of the heroized dead and were thought to be occupied by them while they enjoyed their customary offerings of wine, milk, honey and other nourishment.

146

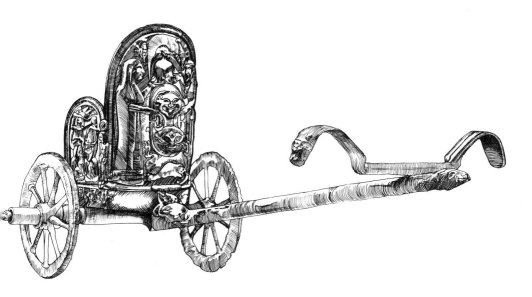

Bronze parade chariot. From Monteleone di Spoleto. New York, Metropolitan Museum

When the final rites had been accomplished, Aranth, Laris Matunas and the priests of the divinities of the underworld ascended the staircase leading from the tomb to the level of the street and the entrance was closed up again with a massive stone slab. The small piazza in front of the tumulus was crowded with mourners, members of the royal household and of the great families of Caisra. Larthi stood by herself, being the only female relation of the king to be present; Veilia, who had remained in the palace, was said to be in a state of complete shock.

Neither Aranth nor Laris Matunas had seen the queen since the lightning had struck. When Aranth reached home from Pyrgoi on the day after the fateful sign from heaven, it was his father-in-law who had received him and reported on the measures he had taken in an attempt to avert the threatening disaster. Together they anxiously calculated the length of time needed for Veilia's messenger to reach the king and warn him, and the earliest possible hour of his return, when two of the royal servants, who had been taking part in the hunting-expedition, rode up on exhausted mules. Their faces revealed the terrible news even before they had

147

been able to speak: the king was dead. On the very day when the hunting-party had observed a distant thunder-storm in the direction of Caisra, the king had been stalking a particularly large boar. For weeks this fierce beast had caused havoc in the fields which bordered the marshes, wallowing in the corn and uprooting newly planted vines. A deputation of the terrorized local farmers had called on the king, begging him to relieve them of the brute. In the afternoon the boar had finally been located and cornered in a swampy spot, accessible only to one man at a time. The king had hurled his first spear which, although it had pierced the creature's flank, did not kill it. Infuriated by the pain, the boar had broken from its cover of reeds and charged at the king, who stood calmly waiting for it with his second spear poised. As he struck, the far away rumbling of thunder was heard by everyone present, followed by the sharp, splintering noise of the royal spear-shaft breaking. The king collapsed, falling backwards under the thrust of the dying beast, fatally wounded by its fearsome tusks.

Reflecting once more on the sinister events of the past few days, Larthi realized with awe that the burden of prophetic vision must have descended on her again. Had she not sensed the imminence of evil when she had abruptly left the lauchumna - the royal house? Was it now the will of the gods that she should return to live there together with Aranth, the heir to the king? She strained her mind as if to penetrate the darkness of the future, but she could see no light. No image of impending happiness in the palace arose before her inner eye. With humility and resignation she accepted that it was beyond her powers to use her gift intentionally - it came from the gods and it was their's to grant or withhold as they saw fit.

She was recalled from her musings by the bard, who had begun pronouncing a eulogy on the dead king in front of his tomb. In resounding phrases he glorified the ancient house of the Velchana and their noble deeds over many generations, culminating in eloquent praise of the departed Velthur: wise in the dispensation of justice, generous to his people, brave and resourceful in war. He extolled the king's deeds of valour as the leader of the army which had fought in Campania some twenty years earlier, his benevolent rule which had increased the wealth and power of Caisra, his skilful

148

diplomacy during his term as federal leader of the Rasenna, his lavish hospitality to his friends and finally his heroic end in killing the monster which had been the bane of his subjects.

Larthi's dejection gave way to pride, as she listened to this account of the family's eminence and merits. Her eyes searched for those of Aranth who stood beside the singer, totally absorbed. She prayed ardently that the son she felt sure she was carrying would continue this illustrious line worthily in the manner of his forefathers.

The oration was to be followed by the traditional funerary games outside the city. Aranth had already set aside valuable prizes from the royal store-house for the victors. But before the mourners left the cemetery to join the common people in the arena, they got ready to witness the age-old ceremony of the game of the Phersu. Larthi remembered from her father's teachings in her child-hood that this rite sometimes ended in the death of one of the combatants, who was usually a condemned criminal or a prisoner of war. It appeared that in the distant past human sacrifices had been performed upon the tombs of royalty and that the Phersu-combat was a survival of this ancient funerary custom.

The mourners now stepped back to make room for the performance and took up positions along the sides of the irregular little piazza. Larthi found a seat on an outcrop of rock at the base of one of the mounds surrounding the open space. A big, muscular man, naked but for a loin-cloth, was meanwhile brought into the centre led by two of the priests. His head was entirely enveloped by a thick piece of material, secured tightly round his neck; it blindfolded him completely. A stout wooden club was put into his hand, which he wielded in a tentative way, turning his head this way and that, as if to anticipate the direction from which his attacker was likely to set upon him. The Phersu was an extraordin-ary-looking character. He now skipped into the circle formed by the spectators, wearing a brief, tight-fitting tunic with short sleeves of a deep red shade. A mass of irregularly-shaped, multi-coloured patches were sewn onto the bodice, which lent a ludicrous air to the garment. The comic aspect of this outfit was however contra-dicted by the sinister head-dress of the Phersu, which consisted of a pointed cap of dark colour, shaped rather like a helmet with

149

Phersu running away. Fresco from the Tomba degli Auguri at Tarquinia

raised cheek-guards. Attached to this was simulated hair, rising stiffly above the forehead, with a bearded mask covering the entire face. Through the holes in the mask Larthi could see the Phersu's eyes darting about rapidly.

He controlled a fierce dog with the help of an exceptionally long leash tied to its collar. Suddenly he released the collar, setting the dog on the victim. With violent barks it flew at the blindfolded man, who tried to defend himself with his club. His frantic efforts to fight off the dog were, however, hampered by its leash held firmly by the Phersu. Its coils gradually enveloped the limbs and body of the man as he spun around, hitting out at the attacking hound, making it more and more difficult for him to move with any speed or aim his blows effectively. The dog's sharp fangs had already drawn much blood from the victim, who by now was beginning to groan while the Phersu continued to incite it to further attacks. Dancing around with fiendish agility, he managed to enmesh the man's legs so that he stumbled repeatedly and was almost brought to his knees. At this point the dog fastened on the condemned man's left thigh and would not let go. Painfully hurt as he was and streaming with blood, he succeeded in gripping the dog's collar and struck the creature on the head so that its skull cracked and it collapsed dead at his feet.

Larthi felt utterly sickened by the sight and covered her eyes with her hands. But the other spectators, who had followed the cruel game with breathless excitement, loudly encouraged the wounded man to remove the cover from his head and take his revenge on the Phersu, as he had now won his freedom. Tugging with his lacerated hands at the ties which fastened the cloth round his neck, he at last managed to tear it off. The sudden light dazzled him, however, and his first blow missed the Phersu, who capered about him mockingly. The man lurched forward once more, again failing to hit his tormentor and staggered after him ineffectively, as the Phersu escaped finally through the crowd.

The nervous tension which had built up in the spectators during this sinister game now released itself in laughter and loud acclaim at the victim's endurance and skill. But Larthi wondered sadly if the man would ever survive the terrible wounds inflicted on him. Although he had triumphed over the demon of death, represented by the masked Phersu and his dog, she feared he would be claimed by the dreaded ruler of the underworld before long.

10

The baby was crying again. With a sigh Larthi got up from the loom where she had been working and bent over the child's basket, vainly trying to calm him. He gripped her finger in his tiny fist but continued to cry.

'Oh, Vel, Vel,' she said wearily, lifting up her son, 'I feel just like you, only it's no use crying - it won't bring your father back to us.'

Ramtha, who was sitting close to the candelabra sewing, looked up and said, 'Let me take him for a while; you must be worn out with lack of sleep. He's teething. I remember what it was like when our Arnza was a baby.' She raised the little boy high into the air; he caught sight of the burning candles and gazed at them in amazement. His wailing ceased and Ramtha turned to Larthi with a delighted smile. Larthi looked at her friend gratefully and settled down to her loom again. How unselfish and helpful Ramtha had been, despite her own unhappiness.

Dandling Vel on her knees, she hummed a little tune to which he responded by kicking his legs, wrapped in swaddling-clothes.

'You are going to be a big boy soon,' Ramtha talked to the baby and managed to hold his attention; 'and one day you will be a big, strong man, just like your father and then you'll help him to get rid of the rabble that has taken over our city and we shall all be happy once again.'

The baby's dark eyes, which had been fixed on Ramtha's face, drifted away, the lids slowly closing. His small thumb found its way back into his mouth and his head crowned with downy black hair sank back into the crook of her arm. Very gently she got up and placed Vel in his basket again.

'Sometimes I cannot believe what has happened to us,' Larthi murmured, as Ramtha took up her sewing once more.

'Unfortunately it's real enough,' she answered, sighing; 'I remember so well years ago when Marce first had to leave us, you told me how you feared that what had been the fate of the Tarquins at Ruma, might well happen in Caisra, too.'

'Did I?' said Larthi, marvelling once again at her insight as a young girl. 'What I did not foresee was that I would be married to a member of the royal family then and that the end of the monarchy would be brought about by that upstart Thefarie Velianas,' she added bitterly.

'I've been thinking about all that so much recently,' Ramtha said. 'Do you remember the day when we went to the temple of Hera to pray for your aunt's life?'

'I shall never forget the menacing face of that slave who attacked me and the hostile crowd surrounding us, who would not come to our help until that man rescued us - it was probably the only decent thing Thefarie Velianas ever did in his life,' Larthi said in disgust, shoving the shuttle so forcefully that it hit the frame of the loom with a loud click. She cast an anxious glance at the baby's basket, hoping that the noise had not wakened him again.

'Oh, but I do feel certain now that in fact it was he who had already tried to incite the common people and the slaves to revolt against the king. Do you remember noticing that he was the only man of any standing in the market-place at that time and that they obeyed him like sheep, when he told them to go home quietly.'

Larthi gazed at her friend with astonishment. 'That had never occurred to me,' she said; 'but you must be right. I remember clearly how we met Uncle Caile who told us that he had heard seditious speeches being addressed to a crowd as he passed on his way to the lauchumna. He probably reported it, and as usual, nobody took any notice of what he said. I suppose Thefarie Velianas must have been testing the mood of the people and, when he didn't find enough support, he postponed his plans, or rather changed them . . .' she looked broodingly into the candlelight.

'Yes,' Ramtha continued, 'he must have feared that his attempt to stir up trouble would get out, which is probably why he left the country for such a long time. We had almost forgotten him, when -'

'When he came back, bursting with his ill-gotten Carthaginian gains with which he thought he could buy me and so insinuate himself into the aristocracy,' Larthi interrupted her, whispering fiercely. 'And to think that he succeeded in the latter, despite my having rejected him!'

'I would never have believed Veilia capable of such treachery,' Ramtha said.

'Nor would I, though I knew she hated me from the moment I married Aranth. His return must have been a blow to her schemes in the first place. I expect she hoped that he would perish abroad and never come home to succeed his father. And then when I became pregnant, she realized that her ambitions for Mamarce were frustrated. That's when she and that kinsman of hers must have put their heads together to devise some scheme and meanwhile, there was Thefarie Velianas, plotting and bribing and rousing that rabble . . .' She held her hands over her eyes. 'How blind we must have been not to have noticed!'

'We were much too preoccupied by the events in our own lives,' Ramtha said. 'Just think of all the things that happened during that period. There was your illness, and then your wedding, and your pregnancy - when the king and Aranth were completely engrossed in reorganizing the army and the fleet. We were all expecting an enemy from abroad, what with Porsenna starting his campaign in Latium . . .'

Ramtha stopped overwhelmed by emotion; her voice became unsteady, her eyes filling with tears. This time it was Larthi who got up to comfort her friend. Standing behind Ramtha's chair, she looked down sorrowfully on her fair, bent head and put her hands on her shoulders, which were shaking with suppressed sobbing.

'Porsenna got just what he deserved,' Larthi said sternly. 'His army was routed and he lost his son Arruns in the battle. But we lost Marce. So the gods gave victory with one hand and ended a life dear to us with the other.'

Ramtha cried bitterly, while Larthi stroked her hair.

'We should be proud of Marce,' she went on. 'I haven't told you yet, because I thought it might upset you, that a secret messenger from Avile Spurinna arrived only yesterday with news. You can imagine how difficult it must have been to get through for any partisan of the Tarquins, or anybody with Greek connections, or indeed anyone related to us - with Thefarie Velianas' spies and henchmen everywhere. That't why it took so long for Avile

154

Spurinna's man to reach us and let us know how it all happened.'

She knelt down beside Ramtha who had pressed the stuff she was sewing against her face, in an attempt to stifle her heart rending sobs.

'Let me tell you how brave he was,' Larthi continued gently. 'We know that King Tarquin, after all his failed attempts to regain power at Ruma with the help of the Rasenna, had sought refuge in Latium with his son-in-law, Mamilius Octavius at Tusculum. Porsenna was anxious to strengthen his own hold on Ruma and eliminate the Tarquins once and for all. He therefore attacked the Latin League, who had sided with the exiled king. The troops under Porsenna's son Arruns managed to drive back the Latin army on Aricia, which is the site of their federal sanctuary, just as Velsena is ours. Besieged though they were within the walls, the Latins were able to send for help to the Greeks of Kyme. The Kymeans dispatched Aristodemos with an expeditionary force. He sailed up with his troops, disembarked on the coast and marched them to

Bronze statuette of a swordsman. From the top of a candelabrum. Oxford, Ashmolean Museum

155

Aricia. From what the messenger told us, it is clear that Marce was one of the envoys who went to Kyme and that he returned with the Greek relief-army. Together with a body of Aristodemos' soldiers he succeeded in separating Arruns from his men; after which, it was Marce himself, in fact, who was responsible for killing Arruns!'

Ramtha raised her head and looked at Larthi expectantly with tear-filled eyes.

'After that Porsenna's troops were quickly routed by the Greeks and the besieged Latins who sallied out from Aricia. Aristodemos' strategy must have been brilliant. Unfortunately, while stripping Arruns' body of his weapons and armour, Marce was killed by some of Porsenna's bodyguard, who had come up too late to save their king's son.'

Ramtha pressed the cloth against her face again with a low moan. The candlelight caught the ring which Marce had given her and made it gleam.

'Look at the warrior on your gem-stone,' Larthi said quietly; 'he is Achilles in the splendid armour his mother, the goddess Thetis, had made for him by Hephaistos, whom we call Sethlans. Achilles was the greatest hero amongst all the Greeks - but despite his bravery and his divine mother's prayers, he had to die, because fate had decreed it so. It is the same for all of us mortals.'

11

Laris Matunas leant over the gaming-board, pondering his next move. Caile, sitting opposite him and waiting his turn, stretched out his clammy hands towards the charcoal-burner on the floor.

'How cold it is!' he said to Larthi, who was nursing her baby.

She nodded and pulled her mantle closer round Vel who sucked contentedly.

'Thresu! Thresu!' Caile shouted, 'bring in some more charcoal - we are freezing!'

Startled by the noise, the child stopped feeding and began to whimper.

Larthi cast an exasperated glance at her uncle. How she wished the weather would improve so that he could get out of the house more. Since he had moved in with them, because he claimed he felt safer in the house of an augur, he had managed to upset not only all their slaves by his demanding manner, but was a sore trial to her father and herself.

'Thresu is helping to slaughter the pig; they are all very busy over there in the yard,' she said, attempting to persuade the baby to go on with his feed.

'It's most annoying that one has got to do everything oneself these days,' Caile grumbled, as he got up to fetch the charcoal himself.

Laris Matunas at last made his move. Larthi noticed with disquiet that he fumbled towards the piece, as if unable to see it properly in the dim light of the winter-day. Was he losing his sight, she wondered. Once or twice recently she had noticed him hesitate on entering a dark room or when walking on uneven ground. He never read in the sacred books now. She had not in fact seen him unfold them since Piana Velavesnas had been proclaimed chief augur. Suddenly she realized how much he had suffered during the upheaval, as much indeed as she had herself; it made her look at him with fresh eyes. How pronounced his stoop had become just recently and how grey his hair had turned within the last year! Even in former days he had rarely smiled, but since her return home during the storm that heralded the king's death, a permanent deep furrow between his brows betrayed his profound despondency. Larthi felt sad and discouraged. She longed to comfort him, to hold out some hope that their condition might get better again one day. At the same time she felt oppressed by the mounting weight of responsibility on her shoulders. If her father were to fail now in health and good council, the burden on herself would become intolerable. It was useless looking to Caile for help and support.

Her mind and body craved for Aranth. She could hardly bear to be separated from him much longer. There had been no further news from him since a messenger had come secretly from Pupluna to report that Aranth had arrived there safely and had found refuge' with his friend Teucer Hermenas. The messenger's instructions were to ask for a couple of homing-pigeons to be handed to him for Aranth's use, but over a year had passed since then and none of the birds had returned. Larthi herself was unable to send anyone to Pupluna for tidings - all their slaves and freedmen were too well known to escape recognition by Thefarie Velianas' spies and she dreaded betraying Aranth's whereabouts. The continued uncertainty however was beginning to wear her down.

Caile returned with a basin of charcoal and put some pieces of it on the bronze brazier, while fanning the smouldering embers with a dry bird's wing.

'There's one advantage, at least, in being deprived of Greek slaves,' he observed, still ruminating on the personal discomforts the change in their fortunes had wrought; 'you do hear far more gossip.'

'How is that?' Laris Matunas asked, looking up from the gaming board.

'Well, as I have to go to the barber's nowadays to be shaved and to have my body hair plucked, I'm thrown together with all sorts of people I would never have dreamt of consorting with before. The place is filthy, of course. Everyone who passes by in the street can see you being done and I loathe the familiarity of Vetu, the owner of the establishment, but you do hear a lot of news.'

'If only you would let Teitu shave you, as he does me, there would be no need for you to frequent such common haunts,' Laris Matunas remarked.

'If Teitu were thirty years younger and less clumsy with the knife and the tweezers, I would certainly avail myself of his services. But he must be as blind as a bat, to judge from the mess he made shaving me the only time I ever tried him.'

'None of us get any younger,' said Laris Matunas, his voice sounding irritated. 'Let's be grateful for our faithful old servants who remain with us in these bad times.'

'Oh, how I miss not being able to choose handsome young Greek slaves! The supply has dried up completely since the pass was sold to the Carthaginians by that man whose name I cannot bring myself to pronounce.'

'Weren't you going to tell us the news you heard at the barber's?' said Larthi, who had put Vel to sleep in his basket and pulled up her chair to the brazier to rake over the charcoal.

'It was nothing special, really,' Caile said, having turned his attention to the gaming-board once more, 'except that I gather a lot of people are becoming disenchanted with the man whom not so long ago they hailed as a better and fairer ruler than Cousin Velthur, particularly all those merchants who now find themselves out of business because of the Carthaginians.'

Staring at the glowing charcoal, Larthi remembered once again the harrowing day of the king's funeral - it was like a recurring nightmare: the terrible confusion everywhere, her mortal fear for Aranth when Cae, the royal steward, had come up breathlessly to the cemetery to warn them, just as they were setting out for the stadium.

Cae had been supervising the preparations for the dinner in the lauchumna, to be served to the mourners after the funeral games, when the house was suddenly invaded by armed men who, though they threatened the slaves and cowed them into handing over the weapons from the armoury, did not show any violence to the widowed queen and her son. The steward managed to escape unnoticed. He threw himself onto a horse and galloped to the stadium, where he expected Aranth to be presiding over the games. Instead he found a waiting crowd of commoners and slaves being harangued into rebellion by Thefarie Velianas, who stood surrounded by his numerous bodyguards, all armed to the teeth. The demagogue was accusing the dead king and his family of tyrannical rule and sympathizing with the Greeks, the inveterate enemies of the Rasenna. He claimed that the gods themselves had signified their rejection of Velthur Velchanas by their dreadful sign from heaven. He claimed that he, Thefarie Velianas, was the only champion and liberator of the oppressed classes and that he would henceforth protect the people and the city. The tumultuous applause which came from a large section of the assembly at the conclusion of this vehement speech, made Cae aware of the extreme danger that Aranth and the heads of the noble families would run, were they to arrive at the stadium without being warned. The mutinous mob was in a very ugly mood.

Cae retreated unobtrusively from the edge of the crowd and hastened to where he had tied up his horse. He reached the ceme-

159

tery just as the mourners were preparing to leave for the games.

On hearing the news, Aranth immediately decided to storm the stadium and call Thefarie Velianas to account. But some of the older noblemen restrained him, pointing out that they were all unarmed and that the troops loyal to them were stationed in frontier-posts too far to reach in time for a concerted attack on the rebellious part of the populace. Utter confusion reigned for a while. Larthi recalled imploring Aranth again and again to save his life and flee the country. He wouldn't listen to her. He frantically cast about for means of raising support to crush the uprising. But when he realized that it was impossible to come to grips with the usurper on the spot, he at last agreed to seek refuge in the north. Most of the other noblemen, too, decided to leave Caisra until it was safe to return.

Laris Matunas, however, declared that he would stay behind to look after Larthi and her child, knowing that, as the chief augur, he would be treated with respect and religious awe. It was this decision which in the end swayed Aranth. Larthi remembered vividly how she had pushed him from her, desperately urging him to mount the horse on which Cae had arrived. The memory made her heart ache. What she would give now to embrace him just for one moment! He did not even know yet that he was the father of a son. Her physical need for Aranth suddenly became so overwhelming that she made up her mind to steal away from the city one night and make her way to Pupluna. The short, gloomy winter days would be an advantage, as few people would be likely to work in the fields at such a time. She would travel light and only take Cupe and a mule with her, thus avoiding recognition. The sooner Aranth was made aware of the situation in Caisra the better, it would enable him to lay plans for the future. The news would come as a complete shock to him, but it was surely better that he should be told it by her rather than some anonymous person. The whole extent of Veilia's treachery, she knew, would seem improbable to him, as it had to them, until they managed to piece together various apparently disconnected events and the reports of Cae and other loyal servants.

It transpired that shortly after the wedding of Aranth and Larthi, Veilia, using Piana Velavesnas as intermediary, had suggested

160

to Thefarie Velianas that, if he were to eliminate the king and Aranth, she would be prepared to marry him and so lend him legitimacy as future ruler of Caisra. The knowledge of his importunate wooing of Larthi had clearly inspired Veilia to do this. It seemed the most promising way of realizing her burning ambition for Mamarce. Thefarie Velianas had accepted this unexpected offer with alacrity, since it provided him with the semblance of a legal claim not only to the succession, but to the vast properties of the royal family. This was all the more welcome for, during his protracted secret efforts to influence popular opinion in his favour, he had given away a great deal of his own fortune in bribes, and his personal wealth was nearly exhausted. By promising to close the ports to Greek shipping, if he came to power, and to exile Greek merchants residing in Agylla, he had already secured the political support of the Carthaginians, who were anxious to extend their own trade and influence in the coastal waters.

Though Thefarie Velianas' well-laid plans depended on removing the king and his eldest son, he could not bring himself to have them assassinated. At this point, Piana Velavesnas, eager to ingratiate himself even further with the future husband of his ambitious kinswoman, suggested resorting to an ancient and dreadful ritual, that of drawing down a fatal thunderbolt on the royal house. On the day of the storm, when Cae was inspecting the vineyards to the north of the city, he had observed Thefarie Velianas and Piana Velavesnas engaging in a rite, the meaning of which escaped him at the time. What had struck him, however, was the clandestine nature of the proceedings, for the two men while performing this arcane ceremony had carefully chosen an isolated outcrop of rock at the far end of the necropolis-ridge which was rarely visited. The darkening sky and the cloudburst which preceded the lightning, prevented Cae from noticing every detail, but the coincidence of their action with the ominous thunderbolt made him suspicious and he consulted Laris Matunas, when Thefarie Velianas had conspicuously rewarded Piana Velavesnas for services rendered, by choosing him as his chief augur and haruspex.

By then too many other proofs of the conspiracy between Veilia, her kinsman, and the usurper had come to light to leave Laris Matunas in any doubt as to the nature of the secret incantations carried out on that ill-fated day in the deserted corner of the cemetery. This discovery however only added bitterness to their circumstances, as they were powerless to denounce or punish this sacrilegious act. Most of the heads of the great families had felt it prudent to retire from the city to remote country-properties or to go abroad, while others, in view of the powerful Carthaginian presence, had acquiesced in the situation and left Thefarie Velianas to rule Caisra without further demur.

The thought of all their misfortunes made Larthi beat the fire-rake on the floor in futile anger. The dull thud caused her father and uncle to turn round. At that moment the door was pushed open hastily and Teitu and Thresu burst into the room, making the three of them jump to their feet alarmed. The servants' aprons were bespattered with blood. Thresu was still clutching the bronze flesh-hook which was used for lifting meat from the boiling cauldron, while a pigeon perched on Teitu's wrist. The bird sidled up his forearm and blinked at the fire uneasily, but it allowed itself to be taken off by Laris Matunas when Teitu had whispered excitedly, 'It's one of the pair we sent to master Aranth!'

Larthi's heart began to pound violently while her father felt for the bird's legs. Teitu explained rapidly, 'It just kept fluttering from one corner of the courtyard to the other until we realized that it wasn't one of our ordinary pigeons and brought it in immediately.'

As Laris Matunas detached a small roll of linen from the bird's leg, unwound it and peered at the writing on it without a word, Larthi said eagerly, 'Oh, do let me read it for you, please!'

'I need more light,' he murmured and Caile sent Thresu for a candelabrum.

'Let me try, father, please!' Larthi entreated and he handed her the strip of linen.

It contained a brief message from Aranth, saying that he was well, but anxious for news from them. He had been engaged in a joint business venture, which took him and Teucer Hermenas north to the mouth of the river Po and promised well for the future. If conditions were favourable, he would visit Caisra secretly, but he needed their advice before attempting it.

'Father!' Larthi exclaimed, when she had read it out, 'we cannot let him run the risk of coming back here.'

162

Laris Matunas nodded in gloomy agreement.

'And neither you nor Caile could leave the city without being noticed, but I could get away easily one night - nobody would know. You could tell everybody that I was ill or that Vel was sick, if people remarked on my absence. Surely, father, you must see that this is the only way we can do it. Please, let me go!' she urged him, as he shook his head doubtfully.

'Father,' she said desperately, 'you know that I must go and anyway I have made up my mind. Peci will look after Vel. I'll take Cupe with me - he knows all the roads and we can travel by night.'

Laris Matunas looked at his daughter searchingly for a moment and then he raised his hands in prayer: 'May the gods protect you and bring you back safely.'

12

Larthi was expecting her second child. Vel's birth five years earlier had been difficult and long drawn-out, despite the skilled midwifery of Teitu's wife. Only after the boy had at last been born, an old maid of Veilia's was discovered squatting cross-legged outside the door with her clothing tied in knots and her fingers locked together, a sign of evil magic which had managed to delay the delivery.

Realizing that she was pregnant again after the last of her secret visits to Aranth, Larthi decided to make a pilgrimage to the sanctuary of the great mother-goddess Uni at Pyrgoi to pray for an easier birth. Laris Matunas insisted on accompanying her on this trip, although his eyesight had by now become extremely poor. Larthi readily agreed, as it was clearly a matter of pride for her father to act as her and Vel's guide and protector. But she could not help smiling, when she considered how short and safe the proposed ride to the city's largest harbour was, compared with the long and dangerous journeys abroad that she had undertaken in the last few years with only a slave to attend her.

This visit would be their first to the sanctuary since it had been enlarged and embellished by Thefarie Velianas and his Carthaginian allies. Had it not been necessary to propitiate the protectress of childbirth, Larthi and her father would have preferred not to have been seen in a place that was now so conspicuously associated with the tyrant. During her repeated journeys north to see Aranth, Larthi had succeeded in escaping detection, partly because of the secrecy with which she had moved and partly because the passage of time had blunted the vigilance of Thefarie Velianas' spies. In any case, the usurper felt unassailable now, since none of the aristocrats remaining in Caisra had attempted to oust him, while those who had fled to other cities did not seem able to raise enough support to carry out a coup.

Thefarie Velianas commanded the loyalty of a broad section of the local people benefitting from trade with the Carthaginians, who now enjoyed exclusive access to the markets formerly dominated by Greek merchandise. However, all those independent ship-owners and sailors who had staked their fortunes on profitable exchanges with Greek cities in the past, were now deprived of their livelihood and suffered great hardship. Some of the better-off managed to improve their agricultural properties and raise new crops, but the landless and the small merchants, whose old-established sources of supply had been cut off, found it difficult to make ends meet. Their hopes for a redistribution of land, which Thefarie Velianas had hinted at when agitating for the overthrow of the king, were disappointed. He had called himself champion of the oppressed classes while relying on their support to gain power, but now seemed to have forgotten his earlier promises and had turned into a more grasping tyrant than any of the previous rulers of Caisra. His protégés and henchmen meanwhile took liberties with the people that would never have been tolerated before.

As the mule-carriage rattled along the great road to Pyrgoi, leading in a north-westerly direction through the coastal plain towards the sea, Vel continuously asked questions of his grandfather, but after some time both had fallen asleep. Larthi recalled what Aranth had said to her, when they had once again discussed the situation in Caisra during her last stay with him.

'Tyrants have a way of over-reaching themselves. I believe that Thefarie Velianas will bring about his own downfall, without any need for us to shed our people's blood. As to Veilia, she has already been punished by the gods in having an idiot son.'

'How I wish we could hasten the end of this tyranny and see you back with us at last!' she had exclaimed impatiently. 'Vel doesn't even know you yet - it's quite unnatural!'

'I long to see my son,' Aranth had replied with passion, 'and I will, when the time is ripe. Believe me, I think of you and him more often than you give me credit for.'

Larthi felt ashamed, for occasionally she suspected that Aranth enjoyed his new life abroad and was in no hurry to give it up. The tall and fair-haired women up there were said to be very beautiful.

Once, though, he had taken her with him on the long and strenuous journey north from Pupluna, a port facing the island of Elba. Looking out from the city across the sea to the west, she remembered seeing the black smoke rising from the smelting-ovens for the iron-ore on the island. A dark haze hung perpetually about its peaks and explained why the Greeks called it Aithalia, the sooty island. Aranth had shown her the furnaces and the bronze- and iron-working establishments in Pupluna itself and the mines in the metal-rich mountains north-east of the city, through which they travelled on their way to Velathri. There, in the wind-swept hill-town with its acropolis ringed by mighty stone walls, they had stayed for a while as the guests of Avele Feluske, a friend and associate of Aranth in the far-flung trading-venture that linked the Tyrrhenian coast with that of the Adriatic.

Teucer Hermenas, the wealthy mine-owner of Pupluna, had been looking for new outlets. In the past Aranth had done much business with him, before shipping to Campanian and more southerly ports had been virtually cut off by western Greek and Carthaginian rivals. As he had travelled and sailed further than any of his friends and had kept abreast of all the new developments, Aranth was able to suggest that they make contact with the Athenian merchants at their emporium in the recently founded harbour-settlement of the Rasenna on the mouth of the river Po. Greek traders called here regularly in search of Tyrrhenian metals, amber from the Baltic and Venetic horses, offering in exchange their finely painted pottery, which they shipped along the comparatively safe and short sea-route of the Adriatic. To transport their own merchandise across the passes of the Apennines was a risky and arduous venture for Aranth and his associates, but the rewards proved high, as there was an ever growing demand for Greek vases in the Rasenna cities.

During their journey Larthi had marvelled at the gaunt mountain chains towering above the paths, treeless, stony and covered by deep snow in winter. As it was early summer, their lower slopes were aglow with flowering broom and the air pungent with the scent of herbs. They had stopped briefly in the newly-built town of Misa in the wooded northern foothills of the Apennines, a strange, uniform-looking settlement on a plateau in a bend of the swift, shingly river. The potters. metalworkers and merchants living there flourished on the trade which passed through on its way to Felsina on the plain and beyond that old city to the Po and its tributaries.

The last stages of their journey were covered by boats, which transported their goods along the more navigable rivers. Larthi was unfamiliar with the seemingly endless plain, shimmering in a heat-haze and punctuated only by silvery rows of willows and elms along the water-courses and canals, accustomed as she was to the richly modulated landscape of her homeland. Aranth told her that the Rasenna had settled in these vast and fertile regions generations ago, draining the soil and then working it and carrying on commerce with the barbarian tribes who inhabited the wild valleys of the Alps.

Finally, at the mouth of the Po, where the broad river split up into a delta of lesser branches between reed-covered islands and sandy dunes, they had reached the city in its lagoon.

Here the low wooden houses were built on piles, driven into the marshy ground and were approached by waterways intersecting the main canals at regular intervals. Though its architecture was modest, this harbour-town was a lively place, where many nationalities met and the talk was of business, politics and wars in distant countries. While feasting her eyes on a marvellous array of beautifully painted Attic vases in the Greek emporium, Larthi heard the Athenians tell Aranth about a revolt amongst the Ionians of Asia, who had risen up against Darius, the Great King of the Persians. Athens had sent twenty ships in support but, after burning Sardis, the Ionians were beaten and following their defeat at

166

Ephesus, the surviving Athenian troops had returned home. Bent on revenge, the Persians were now attacking the rebellious Ionian cities one after the other and subduing them.

Larthi recalled the frightening day in her childhood when she first heard the account of the sack of the Greek city - Sybaris. It had had close ties with Ionian Miletus, which was now threatened itself. Ever since that far-off day she had been conscious of the continuing menace of war, disaster and death . . .

'And what is that, grandfather?' Vel's clear voice penetrated her brooding abstraction.

Laris Matunas gazed intently to where the boy was pointing.

'I'm not sure what you mean, my child,' he answered uncertainly.

'That big mound with grass on top.'

'It's a tomb, Vel,' Larthi said; 'Greeks are buried there.'

'Why?' Vel enquired.

With surprise Larthi heard herself telling her son the grim story of the stoning of the Phocaean prisoners in almost the same words that Aunt Culni had used in the past when relating the same event - an incident so closely bound up with the history of their family.

'And to this day we hold the funeral games here,' Laris Matunas added as they were passing the stadium; 'though I have not attended them for some years now.'

'Why not, grandfather?'

'The man who now presides over the games is not of royal blood and is unworthy of the honour he has assumed. He enjoys neither the recognition of the heads of the great families, nor has he acquired the gods' consent. Without the solemn inauguration, during which the chief augur lays his right hand on the king's head, the power does not pass into him and he is unfit to rule.'

Vel gazed at his grandfather with uncomprehending awe for a moment before asking, 'Shall we be able to go to the games again when there is a good king?'

'Only the gods know what is in store for us,' Laris Matunas said sombrely.

Larthi sensed again how deeply her father had suffered from the reversal of the sacred order of things and the impious flouting of rites hallowed by age-old tradition. For the chief augur also had to be chosen after an auspicium, performed with due ceremony and sanctified by the laying on of the hand of his predecessor, so that the supernatural force passed into him for the safety and benefit of all the people. But the usurper had arbitrarily appointed Piana Velavesnas to the office which, by divine ordainment, had been held by Laris Matunas. Evil was bound to ensue; the gods were bound to punish such sacrilege. Veilia was paying the price for her misdeeds already in full measure: Mamarce, feeble and tearful when a baby, had never learnt to speak as he grew into a boy, but shambled about, slavering and babbling incomprehensively. For years Veilia had tried to conceal the fact, but now it was obvious to everyone that Mamarce was weak in mind as well as body.

Contemplating Vel's sturdy, dark-haired little figure, his clear golden-brown eyes fringed by heavy lashes like his father's, and his alert and inquisitive manner, Larthi felt deeply grateful for her healthy and handsome son.

'Grandfather, look at all those white birds over there!' Vel's sinewy arm pointed into the distance, where flocks of seagulls were following the ox-drawn plough of a peasant turning over the stubble. 'What does it mean when there are so many of them?'

Laris Matunas could hear the screeching of the birds, but was unable to make out their shapes as they swooped down and rose again swiftly from the rich brown ribbon of soil which the plough-share had turned up in the autumnal field.

'It only means that they're hungry, Vel. They are feeding on the worms in the earth,' Larthi said gently. She was thrilled by the child's natural curiosity to discover the significance of the flight of birds and at the same time felt sorry for her father, who could no longer instruct his grandson. She knew how bitter he must feel at losing his sight and how this anguish must be exacerbated by the knowledge that the boy craved for a man, especially a father, to teach him the meaning of everything - and he was failing him.

Silently pondering his misfortune, Laris Matunas wondered whether the gods were determined to make everyone suffer for the crimes committed by only a few.

Bronze group of a ploughman and his oxen from Arezzo. Rome, Villa Giulia

The road now skirted the shore. Vel, who had never seen the sea close to before, jumped up excitedly, pointing at the gentle swell lapping the shore and cried, 'Stop, Cupe! I want to get down. Look at all the shells there!'

Larthi clasped him round the waist. 'No, Vel. We have no time to stop here. When we get to the harbour you can collect shells there.'

Vel sat down reluctantly, pouting - his eyes blazing. But his anger was short-lived. There was too much to distract him by the roadside.

'What's that funny wooden tower over there for?'

'There are lots of them at intervals all along the coast,' Larthi said. 'People watch out for the arrival of the tunny-fish from them. You can see much further from up there than from the ground and when the guard discovers the first sign of a shoal on the horizon, he blows his horn and the fishermen go out in their boats and catch the tunny as they come in.'

169

They passed a cluster of fishermen's huts, flimsy, tent-like constructions made from reeds, below which boats were drawn up on the sandy slope of the beach. There was no one about, only a dog barking perfunctorily at the rattling carriage.

'They've probably all gone to the market to sell their catch. Look, there's Pyrgoi already.' Larthi pointed ahead to where a shallow peninsula jutted out into the calm sea, outlined against the luminous sky by tall towers and temple-roofs.

13

They left their wagon at the northern corner of the sacred precinct and Laris Matunas told Cupe to meet them there again later in the day at the same spot. They followed the paved road here which entered the sanctuary at an oblique angle and led past the length of the temple, the façade of which overlooked the sea and harbour to the west. The whole enclosure was crowded with pilgrims, priests, merchants and sailors and Larthi found it difficult to make her way through the mass of people with her father leaning heavily on her right arm and Vel pulling on her left hand, repeatedly demanding to be told what the sculptures decorating the roof of the temple were and why bronze spikes were fixed on top of them.

'That's to keep the birds off,' she said. 'But wait a moment, Vel; let's go to the front, so that we can look at it properly. It's all so different from what I remember.'

She had to steady Laris Matunas as he was jostled by the passing throng, making him stumble over a crack in the paving.

'When I last visited the sanctuary of the goddess with Cousin Velthur to inspect the progress of the rebuilding, his attendants cleared a way for us. Nowadays nobody seems to respect an aged and infirm priest,' he observed tetchily, tapping the ground with his stick.

'There are so many foreigners about and most of them sailors - they were always a rough lot,' said Larthi trying to soothe him.

They had now reached the open space in front of the temple.

'It's been completely reconstructed with columns all around it,' she said as she began to describe the building in detail to her father. 'They've used our local red tufo from Caisra for the cella walls and plastered it. There's a deep porch and I think that the wooden doors are studded with golden nails. Can you see them glitter, Vel?'

The boy nodded, wide-eyed and breathless with wonder.

'And the great beams of the entablature and the roof are faced with lovely painted terracotta friezes and plaques in relief. Look, Vel, up there: There's Hercle, the Greek hero, with his friend Iolaos, and between them is Hydra, that many headed snake they killed. And do you see those figures on galloping horses at the corners of the roof. And if you look along the edge of the roof you'll see that the end-tiles are decorated with heads of negroes and satyrs and maenads. Isn't it beautiful!'

'What's that round thing with a hole in it used for?' asked Vel, pointing to a circular structure on a low platform of tufo blocks to the left of the temple.

'That's an altar into which the priests pour offerings to Tinia and the gods of the underworld, who are also worshipped here.'

'Will grandfather be doing that now?'

'No, my child,' Laris Matunas said, 'I have no reason to sacrifice to the infernal deities here. Your mother has come to pray to the great goddess Uni and to propitiate her with a gift.'

'Here, Vel, this is what I'm going to give to the heavenly mother so that she may protect me and the little brother and sister I'm expecting.'

Vel gazed up at her as she unclasped the gold necklace with the gorgons' masks that he used to play with when she carried him in her arms as a baby.

'Will the goddess put on your necklace?'

'I think the priestesses will keep it for her. They guard a great many treasures here which other people have offered up to Uni.'

Larthi glanced around her, wondering where she could safely leave her father and Vel while she performed her sacrifice and prayer. Her eyes lit on one of the boundary stones on the seaward side of the precinct and she led them there. Laris Matunas sat down on the block, grateful for not being jostled about by the crowd any longer, but Vel objected to being left there, insisting that he wanted to see the image of the goddess.

'Listen, Vel,' Larthi whispered, 'grandfather needs you to look after him. Please stay with him. He's too frail to come and I can't leave him alone.'

Vel pressed his lips together, torn between his wish to go and the duty he had been asked to perform, which appealed to his pride. After a brief struggle he turned and put his hand on Laris Matunas' knee.

'Grandfather, you needn't worry. I'm going to protect you here.'

The old man smiled. Larthi ruffled Vel's hair affectionately and went towards the temple, turning back twice to wave to them.

Vel began to eye the passers-by attentively. He noticed a middle-aged man with stiffly rising hair, clad in priest's robes. He stopped to look more closely at Laris Matunas. Vel pulled himself up in front of his grandfather and fixed the stranger with a frown.

'Do my eyes deceive me?' the man said; 'is this the eminent and learned master who taught me in my youth?'

Vel cast an inquisitive glance at his grandfather who peered up at the speaker.

'I recognize your voice, Lecne Teithurna,' he murmured, 'though I have not seen you for many years and never shall again alas, as my sight has left me.'

'How is it a venerable teacher and an augur of such renown is sitting here, attended only by a small boy?' - Vel's frown became fiercer - 'Where are your servants? You look tired. Let me take you to my house, which is not very far from here and then you can rest and refresh yourself.'

'Thank you for your kind offer, but we cannot leave this spot, as we are waiting for my daughter to return to us from the temple. She is making a sacrifice to the goddess for a safe delivery.'

'May her prayer be answered with favour by the great mother,' said Lecne Teithurna, a former pupil of Laris Matunas. He raised his hands piously.

'Indeed!' Laris Matunas assented emphatically; 'though I must confess that I'm fearful of the future, for the gods have been hard on my family . . .' His voice faded away.

172

'I have heard of your misfortunes and I feel for you. Let me assure you . . .'

'Perhaps even now,' Laris Matunas interrupted, 'we are spied upon by the informers and you might do yourself harm by showing respect and kindness to one whose kin has been persecuted by the powers that be.'

Lecne Teithurna looked round furtively before bending down towards him and saying quietly, 'Many of us here do not approve of the new forms of our cult which have been introduced into the sanctuary. You would have thought this temple stood in Carthage itself or on Mount Eryx, from the way they address the goddess Uni as Astarte. And instead of worshipping Tinia as her divine husband, they hold a festival in spring to celebrate the wedding between the goddess and the Phoenician god Melkart, whom they represent rather like Hercle. You will have heard that the tyrant and his Punic allies have embellished the temple, but did you realize that Thefarie Velianas actually claims on gold tablets here, to be the ruler of Caisra, thanks to an act of grace by the goddess, who required him to build her a holy place?'

Laris Matunas threw up his hands, horrified. 'What blasphemy!'

'Indeed,' Lecne Teithurna continued, 'these inscriptions - one of which is even written in Phoenician script which I cannot read - are nailed to the shrine, containing the image of the goddess that he dedicated to her in gratitude in the third year of his reign. He has stated quite explicitly on them the provisions for the new cult and expresses the wish that the statue of Uni-Astarte should exist in her sanctuary for as many years as there are stars in heaven.'

'Oh, may the shrouded gods soon punish the man's hybris!'

'I, too, ardently hope that the old order of things will be restored speedily. For not only have they introduced alien priestesses and foreign rites, but they have installed in special quarters a whole host of women for the service of the goddess,' - Lecne Teithurna gestured towards a row of cells along the enclosure wall - 'who practice sacred prostitution according to the habit of the Phoenicians.'

'Let us implore the gods to make the ways of our forefathers those of our descendants!' Laris Matunas exclaimed and both men

173

prayed, while Vel gazed from one to the other with wide-open eyes.

'Have you been to the harbour yet?' Lecne Teithurna asked, when they had finished their imprecation.

'No,' Vel said eagerly, 'but we are going to go there when mother comes back; she promised that I could collect shells there.'

'You won't find many shells there now, my boy. The harbour is bursting with Carthaginian ships and they have built arsenals and warehouses for their goods on the shore. This and the port of Punicum are their most northerly points of support on the Tyrrhenian coast and they guard them jealously against the Greeks. For the next big harbour to the north is that of Tarchuna, whose people have long been friends of the Greeks.'

Laris Matunas nodded, murmuring that his wife had belonged to a renowned family of Tarchuna.

Lecne Teithurna went on, 'Nobody knows better than you, then, that Greek ships have called there for generations and Greek artisans and merchants have settled in the port and built shrines to their goddesses Hera and Aphrodite close to the sea. I myself have visited these sanctuaries and in their neighbourhood I have also seen an inscribed stone anchor, put up by the famous sailor Sostratos in honour of the god Apollo of Aigina.'

'Why was he so famous?' Vel asked, hanging on Lecne Teithurna's lips.

'Because he was the most successful of the Greek merchants who traded with the cities in the west.'

'My father is also a great trader and sailor,' Vel said proudly.

Lecne Teithurna put his hand on the boy's shoulder. 'You do credit to your father and your grandfather. Let us hope that before you reach manhood, the gods will have changed the fortunes of Caisra for the better.'

With those words Lecne Teithurna took his leave of them and it was not long before Vel caught sight of Larthi emerging from the crowd which pressed round the front of the temple.

'Grandfather,' he cried, 'here comes mother and she looks very happy.'

As she approached with a smile, he jumped up and down excitedly, without, however, attempting to abandon his post of duty.

174

'Thank you both for being so patient,' Larthi said, kissing Vel and helping her father to his feet. 'I hope I haven't kept you waiting for too long? I'm so relieved to know that my prayer and my gift have found favour with the great mother. They informed me, that if I thought hard of the goddess during the birth and told her thrice nine times that I remember her, the delivery would be easy.'

For a moment she laid her hand on the curve of her body, which was just beginning to reveal her pregnancy.

'While we were waiting we learnt a lot of interesting news from Lecne Teithurna. I used to instruct him in the sacred rites before you were born. He became augur and haruspex at this sanctuary and still holds this position, despite all the disasters that have overwhelmed us. Perhaps he will live to see justice done and the old order restored,' Laris Matunas ended wistfully.

'Mother, he said I was a credit to my father and grandfather. Will I be able to sail as far as the Greek Sostratos, when I'm grown up?'

'If the gods will it so, you shall,' Larthi said, stroking his dark curls.

The day was now well advanced and they felt hungry and thirsty.

'If you agree, father, we'll go and see if Cupe has come to the gates with the mule-cart. I got Fasti to pack provisions for us so that we could eat on the beach a little way out of the town; there are far too many people for comfort here.'

'Oh yes, let's do that! Then I can collect my shells, too.' Vel exclaimed, skipping alongside Larthi, who was supporting Laris Matunas once more. They had just reached the narrow approach to the entrance of the sacred precinct, when they heard shouting and saw a crowd being driven apart by attendants with sticks to make way for an important personage. They stood aside to let the cortège pass.

A sudden pain in her left temple made Larthi catch her breath apprehensively. As she raised her hand to ease her aching head, she realized that the lady being escorted past them by guards and followed closely by maids, was Veilia. She, too, was pregnant. Larthi's sudden movement caught Veilia's attention and she stopped abruptly, recognizing her daughter-in-law. She stared at

Larthi, looking her up and down, her eyes smouldering with hatred, and exclaimed, 'Did you pray for that bastard you are carrying? Shame on you, who have no husband, but expect a child! You are desecrating this sanctuary!' And with that she passed on.

Larthi's hand dropped from her forehead as she staggered back, ashen with shock. Every eye had been on her as she was insulted by Veilia and all those bystanders who had not followed the queen's procession, now put their heads together and pointed at her, their tongues wagging. Vel threw his arms round Larthi's legs, sensing that his mother was deeply hurt, but not really understanding what had happened.

'Mother, why was that fat lady with yellow hair so angry with you?'

'Who was that person accusing an expectant woman of impiously visiting the goddess's temple?' Laris Matunas demanded sternly. 'She knows nothing of the mercy of Uni, whose concern is for all who give birth.'

Larthi's mind reeled with indignation, shame and impotent fury. Her head throbbed with spasms of agonizing pain. She was barely able to answer. In a hoarse whisper she said, 'That was Veilia - she was speaking to me.'

'May the gods punish that evil woman for all her terrible misdeeds and monstrous insults!' Laris Matunas cried out in a shaking voice.

A growing conviction began to dominate Larthi's troubled mind - that Veilia would not survive the birth of her child by Thefarie Velianas.

As she stared after the train of her attendants disappearing behind the temple, a sudden fearful vision obliterated everything real in front of her eyes. It seemed that the sanctuary, which looked strangely altered in appearance as if it belonged to a future age, was being attacked in the dark of night by foreign soldiers, who had stormed off ships that had come from the south. Having sacked its treasures and slaughtered the priesthood, the soldiers set fire to the temples. Larthi's blood ran cold and she groaned when she realized that the raiders were Greeks - Syracusians - implacably bent on the destruction of the power and wealth of Caisra.

176

14

'Vel, I won't let you go away without your hat in this heat!' Larthi exclaimed, running after the boy as he escaped into the street, where Caile and Cupe stood waiting for him with the dogs and a mule loaded with provisions and-hunting-equipment.

'Oh, mother, I don't need it,' Vel protested, feeling that he was being treated like a small child, for Larthi placed the curly-brimmed, tall straw cone firmly on his head and secured its strap under his chin. Impatiently he clasped his curved throwing-stick for hare-hunting.

Return from the hunt. Low relief on a limestone funerary monument from Chiusi. London, British Museum

'Every good huntsman wears a hat in such weather,' Larthi said resolutely; 'Look at your uncle.'

Vel pouted but suppressed the remark that Uncle Caile, whose hair had become rather thin, needed it more than he. Caile adjusted his own hat with a pat and observed, 'You know Vel, these things look really quite attractive, apart from their useful-ness. However, I think we'd better start before the sun's too high.'

177

They set off, the mule's hooves clattering away over the cobbles which were already glaring. Larthi followed the three of them with her eyes. Just as they reached the corner of the street leading to the seaward gate, Vel turned round and quickly waved to his mother. Smiling, she went back into the house, where Peci was giving Seianthi her gruel.

Larthi's second child, a little girl, was named after her grandmother. Teitu's widow, who had assisted at the baby's birth, insisted from the first moment she saw her, that she looked exactly like Larthi's mother. The child's soft curls certainly had the same chestnut sheen which Larthi remembered on Aunt Culni's hair. Seianthi was now three years old and well advanced for her age. She had learnt to speak early since Vel, who was devoted to his small sister, talked to her a great deal. Ramtha's twin children, only six months younger than Seianthi, but brought up in rural seclusion, had barely begun to be articulate.

It was the day on which Larthi expected Ramtha with little Marce and Ravnthu to visit her. On the infrequent occasions when her husband Sminthe Ecnata, the landowner, came into town for business, Ramtha usually accompanied him so as to see her parents or call on her friend. The Ecnata family lived on a big farm in the tufo country to the north-east of Caisra, not far from the spot where a small river poured in a silvery cascade over the rocky edge of the hillside into a foaming pool deep below. It was fertile land, though eroded by torrents and streams into countless ravines with steep, rust-coloured flanks. In the luscious meadows of the sheltered valley-bottoms the large herds of Sminthe Ecnata were fattened for the market.

Grinding wheels and voices in the street announced Ramtha's arrival. Larthi picked up Seianthi and hurried out to greet her guests. Peci and Fasti followed and each servant received one of the wailing twins as they were handed down by their mother and Vesi, her maid. Ramtha looked rather worried as she climbed from the carriage:

'I only hope the children didn't get too much sun on their heads,' she said, mopping her brow. 'Vesi tried to hold the sunshade over them, but we were pitched about so badly that it wasn't much use, you have no idea how rutted the roads are - and as for the dust . . .'

'I can well imagine,' Larthi said, while Seianthi struggled from her mother's arms into those of Ramtha, who hugged and kissed the little girl affectionately. Instantly the twins' whining rose to a more piercing note.

'Let's all go into the garden,' Larthi suggested. 'It will be nice and cool under the trees there and Fasti can bring you water for a wash and we'll have something to drink.'

They trooped into the orchard and were soon comfortably seated on the grass under some ancient apple trees. While the maids went to fetch refreshments, the three children eyed each other warily for a moment before beginning to play with each other. Seianthi's doll with its moveable wooden arms and legs aroused the twins' curiosity. Holding it out to them, Seianthi allowed Ravnthu and Marce to touch its floppy limbs, but she jealously refused to hand over the doll. There was a renewed chorus of wails. Larthi shook her head at Seianthi: 'Do be a good girl and let them have your doll. I'll go and get you your great-grandmother's little pottery vessels to play with.'

Seianthi immediately surrendered her toy to the twins who quickly quietened down. Chortling contentedly, they bent over the doll, poking and patting it with their podgy hands.

'Do you mind if I get father to come out and sit with us here?' Larthi asked Ramtha. 'It's so miserable for him to be left alone, now that he is completely blind. And in any case, the house is stuffy in this weather and it would be far better for him to be out in the garden.'

'Of course, please do! I should love to see your father again. I do hope he is otherwise well.'

'Actually,' Larthi replied in a subdued voice, 'to be honest, he is in very low spirits. It's not only that he can't see any more, but just lately he's begun to worry about the family's tomb and the continuation of the cult of our ancestors. As he has no son and Caile shows no signs of wanting to get married, father fears that our family may now die out and that there will be nobody to look after the burials and to perform the essential sacrifices. However often I tell him that we shall take care of the Matuna family's tombs as well as the Velchana ones, he will not be reassured.'

'Oh, I do understand his anxiety,' Ramtha said, full of sympathy. 'Let's hope that your uncle will decide to get married. How old is he now?'

'Forty-five. He is leaving it rather late if he intends to have a family. - Well, anyway I'll go and get father now. It will probably cheer him up to hear the children chattering away. No, Seianthi, I won't forget your little pots and pans.'

While Larthi went into the house, the maids appeared with a bronze water-jug, a shallow bronze basin on three lion's paws and some clean linen towels. They helped Ramtha wash her children's dust-covered faces and clean herself up. Thresu now brought a folding-stool for his master, and Larthi carefully guided Laris Matunas over the uneven ground so as to join the company.

He acknowledged Ramtha's greeting and lowered himself onto the stool resting his chin on his hands that were folded over the crook of his stick.

'I hear the voices of your children,' he went on; 'Your husband is indeed fortunate in having a son! Are both your brothers married already?'

'Rasce, the elder one was married last year and his wife is expecting her first child; but the younger one, Arnza - I can't get out of the habit of calling him by his baby-name and he doesn't like it at all - he is still a bachelor.'

'So is my younger brother,' Laris Matunas said with a sigh.

'Look, Seianthi,' Larthi said, untying a little cloth bundle, 'here are great-grandmother's toys. You can play with them now, as long as you are careful, and please see that they don't get broken.'

She spread the cloth on the grass and put on it a set of miniature jugs, bowls, cups and goblets of shiny black pottery. Seianthi clapped her hands with delight and began to re-arrange the vessels in an order that seemed more appropriate to her. Then she raised one of the small pitchers and held it up to Fasti who was just pouring milk into two cups for the twins.

'Milk for my doll,' she demanded and Fasti complied. While Ravnthu and Marce took their drink - rather messily as it happened, for they were accustomed to their spouted feeding-cups at home - Seianthi picked up her doll and pretended that it, too, was being fed.

180

Laris Matunas meanwhile had lifted his head and, with the quickened hearing of the blind, picked up unfamiliar sounds beyond the fence of the orchard.

'Larthi,' he said, 'send someone out to see what's going on - I can hear strangers arriving.'

Fasti was despatched with all speed to find out who might be calling on them unexpectedly. After a few moments she returned looking flustered. Casting a rapid glance round the garden to make sure that she could not be overheard, she whispered, 'It's master's old friend, Avile Spurinna, with just one slave and a bundle, and he looks a pitiful sight!'

Laris Matunas struggled to his feet and exclaimed, 'Bring him here this instant and tell Thresu to prepare a bath and fresh clothes.'

Larthi and Ramtha jumped up from the grass and the children looked up at them with startled faces. Larthi hastened to meet her father's friend and showed him into the garden. She, too, was shocked by Avile Spurinna's appearance. In his lined and haggard face the acquiline nose stood out more prominently than ever, while his hair had dwindled to a few bleached strands. His dusty clothes hung about him in tatters. To cover her dismay, Larthi said to him under her breath, 'You will hardly recognize father - he went blind some years ago.'

With an expression of profound pity Avile Spurinna approached Laris Matunas and seized his hands.

'My friend,' he said, 'the gods have not granted us to meet again as happy men. The last time your hospitable house received me, we were both vigorous and full of hope; now we are old and ill-fated men with nothing to look forward to and deprived of those who would care for our tombs. Cursed as I am, I will not be a burden on you for long, lest my presence bring further disaster upon this roof.'

Laris Matunas, raised his hands in solemn appeal to the gods, imploring them to look upon their families again with favour: 'Whatever our failings, they were trespasses unwittingly committed. We have atoned for them now through our endless misfortune and suffering. Cease persecuting your faithful servants, oh all powerful ones, and smile upon those who are guiltless!' His gesture encompassed the children at his feet. Avile Spurinna, Larthi and Ramtha echoed his prayer with intensity.

After a brief silence Laris Matunas said, 'My friend, a bath is being prepared for you at the moment. While they are getting it ready, some refreshment will be brought to you. You must not think of leaving us again. Please stay here as long as you wish. I only beg you to forgive me for not entertaining you in the proper way. Our situation is not what it used to be; I am sightless now and but a poor host.'

'Your kindness and hospitality are unchanged,' Avile Spurinna replied, 'but I shall not abuse them. When I have rested for a couple of days and recovered my strength a little, I'll continue my way to Tarchuna, the city of my forefathers.'

'Much as I would like to keep you with me for much longer,' Laris Matunas now said in a low tone, 'I fear that it would indeed be safer for you to live at Tarchuna, where things have remained as before and where the Greeks and their friends are still held in high esteem. As to the Tarquins . . .'

'My king is dead,' Avile Spurinna murmured, 'and all I seek now is a place where I, too, can die.'

'How did King Tarquin meet his end?' Laris Matunas asked, visibly shaken, while Larthi and Ramtha gazed at Avile Spurinna in shocked silence.

'You may have heard last year that the king's son-in-law, Octavius Mamilius of Tusculum, leader of the Latin confederacy and the remaining partisans of the Tarquins, was killed by the Romans in a battle near Lake Regillus. The enemy was again helped by reinforcements from Laris Porsenna but after a long and fierce struggle our hopes of defeating the Romans and reinstating King Tarquin in his rightful place were finally destroyed. When the battle was irrevocably lost, the aged king sought refuge with his former champion, Aristodemos of Kyme, who had made himself tyrant of that city on returning there from his victorious expedition against Porsenna at Aricia. I accompanied King Tarquin south to attend him in his continuing exile. Like me, he had now lost his sons, his home and his hopes for ever.'

Tears streamed from Ramtha's eyes as she bent down to pick up Marce, who was whimpering at her feet, upset by his mother's obvious distress. Larthi stroked Seianthi's curls mechanically, while the child clung to her legs, looking up with frightened eyes at the serious faces of the grown-ups.

'Three months ago,' Avile Spurinna went on, 'King Tarquin began to sicken and shortly afterwards died. I did what I could to assist Aristodemos arrange a worthy funeral and I saw to it that all the proper honours to our dead king were observed. But after that, there was nothing left for me to stay at Kyme for. Moreover, Aristodemos' position there is by no means secure. His power as tyrant is based only on the support of the common people. When he made himself master of Kyme, all the aristocrats fled to Volturnum, where they are waiting their chance to return and destroy him. There is bound to be an upheaval before long. As I was now nothing but an embarrassment to Aristodemos, I decided to take my leave of him and try and make my way north to find a last resting place in the land of my ancestors. My journey through the unsafe Latin hill-country was a long and tiring one and I am fully aware of the danger that I run in Caisra as a recognized supporter of the Tarquins. But I longed to see you all once more and tell you what fate had befallen me. Destitute and ragged as I am, I fortunately managed to escape recognition when entering the town by mingling with the beggars and country people coming into market this morning.'

'My poor friend,' Laris Matunas said, 'you must be worn out. Let's go indoors so that you can rest properly and have your bath before a meal.'

Larthi accompanied the two old men into the house and gave instructions to the servants to look after them. Meanwhile, Ramtha wept, comforted only by the children who cried in uncomprehending sympathy with her.

Larthi felt agitated. Her mind was full of conflicting thoughts and plans as she returned to the garden to help Ramtha calm and feed the children. The lonely, tragic end of King Tarquin amongst the Greeks of Kyme seemed to signal a portent from heaven which demanded to be heeded. Were the gods signifying their intention to terminate the rule of all monarchs of the Rasenna? Were the days of those people who clung to their traditional friendship with the Greeks numbered? Even so it could hardly be divine will which had imposed the tyranny of Thefarie Velianas and his Carthaginian allies on their city instead of the temperate rule of her father-in-law. Surely the gods would want the Rasenna to be masters in their own land and to continue worshipping in the time-honoured way. She was struck however, by the strange similarity in the fate of Kyme and Caisra. Both cities had suffered the same plight; power had been usurped by a tyrant who had driven the aristocracy into exile. For a decade now Aristodemos and Thefarie Velianas had managed to quell all opponents within their cities, while keeping the refugees from the ranks of the nobility abroad. Avile Spurinna's account of the heads of the great Kymean families, watchfully biding their time in nearby Etruscan Volturnum, stirred her imagination. There was a lesson to be learnt here as regards their own city.

'As soon as I can get away,' she said suddenly to Ramtha, 'I'll go north again. Aranth must be told what has happened.

15

'What's the matter with you?' Fasti asked Peci who was sitting on a stool by the hearth, chin in hand, staring gloomily into the fire.

'I'm worried about the mistress. Haven't you noticed how thin she's become?'

'You can't say that my cooking's to blame for that,' Fasti exclaimed, pausing as she cut the onions to wipe her eyes with the back of her hand; 'I'm doing my best - though when I think of the old days, it's hardly the same. Mind you, Master Vel is quite good at filling the larder with hares and pigeons, but I can't remember when we last killed an ox.'

'There hasn't been much occasion for feasting,' Peci murmured, while Fasti added the onions and a handful of herbs to the broth simmering on the hearth. 'No,' Peci went on, 'it's nothing to do with lack of food that she looks so wasted. I'm sure of that.'

'What's wrong with her then?' Fasti enquired.

'I think she's given up all hope now. All these years she's carried on so bravely, looking after our old master and the children and what little is left of the property - all without the help of

184

her husband. Ever since she came back from her last stay with him, I could feel that she'd lost heart and she looked as though she had, as well.'

'But why? Nothing's changed here. Why should she be so downcast about everything?'

'That's just it.' Peci answered impatiently; 'It's because nothing has changed she finds it hard to carry on. You haven't got to worry about your husband and haven't any idea what it would be like to be without him. Your Thresu is always around when you need him. But my poor mistress is all alone and has had no one to look after her or stand up for her. Master Caile is no help at all.'

'Don't I know it,' Fasti groaned, as she went over to fetch some oats from one of the large clay storage-jars, 'he's always grumbling about the food.'

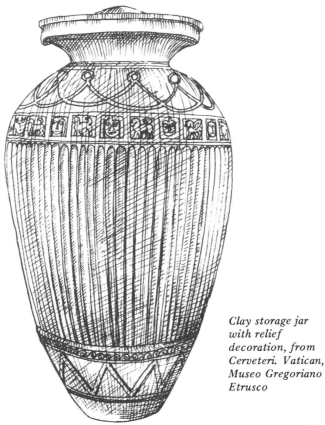

Clay storage jar with relief decoration, from Cerveteri. Vatican, Museo Gregoriano Etrusco

185

'He grumbles about that villainous man Thefarie Velianas as well, but he doesn't do anything about getting rid of him. I can't understand it - none of these great noblemen have the courage to do away with him. They are just sitting about at a safe distance, waiting for someone else to come along and free the city. The fighting spirit seems to have gone out of everyone in this place!' Peci said contemptuously.

'Well, do you really expect to see people risk their lives for nothing? Nobody has a chance against a man who's so heavily protected and his spies would soon find out if there was a plot to kill him.' Fasti had instinctively lowered her voice and cast a cautious glance out of the kitchen door.

'If only he were to fall ill and die,' said Peci, 'but the gods seem to smile on him and his evil deeds and there seems no hope for my poor mistress. Ah, well,' she rose with a sigh, 'you and I can't do anything about it. I'd better go and carry on with my mending.'

Fasti watched the cauldron thoughtfully. 'Wait a moment,' she whispered suddenly, wiping her hands on the cloth tied round her waist; 'Do you know the witch Enicu?'

'Is she that old woman who lives in the cave by the path which leads to the lake? I've never seen her, but I've heard a lot about her.' Peci stopped at the door and made the sign to avert evil. She now turned and looked inquisitively at Fasti who stood with arms akimbo and a determined expression on her broad face.

'That's her,' Fasti nodded. 'I can tell you that she helped me when I wanted Thresu to marry me and he didn't even seem to notice it.'

Peci gazed at her in amazement. 'Well, I would never have guessed it!' she exclaimed; 'though I must say I was surprised when mistress and I came back to live here to find that you had already got your man, when he hadn't even shown that he fancied you before.'

'There was nothing wrong with me,' Fasti said testily, smoothing the apron over her ample hips, 'he just needed it to be put into his head that I would make a good wife for him and so I went to old Enicu one night at new moon . . . she's got ways to make things turn out as you want them to.' She stopped to attend to the fire.

186

'What do you mean?' Peci whispered; 'do you really think she might be prepared to do something about that man?'

Fasti nodded vigorously, and said, 'Of course, though we would have to make it worth her while.' She put her finger to her lips, as Thresu came into the kitchen in search of a chopper. 'It's hanging on the wall over there - large as life!' she said to him, pretending to be annoyed when he pinched her affectionately on his way out. 'I gave her a good piece of woollen cloth I had woven for her pains,' she went on quietly, 'but what she really likes is gold.'

Peci put in quickly, 'I've got that gold ring that was left to me by mistress Culni - would that do?'

Fasti nodded emphatically and said under her breath, 'I'm sure it would. Now, let's see - the moon's waning, which is a good time for such magic. I'll ask her first whether she'd be prepared to take it on. We'll both go together then and see that it's done properly.'

Full of admiration for Fasti's resourcefulness, Peci agreed and left the kitchen, glancing furtively behind her as she went.

Two days later around nightfall, they cautiously made their way out of the gate and turned off the road to the south, down a small path which led eastwards, skirting the foot of the rocky plateau on which the city was built. Fasti strode ahead purposefully, despite the rapidly fading light, while Peci followed with some misgivings as she stumbled repeatedly over the twisted roots.

On their left the precipitous promontory of Caisra loomed darkly overhead, while on the right the valley and the stream murmuring through the fields could still be made out in the twilight. Beyond it rose the low ridge of the southern cemetery. Peci shivered apprehensively. A breath of chilly air wafted down from the dank rock-face towering above them. In its crags hung clumps of fern and ivy, fed by dripping water. Frogs croaked in the shallow pools at the bottom of the gullies.

'I'm not sure that the old master would approve of what we're doing,' Peci panted, trying hard to catch up with Fasti.

'It's too late to think of that now,' Fasti replied. 'Old Enicu made me hand over your ring before agreeing to prepare anything for tonight. You don't suppose she would ever give it back after all the trouble she's been put to!'

'Don't hurry so!' Peci implored her, 'I've never been along here before and I can't see my way at all - help!' She slipped perilously on the muddy ground and clutched Fasti's arm for support.

'It's not much further now,' Fasti encouraged her, 'but we have to get there before it's completely dark, so that we don't miss the stepping-stones which cross the stream.'

Peci steadied herself, pulling her mantle about her shoulders, which had got caught on a trailing branch of a creeper. Having adjusted her garments, she went on with more assurance.

The river meandered towards the foot of the plateau where it blocked the path. They stepped carefully across it on a series of flat stones lapped by dark swirling waters. A dim glimmer of light emerged from behind a huge overgrown boulder that had once formed part of the rock-face above.

'Here we are at last,' Fasti whispered as they made their way around it.

The jagged mouth of a cave was lit up from within by a flickering fire. Beside it, with her back towards them, crouched the old witch, a raven perched on her shoulder. She cackled at the bird, while stirring a mixture in a bronze pot with a blackthorn stick.

'Those stupid women are late - they'll spoil our magic if the moon sets before we've dealt with him.' She turned her face and jerked her hawk-like nose towards the small wax image of a naked man, tied with his hands behind his back to a wooden stake and propped up against an altar-like block of stone.

'Enicu,' Fasti said, cowed by the eerie sight, 'we have arrived.'

'Not a moment too soon,' the witch grumbled. 'Look at the moon!'

Peering out into the night sky, the maids saw that the pale sickle stood low on the horizon. Peci kept as close as possible to her companion, eyeing the old woman and the contents of the cave with profound unease.

'Keep still and don't speak, whatever you see,' the witch commanded, throwing some strange-smelling twigs onto the fire which flared up with a menacing hiss. Murmuring indistinct incantations, she raised her hands three times towards the moon, seeming to pull its faint rays towards the waxen image.

188

'Take him down with you, down, down to the infernal deities to whom I pour my libation,' she continued and emptied the contents of the pot, a sinister-looking, dark red liquid, into the circular opening of the altar-stone which communicated with the soil.

Peci noticed with a shudder that a number of huge toads squatted on the damp floor beside the wax figure, their bulging eyes glittering with the reflection of the fire.

Enicu seized the image with her left hand and aimed a bronze pin at its chest with her right. As she was about to pierce it in the region of the heart, the raven suddenly rose from her shoulder with a penetrating screech and flew into a far corner of the cave. The pin missed the left side of the figure's chest and perforated its shoulder instead.

'We're out of luck,' the witch said grimly; 'some demon's protecting the man - I don't know if my magic will work.'

Staring at the figure with a frown, she brooded for a moment. Then she shook back the greasy, grey strands of her hair and murmured darkly, 'I'll do for you yet!'

She dipped her finger into the bottom of the pot and smeared the remaining red liquid first over the hole in the figure's shoulder and then all over the body.

'Down! Down! Down!' she whispered with terrifying intensity and finally flung the image into the fire and watched it dissolve.

'You can go now,' she said, addressing the maids who stood petrified, clinging onto each other. 'Don't speak until you get home and never mention this to anyone,' she added hoarsely, 'lest some very unpleasant fate befalls you.'

16

Larthi lay sleepless. A broad streak of moonlight fell across the bed, illuminating Aranth's bare shoulder and arm resting across her slight body. His deep, regular breathing filled the room: it was a familiar and reassuring sound, for his shadowy face, pressed against her breast, was indistinct and the grizzled hair and beard could easily have been that of a stranger.

He had returned home the previous day. But instead of being able to rejoice, Larthi had felt emotionally and physically drained. The years of impatient waiting had been too many, the deprivations of recent months debilitating. Aranth's ardour, on the other hand, was unquenched by their long separation and the rigours of his journey. Protracted want and hunger were unknown to him, for the northern regions of the country had been spared the famine afflicting south-western Etruria and Latium. His powerful torso with its smooth, firm skin still seemed that of a young man. For a brief moment earlier in the night the passion of his embraces had succeeded in melting the tenseness of her body and they had been united as in years past. But now that he had sunk into heavy slumber, she felt exhausted and utterly remote. Her mind flitted restlessly over the events of the four years which had elapsed since she had last lain in his arms.

He had convinced her then that there was little merit in his returning to some city nearer home from where to watch developments at Caisra. She had urged him to come and stay with Avile Spurinna and his kinsmen at Tarchuna who were distantly related to her through her mother's family. But he was quick to point out that it would be virtually impossible for him to carry on his business from there. To abandon the profitable new trade-connections he had built up over ten years of hard work just in order to lead a life of inactivity in a nearby city, seemed folly to him. And the futility of attempting to regain power with insufficient support at home had been made only too obvious to him by the failure of the Tarquins at Ruma. As long as Thefarie Velianas could rely on the

190

common people in Caisra while enjoying the protection of the Carthaginians at sea, there was nothing anyone could effectively do to oust him. Aranth professed himself profoundly grateful to the gods that the tyrant, because of religious scruples, had abstained from further persecution of the Matuna family, especially since Veilia's death in childbirth.

Larthi returned to Caisra disheartened by the prospect of a further long period of lonely waiting for things to change. Violent changes did occur however, not at home, but in distant Asia, and rumours and repercussions of these events ultimately reached them, too.

Darius, the Great King of Persia, determined to put an end to the revolt of the Ionian Greeks, had concentrated his vast fleet in an effort to blockade Miletus. A battle took place near the offshore island of Lade, in which the smaller and ill-disciplined naval contingents of the Greek cities involved in the rebellion were defeated by the enemy's superior strength and the widespread desertion in their own ranks. Miletus was taken by storm and its inhabitants slain or taken as slaves to the capital of Susa. The terrible fate of this rich and powerful city deeply moved the Athenians, who were themselves of Ionian stock, while all the Etruscans, who had enjoyed long-standing trade-relations with Miletus and had already suffered severely through the earlier destruction of her partner Sybaris, were greatly affected.

However, a band of Samian defectors and groups of Milesian refugees who had escaped from the rout at Lade sailed west in search of new homes. They were encouraged by Anaxilas, the Greek tyrant of Rhegion, to occupy Zankle on the Sicilian side of the Straits. It formed part of the dominion of Hippokrates, the ruler of Gela, whom Anaxilas wished to spite. The arrival of friendly Ionian settlers at the Straits encouraged the Etruscan merchants to hope for the establishment of a much needed outpost for their shipping; for the fall of Sybaris and the resulting loss of the safe overland route to the Ionian sea had meant that Etruscan seaborne trade had to use the Straits, which was an area menaced by hostile Phocaean and Chalcidian Greeks.

The Carthaginians meanwhile firmly established in western Sicily, were eager to extend their control over the coastal waters

191

of the eastern part of the island as well. But Cnidian Greek colonists on the Aeolian islands proved a thorn in their flesh. Their raids and piratical acts from Lipara, off the north-eastern point of Sicily, created a perpetual danger to safe passage. As the ships of Caisra had also suffered from such attacks, Thefarie Velianas was persuaded by his Carthaginian allies to mount a punitive expedition against Lipara.

This diversion from the deteriorating conditions at home was not an unwelcome change for him. Trade had been stagnating since the Carthaginians managed to appropriate more and more privileges and markets for themselves, and there was widespread discontent in Caisra amongst those classes who had once been his stout supporters.

At the same time, alarming portents were reported from the countryside, which was much affected by drought: fires blazed in the sky, a rain of stones fell on the temple of Uni, the lake to the east of Caisra seethed like a cauldron and a cow was heard to talk. Nor was this all. At Pyrgoi a woman had given birth to a two-headed monster, who had survived for seven whole days before being drowned in the sea in the prescribed manner. These ominous signs increased the agitation of the populace. Even Piana Velavesnas could not interpret them as anything but dire warnings of the gods' disapproval of the existing state of affairs. Thefarie Velianas had conducted a solemn procession to the harbour-sanctuary to sacrifice to his protectress Uni, at which he decided to announce that the goddess had ordered him to sail to Lipara to eradicate the pirates. Troops and sailors were mustered hastily and the neglected war-ships got ready. The tyrant himself took command of the force.

As a result of these measures the people were distracted from their grievances and the portents were for the moment forgotten. Moreover, a large body of openly disgruntled men were removed from the city to do service as rowers and so the unrest began to die down. Thefarie Velianas set out with the fleet, confident of victory and an enhanced reputation. However, though an experienced commander of bulky merchant-vessels, he had never before conducted an armed raid and lacked all knowledge of naval tactics.

Larthi, resigned to her fate, gloomily watched from her look-out at the end of the garden, the sluggish sails as they slowly moved south over the horizon and out of sight. Nothing was heard from the fleet for many weeks.

Meanwhile the drought continued. The city now suffered from an incursion of mice and rats which wrought havoc in the surrounding fields. The crops, already meagre from prolonged lack of rain, were totally destroyed and rodents devoured most of the stored provisions. Starving peasants from the countryside began to pour into the city in search of food for themselves and their emaciated animals. Overcrowding, contamination of the wells and the heat of August, added to the inherent dangers of the vermin, eventually led to an outbreak of the plague. The streets were full of the dying and the dead, for whom no proper burial was possible, as they were far from their homes. The citizens themselves were soon no longer capable of giving the traditional funerals to so large a number of victims. While the people from the country and slaves had crowded into the city, the few remaining aristocrats either kept to their houses to avoid contact with the sick, or had left for more salubrious regions in the mountains.

Laris Matunas, however, refused to move from Caisra. For some days Larthi had been torn between her duty to respect his wishes and look after him, and her anxiety for the safety of the children, particularly Seianthi, who was in the seventh year of her life, a period considered particularly perilous to the young. In the event, Larthi decided to remain with her father and sent Peci with Vel and Seianthi to stay with Ramtha's family in the cooler and less ravaged hill-country.

Teitu's widow, who had worked tirelessly with the sick in the neighbourhood, suddenly caught the disease herself and died, while Cupe, after returning with the empty carriage from the Ecnata farm, went down with it as well, but eventually recovered.

Larthi was frantic for news of the children, but also preoccupied by the immediate necessity of having to find something edible for her father. Caile and the remaining servants could think of little beyond the task of trying to keep themselves alive. As her store of pulse had long since run out, Larthi was now reduced to stripping the leaves off yellowing nettles at the far end of their parched garden to cook as food. All their poultry had already been slaughtered and there was hardly a wild bird left in the city; boys with catapults hunted for them everywhere. Fear of the plague had kept the coastal fishermen from calling with their catch as they had formerly done. Caile, however, had managed to capture a large eel at the muddy bottom of a dried-up stream, a feat he boasted of for weeks. Starvation in the city grew to catastrophic proportions and not a drop of rain fell from the pitiless sky.

The circumstances were so desperate that Laris Matunas felt impelled to do something. He commanded Caile to lead him to the chief priest of Tinia. His old authority seemed to have returned to him as he addressed the ailing priest, who had still not recovered from an attack of the disease. Interpreting the recent ominous signs precisely, Laris Matunas demanded that special sacrifices be offered up to the ruler of the sky and that all the citizens supplicate heaven for a remission of their sorrows. His instructions were followed religiously. He was the only augur of any standing left in the city, for Piana Velavesnas had accompanied the expedition to Lipara.

On the day of general prayer, clouds suddenly appeared in the evening in the north-eastern quarter of the sky and before long beneficial rain began to fall. Amid universal relief, Laris Matunas ordered all the able-bodied men to help bury the corpses of the victims of the epidemic and to clear out all the polluted wells and cisterns. The vegetation of the countryside started to revive as the rain continued and the remaining peasants returned to their abandoned fields.

Shortly afterwards the virulence of the plague abated. Larthi, with her father's approval, sent Cupe to inform Aranth of the events at Caisra, while she herself fetched the children home with the help of Thresu. Vel and Seianthi were safe and had fared much better on the remote farm under Ramtha's care than they would have done in the starving and infected capital.

It was at this point that a Carthaginian vessel landed at Pyrgoi bringing news of the disastrous end of the expedition against Lipara. On approaching the island the fleet had run into a storm and been dispersed. A large number of the ships had sunk and others were attacked and captured by the highly skilled and ruthless

194

Greek sailors, who had bided their time until the sea calmed suffic-
iently and the exhausted survivors were quite unable to withstand
them. Thefarie Velianas was wounded in the left shoulder by a
splinter from the mast which had snapped off, but managed to
escape alongside two other vessels. They were expected to reach
port within the following few days.

There was general lament in the stricken city at this further
huge loss of life. At the same time indignation against the tyrant,
who had so recklessly set out on this raid and was responsible for
all their misfortune, began to rise to new heights. How had this
man, who never before commanded an army or naval squadron,
dared to assume leadership of such a dangerous enterprise, when
officers with experience and tactical skill in the past came exclusively from the highest-ranking old families? Voices were heard demanding the punishment of Thefarie Velianas and even the restitu-
tion of the monarchy. Members of the aristocracy, who until now
had lived in exile, began to drift back into Caisra and fan the anger
of the populace by judicious speeches. On the day the wounded
Thefarie Velianas was brought back to the city in a litter, accompanied by his few surviving supporters, the doors of all the great
houses remained firmly shut. Not a single well-wisher came forward to receive the tyrant and commiserate with him. Scattered
groups of people watched him pass by in resentful silence, or they
called out bitterly to him to restore their lost husbands, fathers,
sons and brothers. Thefarie Velianas, pale with suffering, covered
his head with his mantle and had himself carried into the lauch-
uma. Only a handful of his slaves remained there, the rest of the
household having died of the plague. Mamarce, Veilia's feeble son,
had also fallen victim earlier on.

As the decimated, grief-stricken inhabitants of the city struggled to restore their fields to productivity, while trying to appease
the restless spirits of the drowned and slain, Thefarie Velianas lay
in the royal residence almost completely abandoned. Those of his
henchmen who had survived knew that the tyrant's days were
numbered and sought to save themselves by timely flight.

A week after his ill-starred return to Caisra he succumbed to
the gangrene which had set in. The desolate rooms of the lauchumna rang with the wailing of the two slaves who attended their

master to the last. It was they, who carried him to his grave, escorted only by a reluctant pair of funerary priests. The few who happened to meet this miserable cortège on its way to the cemetery turned away muttering curses. Laris Matunas and Larthi had meanwhile become the object of much attention from the aristocrats who had come back and were anxious to restore public life to normality. Aranth's arrival was eagerly awaited by all of them.

Three days after the death of Thefarie Velianas a large vessel loaded with grain berthed at Pyrgoi. Aranth had delayed his return only so long as it took him to procure supplies for the needy city. Cupe's account of the recent famine had made relief for the starving Aranth's foremost concern. His progress from the harbour up to Caisra was triumphal. He was hailed by the common people as their saviour, and welcomed by the heads of all the great families as the rightful king of Caisra. In a brief speech he thanked his peers for their reception and called upon the gods to protect them all from further suffering and tyrannical rule.

'Never again,' he promised amidst general astonishment, 'will the fate of the many depend on the arbitrary power of one man.'

He asked the nobles to attend a meeting in which the future of the city would be discussed. He then withdrew to the house of his father-in-law to be reunited with his family.

Moonlight travelled across the room and lit up Aranth's corselet, his bronze helmet and his weapons which he had cast down in the corner. Both his face and his body were now plunged into deep shadow.

Larthi sighed. Darkness equally enveloped what the gods held in store for both of them now that the tyrant was dead and they were reunited at last. She turned towards Aranth and cradled him in her arms protectively.

An owl screeched repeatedly in the orchard and a dog howled from the direction of the lauchumna. Larthi did not hear these baleful sounds, for she had at last fallen into a troubled sleep.

196

*Bronze statuette of a
warrior. From Falterona.
London, British Museum*

17

'Father, why won't you be king?' Vel asked, looking up at Aranth as they were walking towards the former royal residence. Everyone they met in the streets stopped to cheer the recently returned head of the Velchana family and express their goodwill.

'They all seem to want you to be the lauchume.'

Aranth responded to the people's greetings with friendly dignity before answering his son with much seriousness. 'Listen Vel,' he said, 'in the lives of all nations there are periods during which the gods sanction certain political institutions. These run their course for the time allotted to them by heaven. The monarchy has served our people well in centuries past, but the events we have witnessed over the last decade in our city and elsewhere are a clear indication that divine will demands a change. The fate of Thefarie Velianas is a sign that great power should never remain long in the same hands. It is for this reason that I decided to divest myself of the title and position held by my forefathers and hand over the control of the affairs of the city to a body of magistrates annually elected from amongst my peers. The heads of the other great families have agreed to my proposition, provided that I, too, offer myself as a candidate each year, which I have promised to do. To the few amongst them who doubted the wisdom of my decision, I pointed out that the twelve peoples of the Rasenna do already elect their federal leader from amongst their rulers in accordance with a long-standing custom. This practice, which has benefitted the entire nation, is bound to result in the common good for our city as well.'

'I'm sure you are right, father. May the gods bless the new order.'

Aranth put his arm round his son's shoulder. 'There will be much to put in order here, too.' He pointed at the royal residence which they were now approaching.

The lauchumna looked indeed badly neglected. In Aranth's memory it had always been a stately and handsome building. Not

198

having set eyes on it for many years, he suddenly became aware of its comparatively modest size and old-fashioned aspect. It consisted of several structures which had been added to and altered during the course of the century, forming a building-complex of irregular plan and awkward shape. Close to its front lay the bidental, a small, roof-shaped stone construction marking the spot where the lightning had struck on the fateful day of Velthur Velchanas' death.

'To be honest,' Aranth went on, 'I've made up my mind to pull down our former home. It has been desecrated by the crimes committed by that usurper and the worthless woman responsible for my father's doom.'

'Will you have a new house built for us, father?' Vel asked eagerly.

'Indeed I will, because we cannot all go on living in your grandfather's house, hospitable though he is.'

'Could you have some fairly large stables built as well?'

Aranth smiled at Vel's ill-disguised longing for horses, but he quickly grew sad when he remembered how deprived his son had been during these past years of all the sports and entertainments which he had taken for granted as a boy. He was determined to make it up to him: Vel would have a pair of good horses, young squires and plenty of opportunity to practise for the game of Truia. He would have to have suitable weapons and armour made for him as well.

'Naturally we shall need stables big enough for your horses and mine and all our mules,' he said. Vel's eyes sparkled.

They now stepped into the abandoned lauchumna, followed by Thresu and Cae. The former royal steward who had retired to a lonely farm in the hills during Aranth's exile, had returned to the city again to offer his services to his dead master's son and Aranth had welcomed back with gratitude the faithful freedman and allowed him to live amongst his retainers.

The autumn wind whistled down the chimney and a loose door banged in a distant part of the building. It was an eerie place to visit, in the gloom of an overcast day. The walls of the central hall were decorated with smoke-blackened frescoes on large terracotta panels. Vel looked around with a mixture of curiosity and awe. He had never before set foot in the house of his ancestors, as it had been ruthlessly appropriated before he was born. Aranth went through every room, identifying his property with Cae's assistance, while Vel gazed awestruck at the paintings, wondering what they represented. All that had belonged to Thefarie Velianas was to be collected and put up for auction, the proceeds of which would be dedicated to Tinia in gratitude for the supreme god's help in freeing the city from the rule of the tyrant.

Aranth was particularly anxious to discover if the inscribed linen rolls - the family's archives - had been preserved. They were documents of the greatest importance for the house of the Velch- ana and sacred to its tutelary spirits. After an intensive search of the storage-rooms he came upon the large wooden box with bronze hinges and handles which he remembered as containing strips of linen on which the names and deeds of his forefathers were recorded. On opening the dusty, creaking lid, he saw, with relief, that the precious documents had survived. Much of the furniture and household equipment that he was familiar with in his youth had also been preserved, though ill cared for. It appeared that Thefarie Velianas had made a serious attempt to secure a sem- blance of legitimacy for himself by retaining all the outward signs and attributes of the former king, as well as his personal property. The fact that Veilia, in her role as wife to the tyrant, had been bent on the same aim, had helped to keep the royal residence much as it had been in the old days.

'Father, do tell me what the figures on the walls in the great hall mean. I can't make them out.'

Vel had rejoined Aranth in the room where he had discovered the family archives. It contained a great many household utensils and Greek pottery vessels.

'Oh, what beautiful painted vases grandfather had!' he ex- claimed when his eyes had become accustomed to the poor light; 'I wish I knew who all these people were and what that funny dog with three heads was.'

'Your mother can explain that to you much better than I can,' Aranth replied quickly, preoccupied with his survey of all the chattels, 'she's promised to come and help us shortly. In fact, I think I can already hear her talking to Seianthi outside.'

Vel dashed out from the storage-room to meet them, eager to question Larthi about the wall paintings.

'This is where your grandfather used to sit and dispense justice,' his mother reflected, as she pointed to the ivory throne behind which were painted two heraldically opposed sphinxes, crouching, winged lionesses with women's heads, each raising a forepaw in a protective gesture.

'Which was yours and father's room?' Seianthi asked.

'It was over there - in the other wing,' Larthi answered musing over those distant days thirteen years ago, when she had lived in this house. And now here was Vel, who had been conceived in that room, in the broad bed at the back of the alcove, which had briefly been Aranth's and her private world, away from the busy public routine of the royal household. Vel now stood before her impatiently, wanting to know all about the scenes on the frescoed wall-panels.

'Look,' she said at last, 'Let's start here. These figures show the judgement of Paris. Did I ever tell you about that old Greek story? This is Paris, the son of King Priam of Troy. He is being approached by the god Hermes, whom we call Turms. He is leading the three goddesses to the prince so that he may settle the dispute as to who is the most beautiful of them. Here then is the war-like Athena, our own Menerva and then comes the goddess Hera, whom we know as Uni and behind her walks the goddess of love, Turan, whose Greek name is Aphrodite. Paris will eventually decide in favour of her, as the fates have decreed that he must do. His reward from Turan will be Helen, the lovely wife of the Greek hero Menelaos, but her abduction by Paris from her husband's home in Sparta was to start the long and terrible war terminating in the sack of Troy by the Greeks. One of the few Trojan survivors was Aeneas, who fled with his small son from the burning city, carrying his ancient father and their household gods on his shoulders. After a long and dangerous voyage they reached our shores, or so the story goes, not far from Ruma.'

The children had listened spellbound to her tale, when Aranth could be heard calling for Larthi: 'Come and look at all the things in here! It's amazing how many of our possessions have survived,' he said when they had joined him. 'The gods must have

The judgement of Paris. Painted terracotta slab from Cerveteri. London, British Museum

meant me to inherit all the belongings of my ancestors, but I feel certain that they did not want me to inhabit this house which has been defiled by my father's enemies.'

'I agree that it would surely offend the spirit of Velthur Velchanas, as well as all the divinities, if we were to live within these polluted walls,' Larthi said with deep conviction.

'I shall have the place pulled down,' Aranth decided, 'and when a purification ceremony has been performed, we shall rebuild a house for ourselves a little further away from the bidental.'

'Father has promised me that we'll have stables for lots of horses,' Vel put in eagerly.

Larthi ruffled his hair affectionately.

202

'Mother will there be room for my dolls and for Peci?' demanded Seianthi, tugging at Larthi's chiton for attention, as her mother seemed lost in thought and unaware of her.

Larthi was indeed contemplating the prospect that, for the first time in her life, she would be mistress of her own house. Though she was still weak from recent privations, it was a wonderful thought which filled her with a sudden upsurge of happiness and energy.

'Of course, there'll be room,' she said, smiling down at Seianthi, 'and if grandfather wants to come and stay with us rather than in his own house, we shall be able to offer him rooms.'

'What about Uncle Caile?' Vel asked, sounding a little doubtful.

'He may want to live on in grandfather's house, which is the old home of the Matuna family.'

Aranth had moved on to the next room with Thresu and Cae, who noted down on his wax-tablet what was to be taken away as the property of Thefarie Velianas. Larthi was about to follow them when Vel remembered his questions, 'Oh, mother,' he said, 'tell me what the story is about on the water-jug here.'

'Oh! That one represents one of the deeds of Herakles. Don't you remember the wicked king Eurystheus, who made the hero perform all sorts of difficult labours? Here you can see the king as Herakles is bringing him the captured guardian of the underworld, the three-headed hound Cerberus. Terrifying, isn't he? Snakes growing from all over his front parts. Eurystheus is so frightened by the monster that he has jumped into a big storage vat and holds up his hands in horror.'

'Doesn't he look funny!' Vel exclaimed. 'His mouth is wide open; he looks as though he's shrieking for help.'

Larthi nodded. 'Aunt Culni owned some water-jugs like these, too. They were all made and painted in the workshop of a Phocaean Greek who had settled here many years ago and was fond of depicting the old Greek stories as if they were all rather comic. I personally prefer the vases painted in Athens, like this mixing-bowl by Euphronios. Look, there's Heraklés again. This time he's wrestling with the giant Antaios, whom he has almost strangled. How

Waterjug, so-called Caeretan hydria, painted with a representation of Herakles bringing the dog Cerberus to Eurystheus. Paris, Louvre

204

beautifully their bodies are drawn with all those fine lines,' Larthi said lovingly.

'I don't like these pictures of fighting,' Seianthi protested; 'and the ladies on this vase are running away - they don't seem to like it either.'

How like Aunt Culni she is, Larthi thought with surprise, as she seized Seianthi's hand saying, 'You are quite right. Now let's go and see if father and Cae have finished their work and then we can all go home.'

'Father,' Vel said when they had left the lauchumna, 'have you ever been to Athens? I should love to go there and see where they make all those pots and other beautiful things.'

'No, I haven't; but I hope to go there one day and then I'll take you with me. We have made many Athenian friends in the emporium on the mouth of the river Po.'

'How soon do you think we can go there?'

'That's in the lap of the gods,' Aranth said, 'for the Athenians and the other Greeks are being intimidated by the Persians at the moment. The Persian king has threatened to march against them with a huge army to punish them for the help they gave to their Ionian brethren some years ago. We must wait and see what happens and pray that the gods won't let Athens come to any harm.'

Vel, imitating his father, made the sign to avert evil.

As they got within sight of home, they saw Caile rushing out to meet them with an air of self-importance. 'You won't believe the news I've just heard,' he panted. 'Your agent Paie has just arrived with it from Pyrgoi, where he ran into an acquaintance who had just landed from a ship that had encountered another from Kyme!'

'Well, what is it?'

'That man Aristodemos is really getting above himself. Do you know what he has done? You would hardly think it possible!'

'Would you mind telling us what's happened, please!'

'Well, apparently he has confiscated some cargo vessels which the people of Ruma had sent to Campania and Sicily to buy grain for their starving city. These ships had put into Kyme to negotiate a deal there, when Aristodemos suddenly declared that he was the legal heir of the Tarquins and that he was going to confiscate the ships in partial compensation for the property the Tarquins were deprived of in Ruma. Can you imagine it? The heir of the Tarquins, indeed - when he hasn't a drop of Rasenna blood in his veins!'

'What high-handed behaviour,' Aranth said indignantly. 'But have no fear, Aristodemos will soon regret his excesses, for the gods do not let hybris go unpunished.'

18

'My chicken won't eat anything, mother,' young Laris cried out, as he came in from the yard into the spacious hall of his father's new house. He still clasped the bag of grain from which he fed his pet birds every morning. 'I've never known that to happen before. They usually all come running when I scatter the first handful, but today they only scratched about a bit without wanting to pick it up. Whatever can it mean?'

Larthi slowly turned from her wool-basket to her youngest son. While her fingers continued to work mechanically, her mind had been wandering. Aranth and Vel were once again spending a prolonged period up in the north, looking into their flagging business. How many more years of her life, she contemplated, was she destined to pass without her husband, running the house for him, bringing up his children and nursing her old father, while he travelled overland to visit his business partners or sailed to distant harbours?

Trade in the south had, however, languished in recent years. Since the fall of Sybaris it had flourished again only briefly while the ships of Caisra were able to pass through the Straits unhindered, thanks to the support of friendly Milesians at Zankle on the Sicilian side. But Anaxilas, the tyrant of Rhegion on the opposite shore, had reconquered Zankle some years ago and settled it with Messenians. Having lost the city as a base, the Etruscans had looked for some other point of support on the coast of Southern Italy

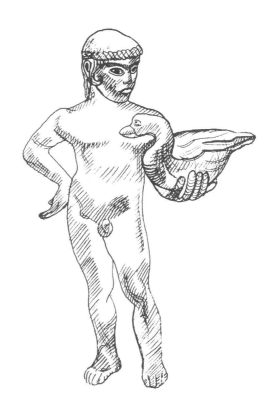

Bronze statuette of a boy holding a goose. London, British Museum

and had unsuccessfully attacked Skyllaion which Anaxilas had fortified. Meanwhile - and this proved more dangerous than anything else - Syracuse, under the leadership of the tyrant Gelon, progressively extended her influence north. A large naval force from Caisra had attempted to take the Aeolian islands in a renewed effort to prevent the invasion of the Tyrrhenian Sea by the Syracusans and secure a vital base for Etruscan shipping near the Straits. They had hoped to succeed where Thefarie Velianas had failed, but this enterprise, too, had ended in disaster and the victorious fleet of Lipara was able to dedicate a thanks-offering at Delphi to celebrate the defeat of the Etruscans. It was a crushing blow which severely damaged the power and prestige of Caisra.

Larthi vividly remembered the black day, some four years earlier, when the few battered ships that had escaped destruction returned to Pyrgoi. Again Caisra lamented its dead: all those who had been killed or drowned, including Arnza, Ramtha's youngest brother. The decision to try and halt the expansion of Syracusan influence into the waters that had for centuries been under Etruscan domination, was taken by the assembly in the recently constructed meeting-place, guided by the magistrates of Caisra who held office during that year. Aranth had repeatedly been elected chief magistrate on his return from exile, but was not serving at the time, being absent from the town. He had gone north with Vel to initiate him into the business and introduce him to his partners.

Larthi never ceased to thank the gods for having spared the lives of her husband and her eldest son, who would certainly have participated in the attempt on Lipara, had they been at home. Perhaps their frequent absence was the price she had to pay for their survival.

Gratefully she looked up at Laris, who was as yet only nine years old and resembled her more closely than any of her other children. He was like her and her father, after whom he was named, in that he was sensitive to the messages from the gods, which manifested themselves in omens and natural events, and he was forever enquiring into their meaning.

'I can't tell you, Laris, why your chickens aren't hungry today. Did you ask the servants whether anyone had fed them already?'

'No, I didn't; but I'm sure nobody would have done so, because that is my responsibility.'

'I wonder if grandfather would know what it means?' Larthi said tentatively. She was anxious to encourage the boy to ask advice again from her father, who had recently become bedridden, depressed and uncommunicative; for ever since Laris had begun to speak, he was inseparable from his grandfather, whose store of fairy-tales and myths seemed as inexhaustible as his patience. In the years following Aranth's return, Laris Matunas's guidance had again been sought by everyone of importance on questions of ritual and on the interpretation of portents, but his blindness had made it difficult for him to consult the sacred books on the more obscure

208

points. His grandson, however, learnt to read early and was soon able to decipher the difficult, old-fashioned writing on the linen rolls. Once young Laris had mastered this art, he proved of the greatest use to his grandfather in the execution of his duties. At the same time he was absorbing the traditional lore and all its subtle meanings and becoming familiar with the large and complex treasure of ancient rites and prescriptions. He already handled the instruments of the cult - the libation bowl and ladle, the bronze axe, the censer and the iron sacrificial knife - with a confidence born of instinct, which was far in advance of his age. Larthi was well aware of the profound satisfaction her father derived from passing on his arcane knowledge and manifold skills to his grandson in the hope that he would be his successor. The old man's sudden lack of interest in imparting his augural science disquietened her deeply.

'I'm certain he could explain it to me,' Laris said, 'but I don't know that he wants to any more.'

'Why don't you try and ask him? He's awake now - I took him his breakfast not so long ago.'

'Yesterday I wanted to find out what it meant when a ram with a beautiful reddish-gold fleece rubbed against me while I was looking at the flocks with Cae. I went into grandfather when I got back and asked him, but he just turned to the wall and wouldn't answer me.'

'Perhaps he was tired. Why don't you try once more.' Larthi gave him an encouraging smile and the boy went thoughtfully across to his grandfather's room, while Larthi secretly rejoiced. She recognized the portent of the ram: it meant future greatness for Laris.

'How are you feeling today?' the boy asked as he approached the bedside, aware that the breakfast stood still untouched.

'My heart is heavy and my body feeble,' the old man said.

'But grandfather, if you don't eat you will get weaker still. Let me break the bread into your milk and help you with it,' Laris said cheerfully.

'Why should I keep my body alive if my mind is no longer any use to anyone?'

'How can you say that, grandfather, when you know so much and are teaching me all you know?'

'My time is nearing its end,' Laris Matunas replied quietly. 'I can feel it. I have just passed my seventieth year - the gods do not send signs to anyone beyond that age.'

Laris felt troubled by the seriousness of his grandfather's tone and said anxiously, 'I will pray to the gods to prolong your life - we all need you and I have so many things to learn still.'

With a wintry smile Laris Matunas felt for his grandson's hand and held it between his gnarled fingers. 'My child,' he said, 'should I die before long, you must get Lecne Teithurna, a pupil of mine many years ago, to instruct you in all those things which I have not yet passed on to you. But I am convinced that much knowledge and virtue has entered you already. Remember that youth sometimes goes hand in hand with great wisdom. Tages,the prophet, who was miraculously ploughed up by a peasant of Tarchuna, had the features of a boy. But despite his youthful looks his hair was grey and his wisdom considerable; for he soon began to sing out to the peoples of all Etruria, who had run up when the ploughman had cried out in astonishment. They took down all the words he uttered and they became the sacred books. When he finished his revelations he vanished, but the texts remain with us today for our guidance and instruction.'

'But quite often I don't know where to look in them for an interpretation of a sign, so I still need all your help,' Laris said. 'And even if the gods don't send you messages any more because of your age, you still know how to make sense of those they send to others. Please, help me,' he went on, withdrawing his hand and beginning to give the old man his bread and milk. Just take this morning, for example, my beautiful Greek chickens, the ones father brought me back, wouldn't take their corn. They only scratched about and then turned their heads first to the south and then to the east and ran hither and thither. Surely, it must signify something, but I can't think what.'

Laris Matunas stopped eating and listened attentively. 'Did they all remain together?' he asked.

'At first they did, but after a bit, one half of them went to the east, amongst them the cock crowing triumphantly and the other half huddled together in the south as if afraid of something.'

210

Laris Matunas moved his hand across his forehead. 'It is difficult to interpret,' he murmured, 'but I believe that two great battles will shortly take place   in both of which Greeks will be fighting successfully against armies of foreign invaders. And while we Rasenna will welcome their victory in the east, their triumph in the south will finally bring us much sorrow.'

He lay back on his bed with a sigh. 'No more,' he whispered weakly when Laris held the spoon to his lips again. 'Leave me alone, my child - I am tired out.'

19

Vel's wedding-ceremony was over. He and his young wife, Thancvil Catharnai had left, but the two families and their numerous guests still remained to enjoy each other's company in the festive setting. Larthi looked around at the familiar faces, grateful that so many of them, even from remote places, had been able to attend. There was Tute Velthina, a sturdy young man, the eldest son of one of Aranth's partners, who had come south partly on business and partly for the celebration. He would soon be getting married to Seianthi who looked more like Aunt Culni by the day, and who primly shared a couch with him. Although she gave her fiancé only an occasional quick smile, Larthi knew that her daughter was happy and felt confident that Tute would make her a good and steadfast husband.

Vel, too, had been fortunate in his choice of wife. Thancvil was delicate and beautiful and came from one of the most distinguished and well-to-do families of Caisra. They had both looked radiant as they sat on their stools opposite each other during the rite which joined them together. Vel was the image of his father in his younger days, though a little slighter in stature.

Larthi's mind went back to her own wedding, some twenty-six years earlier and she turned gratefully towards Aranth who was still handsome and strong, despite his grey hair and beard. He responded to her wistful gaze with an amused wink but continued to give some instructions to Cae. Her eyes wandered on to Caile next to Hasti Afunei, his large and motherly wife. He had hardly changed in appearance. His marriage ten years ago had been a great comfort to Laris Matunas, as Hasti was considerably younger than Caile and soon bore him two children. Avle and Thesanthei now guaranteed the continuing existence of the Matuna family.

How happy her father would have been on this occasion, too, thought Larthi. It was a pity that he had not lived to share their joy. Yet there was every reason to be grateful to the gods for the long life-span they had granted him. Laris Matunas had died the previous year at the age of seventy-one, having first placed his hand on the head of young Laris and in so doing transmitted his priestly virtue to him. He had already passed on to him his augural staff, as well as all the other ritual objects, in the presence of Lecne Teithurna and two other priests.

Laris stood beside the couch of Lecne Teithurna, deep in conversation with his new teacher. The boy's soft brown hair was cut short above the forehead and fell down in a smoothe curve over the nape of his neck. He had Larthi's dark eyes, finely arched brows and mobile features. She looked at him lovingly; it was good to know that he would remain at home with them for many years to come, as the others had already flown the nest. He was only eleven, but looked more mature as a result of the responsibilites thrust on him.

Ramtha and her husband were now surrounded by a swarm of little grandchildren; their twins, Marce and Ravnthu, had both married and produced offspring very young. Caile's children, being the eldest present, presided benevolently over the games the younger ones were playing round the legs of Ramtha's couch. Ramtha's blonde hair had somewhat faded over the years but her face was still pink and fair, and her expression one of serene kindness. No wonder, Larthi reflected, that all children were drawn to her. There had always been something irresistibly warm and protective about her nature. Ramtha was wearing traditional clothes and her hair was done up in a tutulus like Larthi and Hathli Alsinei, Thancvil's mother; but the bride and Seianthi followed the latest Athenian fashion in dress, and their hair was worn in natural ringlets to their shoulders and crowned with festive wreaths.

212

'I hear you've been to Athens recently,' Caile remarked. Tute Velthina, a reticent young man, assented with a nod and Seianthi interjected, 'I hope you noticed my dress. Tute brought it from Athens.'

Hasti Afunei duly admired her grand-niece's new chiton, while Caile continued, 'It's surprising how quickly they seem to have recovered from the devastation of the Persians. Did you notice any signs of war-damage?'

'Indeed, I did! The temples on their acropolis are lying in ruins but they've decided not to rebuild them so as to constantly remind them of the invaders' impiety.'

'I suppose that man Themistokles can think of nothing but building ships and yet more ships after his victory in the bay of Salamis.'

'The more ships they have, the better it is for our trade,' Tute replied.

Aranth, having overheard their conversation, now called from his couch, 'Quite right! We have to make up for the ten lean years we've had between the two attacks on Greece by Darius and Xerxes. Our Athenian trading-partners were preoccupied by these invasions, but things are now beginning to get better at last and they are coming up the Adriatic again. Tute's journey has been most productive.'

Thefre Catharna, Thancvil's father, a great landowner in Caisra, now said pensively, 'It's strange how the gods granted victory to the Greeks over the Persians at Salamis on the same day as they granted victory to the forces of Syracuse and Acragas against the Carthaginians at Himera.'

'I do wish the Sicilian Greeks hadn't triumphed!' Aranth said with feeling. 'I've never been a special friend of the Carthaginians; but since fate delivered us from their puppet Thefarie Velianas, they haven't attempted to interfere in our affairs again, whereas the Deinomenids . . .'

'Aranth!' Caile interrupted him suddenly, striking his forehead with frustration, 'I meant to tell you, but it completely went out of my mind with the wedding and all the excitement . . . I had a visitor from Campania call on me yesterday who brought news that Gelon, the son of Deinomenes, has died from some illness at

Syracuse. They buried him with the greatest honours and worship him as though he were a hero there. Odd, when you think of it, as he wasn't Syracusan at all, but just an usurper from Gela who treated the people in the most tyrannical fashion.'

'But who succeeded him?' said Aranth, his face serious.

'His brother Hieron, though there seems to have been some disagreement over the succession with the younger brother, Polyzalos. But you know, in truth, one of these Deinomenids is as bad as the other; they are all aggressive and grasping.'

'And a clever scheming lot too,' added Aranth thoughtfully. 'Remember how Gelon made it up with Anaxilas and Terillos directly after his victory at Himera, although it was they who had called in that vast army of Carthaginians under the command of Hamilkar to help them against him. In that way Gelon managed to unite all the Greeks of western Sicily under the rule of Syracuse. The size of their combined fleets is quite intimidating now and I feel Hieron is bound to carry on his brother's policy. We shall be in for a bad time if they continue to push north into our waters.'

'And particularly,' Thefre put in, 'as the Greeks of Kyme have turned so hostile to us again since Aristodemos was killed by the aristocrats he exiled. The Rasenna in Campania are already hard pressed.'

'And there is little we can do to help them,' said Aranth dejectedly, 'the Latins having cut our roads there by land. There only remains the sea . . .'

Larthi had listened to the last part of the men's conversation with growing apprehension. Something like a cold hand seemed to grip her heart.

'Let us pray, Laris,' she whispered to her son, who had just come across to her; 'May the gods protect us all!'

214

20

Vel, assisted by Cae, supervised the slaves who were carrying out the little-used armour and weapons from the store-room in Aranth's house.

'We shall have to tell Cneve and Punpu to clean and sharpen the blades,' Vel said, having inspected a couple of rusting iron swords.

'The lining of some of the helmets also needs renewing, master,' said Cae, pointing to the frayed pieces of sweat-stained leather covering the inside of the bronze helmet he held in his hand.

'Tell Ana to look into that,' Vel replied; 'there must be enough hides left.'

Cae consented to do so, while testing the points of some lances that were being carried past him.

'While he is at it, he may as well check that all the metal tabs are firmly attached to the leather-corslets. Some seem to be loose and the straps of the shoulder-pieces are torn or missing on a number of them,' Vel observed.

They were just making certain that the arm-bands on the inside of the great round shields were safely riveted, when little Aranth ran up to them, crowing with delight. The clang of the bronze shields as they were being inspected had attracted his attention, where he had been playing in the yard. He dropped his hoop and stick and started to hammer with his small fists on one of the shields, pressing his ear against the surface to listen to the booming reverberations. Vel smiled indulgently at his son who at the age of three seemed more interested in his father's armour than in his own toys.

'If you like the sound of bronze, my boy, just listen to this,' he said and seized one of the great curved war-trumpets which were being brought out at that moment from the store. 'This is the one your great-grandfather's trumpeter used when they went into battle against Kyme fifty years ago. Let's pretend that we're coming after them again! The Greeks have always been afraid of the sound of this horn which the Rasenna invented.'

He put the mouthpiece to his lips. Aranth looked up with amazement at his father's inflated cheeks. A strangely plaintive, muffled sound wrung itself from the instrument.

'I can't make it work properly - it's been out of use for so long,' Vel said displeased, and handed it back to the slave who was holding another one of the trumpets with a curved, flaring mouth. 'They all need cleaning and tuning.'

Cae noted it down on his tablet with the rest of the things that had to be attended to. But Aranth, disappointed at not seeing the splendid spectacle of someone blowing the horn, tugged at his father's mantle in vain and finally burst into tears. Vel was too busy, however, to take any notice. After a while, the child's persistent crying began to irritate him and he angrily told Aranth to be quiet. Aranth's response to his father's reprimand was to shriek even more, as he had inherited Vel's quick temper.

Larthi, who had been sorting through the men's clothing with Peci, heard him crying and hurried from the house. She took in the situation at a glance.

'Arnza!' she called, 'let Peci show you the piglets that were born yesterday.'

He looked up at his grandmother with a long wail, still sustained when she picked him up and carried him a few steps talking quietly to him in a soothing voice.

'You'll love those piglets. There are six of them, all nice and pink. Peci will take you over to the sty now, because we mustn't disturb the men here, must we? They've got to get everything ready in time. Your father is seeing to all the weapons and armour for the fighting men and your grandfather is down in the harbour supervising the war-ships being fitted out. He's been appointed by the magistrates to lead the expedition against Kyme. You see the Greeks have been attacking our brothers living down there and they won't allow our merchant-ships to pass peacefully either. We must, therefore, come to the rescue of all the Rasenna in the south and defend our freedom on the sea.'

Larthi took a corner of the child's tunic and wiped the last tears from his cheeks before handing him to Peci. With a sigh she turned to Vel, who had come over earlier from his own house, bringing little Aranth with him.

216

How is Thancvil?' she asked her son, as he was testing the fit of some greaves.

'Not very well. This second pregnancy is giving her trouble - and she doesn't like my going away now.'

He forced the greave off his shin; it was slightly bent.

'I shall keep an eye on her,' Larthi said quietly, putting her hand on Vel's arm.

He smiled at her gratefully.

'Mother, I know how you feel about father taking part in this campaign at his age, but he is determined to do it, whatever any of us say, because he's been put in command. No one, as you know, is more experienced and able than he is and I promise to protect him, so that you get him back safely.'

Larthi put her head on her son's shoulder and he stroked her back in a comforting embrace before turning again to his task.

She, too, had duties to attend to. Walking towards the house past the mass of waiting armour, she noticed Aranth's bronze helmet. She remembered so clearly the last time she had seen it - glimmering in the moonlight after his return from exile, so many years ago. She bent down and picked it up and lovingly carressed the proud curve of its smooth, brownish-gold surface. As she gazed at the helmet for a while, an agonizing pain began to pierce her left temple, almost blinding her. Suppressing a groan, she reached for her head and tried to focus her eyes which seemed to be swimming. Fitfully at first and then with cruel clarity, she saw three lines of a Greek inscription suddenly appear engraved on Aranth's helmet:

Ἱάρων ὁ Δεινομένεος
Καὶ τοὶ Συρακόσιοι
Τῷ Δὶ Τύραν' ἀπὸ Κύμας

Her hands trembled as she took in the meaning of this votive inscription:

Hieron, son of Deinomenes
and the Syracusans
to Zeus for victory over the Tyrrhenians

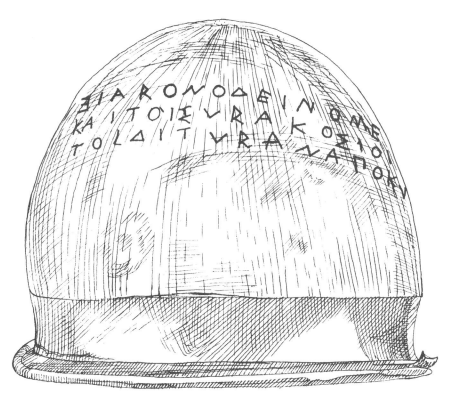

Etruscan bronze helmet with Greek votive inscription. From Olympia. London, British Museum

At that moment the helmet felt burning hot and she dropped it with a harsh clatter to the ground. She stared at it lying at her feet . . . but there was no inscription on it!

Larthi supported herself against one of the wooden pillars; her knees were giving way. The message from the gods, for that was what she recognized the apparition of the writing to have been, had penetrated her mind and made her heart contract in unbearable pain. She realized the inscription meant that Aranth would be killed in the coming battle and stripped of all his armour by the victorious Syracusans, in alliance with the Kymean Greeks. And triumphant Hieron would dedicate the spoils from his most prominent adversary to Zeus in the god's sanctuary at Olympia.

She summoned all her strength to return to the house, when she saw Peci, pale and distressed, leading the weeping Arnza towards her.

'Mistress, something terrible has happened!' she stammered, 'when we got to the sty, the sow had killed all the piglets - only one had survived. It was a dreadful sight!'

Larthi sank to the ground with a moan, unconscious. Peci shrieked in dismay, and Vel and Cae rushed to Larthi's side and carried her indoors.

A week later she stood by the parapet at the edge of the garden of her father's house with Laris beside her. In silence they searched the horizon with their eyes. The city was nearly deserted. Most of the families, whose men had set out with the fleet, had accompanied the departing troops as far as the harbour to see them off. Larthi had not felt strong enough to come to Pyrgoi with her other relations, but had forced herself to walk as far as her childhood home, so as to follow the departure of the ships from her old lookout post.

Laris was now fifteen and eager to go into battle with his father and brother. But his youth had ruled him out from taking part in the expedition. He was bitterly disappointed; Aranth had asked him to stay at home with his mother instead of coming to Pyrgoi to watch the army embark.

Larthi had gone through a harder and more lonely struggle. When she came to herself again after her overwhelming premonition of the future, she realized that any attempt to implore the gods to alter the fate of Aranth and Vel would be hopeless. With an immense effort she had willed herself into appearing calm and confident of the successful outcome of the war. No word which might have betrayed her dreadful apprehension escaped her and she succeeded in bidding farewell to her husband and eldest son without showing any more than the usual emotion natural to such a parting.

The men were light-hearted as they left and looked forward to the chance of settling accounts with the Greeks, for the tension and uncertainty of the last years had been too protracted. It was a liberating experience for them to finally go to war against a people who were strangling their commerce and attempting to take over their nation's southernmost outposts.

The sea glistened like burnished metal under the slanting shafts of the late afternoon sun. Cloud-shadows travelled intermittently over the rippled surface, plunging large stretches of water into fleeting darkness. At last the ships came into view, sail after sail moving south in steady formation.

Laris sighed in frustration. 'What a marvellous sight they are! Oh, why wouldn't you let me go with them?'

'Because you alone are destined to survive and carry on your father's ancient line and my father's sacred traditions,' whispered Larthi, her eyes fixed desperately on the leading ship which was gradually diminishing in size and then suddenly swallowed up in the sombre shadow of a huge cloud-bank. As she strained to catch a final glimpse of its sails, a sudden cold wind blew up, which violently shook the trees of the garden and made them both shiver.

Laris turned towards his mother, profoundly moved by her unexpected words. With unseeing eyes she now listened to the ever-increasing wind, her body tense and her heightened consciousness aware of some further message imminent from the gods.

Above the soughing of the branches and the whistling of the gathering storm they suddenly heard the penetrating blast of a trumpet out of the southern sky.

Larthi gripped Laris' arm. 'This is the sound from heaven that announces the end of our saeculum,' she said with bloodless lips. 'The fate of Caisra is fulfilled - its greatness past. May the gods be more merciful to future generations.'

THE END

Glossary

Glossary

Achaeans	Greeks from the northern Peloponnese who settled colonists in Sybaris, Kroton and other southern Italian cities.
Achilles	Hero of Greek mythology and son of Peleus and Thetis, one of the protagonists in Homer's *Iliad*.
Aeneas	Hero of Greek mythology, son of Anchises and the goddess Aphrodite; the only Trojan leader to escape from the general destruction of Troy.
Aeolian islands	Volcanic islands 25 miles north-east of Sicily, including those nowadays called Lipari, Stromboli, Vulcano and Salina.
Agylla	Greek name for the Etruscan city of Caisra or Caere, the modern Cerveteri
Aigina	Greek island in the Saronic gulf.
Akragas	Greek city in southern Sicily, founded by Geloans ca. 580 B.C., the modern Agrigento.
Alalia	Greek city founded by Phocaeans on the east coast of Corsica, the modern Aleria.
Anaxilas	Greek tyrant of Rhegium (modern Reggio di Calabria), 494-476 B.C.
Aphrodite	Greek goddess of love.
Apulu	Etruscan form of the name of the Greek god Apollo.
Arethusa	Greek nymph and fountain at Syracuse in Sicily.
Aricia	Latin city 16 miles south-east of Rome at the foot of the Alban mountains, the modern Ariccia.
Aristodemos	Son of Aristokrates of Kyme (Cumae). After his victory in the battle of Aricia about 505 B.C., he made himself tyrant of Kyme and still ruled in 492 B.C.
Arruns	Son of king Laris Porsenna of Clevsina, who was killed in the battle of Aricia about 505 B.C.
Astarte	Phoenician goddess, identified at Pyrgoi with the Etruscan Uni
Athena	Warlike Greek goddess, patroness of Attica and of the arts and crafts.
Augur	A religious official who interpreted omens derived from the flight, singing and feeding of birds and from the appearance of the entrails of sacrificial victims and advised upon the decisions in public business in accordance with such omens.
Auspicium	Term used by the Romans for certain types of divination, especially from birds, but also from other phenomena.

Bidental	The ritual burial-place of a thunderbolt. It was Etruscan custom, when lightning had struck, to collect the supposed fragments of the bolt, bury them and wall the place in, while a religious formula was pronounced.
Calu	Etruscan god of the underworld.
Campania	Fertile volcanic region of South Italy between the Apennines and the Tyrrhenian Sea, bordered by Latium in the north and by the Sorrentine peninsula in the south.
Carthaginians	Inhabitants of Carthage, a Phoenician colony on the Tunisian coast, traditionally founded from Tyre in 814 B.C.
Caisra	or Caere. Important Etruscan city north of Rome, the modern Cerveteri.
Cerberus	In Greek mythology the three-headed hound who guarded the underworld and was captured by Herakles as one of his twelve labours.
Chalkis	Greek city on the island of Euboea. Many Chalcidian colonies were planted in south Italy and Sicily in the 8th century B.C.
Charu	or Charun. Etruscan demon of the underworld.
Charybdis	A whirlpool in a narrow channel of the sea (later identified with the Straits of Messina), according to the *Odyssey* located opposite the monster Scylla (q.v.)
Clevsina	or Chamars. Roman Clusium, the modern Chiusi in the province of Siena. Important northern Etruscan city.
Cnidos	Greek city on a long peninsula at the south-west corner of Asia Minor, traditionally founded by Spartans.
Cottabos	An originally Greek game played at drinking-parties, the players flinging dregs of wine from their cups and trying to dislodge a target from a bronze stand.
Darius I	Achaemenid king of Persia, 521-486 B.C.
Delphi	Greek sanctuary on the slopes of Mount Parnassos, a famous oracle of Apollo.
Demaratos of Corinth	Greek refugee who settled in Tarquinia and married a noble Etruscan lady.
Elea	Greek city on the Tyrrhenian coast of southern Italy, founded about 535 B.C. by Phocaean colonists; the modern Velia.
Ephesos	Important Ionian Greek city on the mouth of the river Kaystros in western Asia Minor.
Euphronios	Greek potter and vase-painter in Athens, active during the late 6th and early 5th centuries B.C.
Eurystheus	In Greek mythology a king of Tiryns for whom Herakles had to perform the twelve labours.

Gabii	Ancient Latin city twelve miles east of Rome.
Gela	Greek city on the south coast of Sicily, founded about 688 B.C. by Cretans and Rhodians.
Gelon	Son of Deinomenes (c. 540-478 B.C.) Greek tyrant, first of Gela and then of Syracuse.
Gorgo Medusa	In Greek mythology a snake-haired female monster, the sight of whom turned men to stone.
Groma	An instrument for surveying land.
Hamilkar	Carthaginian general who commanded a large army and fleet against the Sicilian Greeks. He was beaten and killed by the troops of Gelon at the battle of Himera in 480 B.C.
Haruspex	Plural haruspices. Diviners who interpreted natural phenomena as the expression of the will of the gods.
Helen	In Greek mythology the daughter of Zeus and Leda. In the *Iliad* and *Odyssey* she is the wife of Menelaos, who had been carried off to Troy by Paris.
Hephaistos	Greek god of metalworking.
Hera	Greek goddess, the wife of Zeus.
Hercle	The Etruscan form of the Greek hero Herakles.
Hermes	Greek god of fertility, of the flocks; the messenger of the gods and guide of the souls to the underworld.
Hieron I	Son of Deinomenos. Was appointed ruler of Gela when his brother Gelon became master of Syracuse and succeeded to the Syracusan tyranny in 478 B.C. Allied to the Kymean Greeks, he destroyed Etruscan sea-power in the naval battle of Kyme in 475 B.C.
Himera	Greek city on the north coast of Sicily, founded c. 649 B.C. by settlers from Zankle (Messina).
Hippokrates	Greek tyrant of Gela, succeeded his brother Kleandros c. 498 B.C. and fell in battle about 490 B.C.
Hydra	In Greek mythology a many-headed, monstrous snake, killed by Herakles as one of his twelve labours.
Iolaos	In Greek mythology the nephew and companion of Herakles.
Ionia	The central part of the west coast of Asia Minor, named after its Greek settlers, the Ionians.
Kameiros	Greek city on the north-western coast of Rhodes.
Kleoboulos	Tyrant of Lindos on Rhodes (6th century B.C.)
Kos	Greek island off the west coast of Asia Minor.
Krathis	River near Sybaris, the modern Crati.
Kroton	Greek city of south Italy, founded about 710 B.C. by Achaean colonists.
Kyme	(Cumae) Greek colony near Naples, founded after 750 B.C.

Lade	Small island near the city of Miletus on the west coast of Asia Minor, nowadays joined to the mainland as a result of the alluvial deposits of the river Maeander.
Laos	Greek harbour town on the west coast of south Italy, founded as colony by Sybaris.
Lasa	Female figure in Etruscan art, usually winged, which may represent a nymph of beauty.
Lauchume	Etruscan for king, ruler.
Lauchumna	Etruscan for king's residence.
Lindia	A goddess, identified with Athena, worshipped at Lindos on Rhodes.
Lindos	Greek city on the south coast of Rhodes.
Lipara	A volcanic island north-west of Sicily (modern Lipari), settled by Cnidian and Rhodian colonists between c. 580-576 B.C.
Lucumo	The Latin form of the Etruscan word lauchume = king, ruler.
Manlius Octavius	of Tusculum; Latin son-in-law of king Porsenna.
Maris	Etruscan god identified with the Greek Ares and the Latin Mars.
Menelaos	In Greek mythology the younger brother of Agamemnon and husband of Helen.
Menerva	Etruscan goddess identified with the Greek Athena and the Roman Minerva.
Messenians	The Greek inhabitants of the south-western region of the Peloponnese.
Miletus	Important Ionian Greek city on the west coast of Asia Minor.
Misa	Probable name of the Etruscan city (the modern Marzabotto) on the river Reno south of Bologna.
Nethuns	Etruscan god identified with the Greek Poseidon and the Roman Neptune.
Netšvis, Netsviš	Etruscan for haruspex (q.v.).
Nortia	Etruscan goddess of destiny.
Paris	In Greek mythology a son of Priam and Hekuba, who abducted Helen from Sparta to Troy.
Phersu	Etruscan for mask, masked person (= Latin perso-na).
Phocaeans	Greeks from the Ionian city of Phocaea in Asia Minor who explored and colonized the western Mediterranean in the 6th century B.C.
Pithekoussai	Modern Ischia, island in the Gulf of Naples, colonized by Euboean Greeks in the first half of the 8th century B.C.
Polyzalos	Son of Deinomenes, brother of Gelon and Hieron (q.v.)
Porsenna	Laris, Etruscan king of Clevsina (Chamars), or Clusium, the modern Chiusi.

225

Poseidonia	Greek city in Campania, = Paestum; founded about 700 B.C. by Sybaris.
Priam	In Greek mythology the son of Laomedon and king of Troy.
Promanteia	The right of precedence in the consultation of the Delphic oracle.
Punicum	One of the harbour towns of the Etruscan city of Caisra.
Pupluna	Etruscan harbour and mining-city, the modern Populonia, opposite Elba.
Pyrgoi	Modern Santa Severa north-west of Cerveteri, once a harbour of the Etruscan city of Caisra with a famous sanctuary of Uni - Astarte.
Pytho	The oldest name of Delphi (q.v.)
Rasenna	Greek form of the Etruscan word rasna = Etruscans.
Ruma	Etruscan form of the Latin Roma, modern Rome.
Salamis	Greek island in the Saronic gulf, where the Persian fleet was decisively defeated by the Greeks in 480 B.C.
Samos	Greek island off the west coast of Asia Minor.
Sardis	Capital of Lydia in western Asia Minor.
Scylla	Many-headed sea-monster of Greek mythology which lived, according to the *Odyssey*, in a cave opposite the whirlpool of Charybdis (q.v.)
Selvans	Etruscan god identified with the Roman Silvanus.
Servius Tullius	The sixth king of Rome (traditionally 578-535 B.C.), of Latin origin, who ruled between the reigns of Etruscan monarchs, the Tarquins.
Sethlans	Etruscan god of the smithy, identified with the Greek Hephaistos.
Skidros	Greek harbour city in western south Italy, founded as colony by Sybaris.
Skyllaion	A Greek harbour town on the west coast of south Italy.
Sostratos	A successful Greek merchant, mentioned by Herodotus, who traded in the western Mediterranean.
Sparta	Greek city in the central Peloponnese. In mythology the home of Menelaos and Helen.
Spurius Larcius	Consul at Rome with Titus Herminius in 506-505 B.C., of Etruscan descent.
Suri	Etruscan divinity, identified with Apollo.
Susa	The capital of Elam in southern Persia.
Sybaris	Greek city in south Italy, founded by Achaeans and Troezeneans about 720 B.C. and destroyed completely by the rival city of Kroton in 510 B.C. The site is near the modern Sibari.
Syracuse	Important Greek city on the east coast of Sicily, founded by Corinthian colonists c. 734 B.C.

Tages	A mythical Etruscan prophet, miraculously ploughed up from a field at Tarchuna (modern Tarquinia), whose revelations formed the body of the sacred books called after him.
Tanaquil	Noble Etruscan lady of Tarquinia who married Tarquin, the son of a Corinthian refugee, Demaratos, and an Etruscan wife.
Tarchuna	Important city of southern Etruria, the modern Tarquinia.
Tarentines	Inhabitants of Tarentum (Greek Taras) in south Italy, a city founded, according to tradition, about 706 B.C. by Spartans.
Tarquin	The son of Demaratos of Corinth. He married at Tarquinia the Etruscan lady Tanaquil, who persuaded him to migrate to Rome.
Terillos	Greek tyrant of Himera who called in the Carthaginians to help him when he was expelled by Theron of Akragas. But the combined forces of Gelon and Theron defeated the Carthaginian army at Himera in 480 B.C.
Thanur	Etruscan divinity.
Themistokles	c. 520-462 B.C. Athenian democratic statesman who commanded the fleet of Athens against the Persians in 480 B.C.
Thetis	Nereid of Greek mythology, the wife of Peleus and mother of Achilles.
Tinia	Etruscan god identified with the Greek Zeus and Roman Jupiter.
Titus Herminius	Consul at Rome with Spurius Larcius 506-505 B.C.; of Etruscan descent.
Troezen	Greek city in the north-eastern Peloponnese.
Troy	City in north-western Asia Minor, according to Homer's *Iliad* destroyed by the Greeks after a long siege.
Tuchulcha	Etruscan demon of the underworld.
Turan	Etruscan goddess of love, identified with the Greek Aphrodite and the Roman Venus.
Turms	Etruscan god identified with the Greek Hermes and Roman Mercury.
Tusculum	Latin city 15 miles south-east of Rome, near modern Frascati.
Tutulus	An Etruscan female head-dress, fashionable during the 6th and early 5th centuries B.C.
Tyrrhenoi	Greek name for the Etruscans. Hence the name Tyrrhenian Sea for that part of the Mediterranean which borders Etruria.

Uni	Etruscan goddess identified with the Greek Hera, the Roman Juno and the Phoenician Astarte.
Vanth	Etruscan demon; a winged female figure often carrying a torch.
Vecui	or Vegoia. A mythical Etruscan nymph whose prophecies were collected in sacred books bearing her name.
Veii	Important Etruscan city 9 miles north of Rome.
Velsena	Etruscan name of the city called Volsinii by the Romans. The archaic city was probably sited at modern Orvieto rather than at Bolsena.
Vetluna	Etruscan city, the modern Vetulonia north of Grosseto.
Voltumna	Etruscan divinity at whose sanctuary the annual federal meeting of the twelve Etruscan cities took place.
Xerxes	Achaemenid Persian king 486-465 B.C. Son of Darius and Atossa. His fleet was defeated by Themistokles at Salamis in 480 B.C.
Zankle	Greek city on the site of modern Messina in Sicily, founded c. 724 B.C. Its name was changed to Messana in the early 5th century B.C. when it was occupied by immigrants from Greek Messene.
Zilath mechl rasnal	An Etruscan title with the probable meaning: supreme magistrate of the Etruscans.

PO

Atria

Spina

Misa
(Marzabotto)

Felsina
(Bologna)

ADRIATIC

SEA

(Pisa)

(Florence)

ARNO

Velathri
(Volterra)

TIBER

Pupluna
(Populonia)

Clevsina
(Chiusi)

Vetuna
(Vetulonia)

Velsena
(Orvieto)

Aithalia
(Elba)

Tarchuna

ITALY

COR-
SICA

Alalia
(Aleria)

Pyrgoi

Tarquinia

Veii

Caisra
(Cerveteri)

Ruma (Rome)

Tusculum

Volturnam
(Capua)

SARDINIA

Kyme
(Cumae)

Neapolis
(Naples)

Pithekoussai
(Ischia)

Poseidonia
(Paestum)

Elea (Velia)

Taras
(Taranto)

TYRRHENIAN SEA

Laos

Skidros

Sybaris
(Sibari)

Kroton
(Crotone)

AEOLIAN ISLANDS

Lipara
(Lipari)

Rhegion
(Reggio)

Himera

Zankle
(Messina)

SICILY

Akragas
(Agrigento)

Gela

Syrakoussai
(Syracuse)

Carthage

NORTH AFRICA

229

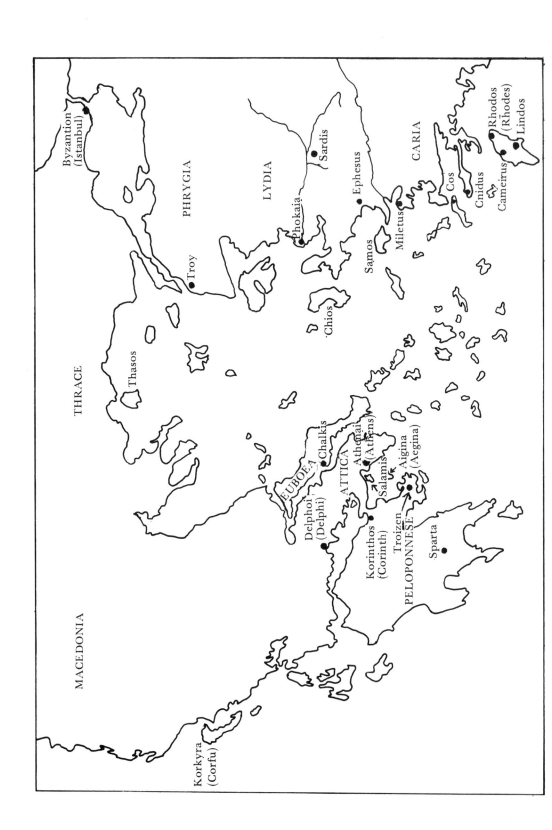